THE ENGLISH ISLES

The English Isles

*Cultural transmission and political conflict
in Britain and Ireland, 1100–1500*

Seán Duffy and Susan Foran

EDITORS

FOUR COURTS PRESS

Set in 11 on 13 point Ehrhardt for
FOUR COURTS PRESS LTD
7 Malpas Street, Dublin 8, Ireland
e-mail: info@fourcourtspress.ie
www.fourcourtspress.ie
and in North America for
FOUR COURTS PRESS
c/o ISBS, 920 N.E. 58th Street, Suite 300, Portland, OR 97213.

A catalogue record for this title
is available from the British Library.

ISBN 978–1–84682–223–0

Printed in England
by Antony Rowe, Chippenham, Wilts.

Contents

Abbreviations

ANS	*Anglo-Norman Studies*
CDI	*Calendar of documents relating to Ireland, 1171–1307*, ed. H.S. Sweetman, 5 vols (London, 1875–86)
CMCS	*Cambrian* [formerly *Cambridge*] *Medieval Celtic Studies*
EHR	*English Historical Review*
IHS	*Irish Historical Studies*
JGAHS	*Journal of the Galway Archaeological and Historical Society*
JRSAI	*Journal of the Royal Society of Antiquaries of Ireland*
SHR	*Scottish Historical Review*
TRHS	*Transactions of the Royal Historical Society*
ZCP	*Zeitschrift für celtische Philologie*

Introduction

The first medieval conference from Trinity College Dublin's Centre for Irish-Scottish and Comparative Studies was organized by Seán Duffy and Susan Foran in cooperation with the Department of Celtic and Scottish Studies in the School of Literatures, Languages and Cultures at the University of Edinburgh in March 2003. The highly stimulating papers and discussions arising from that conference led to the volume entitled *The world of the galloglass: kings, warlords and warriors in Ireland and Scotland, 1200–1600*, ed. Seán Duffy (Dublin, 2007).

Publication of the latter coincided with a second conference organized by Seán Duffy, Susan Foran and James Walmsley on a related theme. In this case, leading medieval scholars gathered at Trinity College Dublin on 14–16 September 2007 to debate and offer a new perspective on the origins of England's empire: papers congregated around the theme of the impact of medieval English imperialism and the ways in which English and wider European cultural norms were transmitted outwards towards Ireland, Scotland and Wales from the Norman Conquest onwards. The proceedings are published in this important interdisciplinary collaboration.

In the chapters below, John Gillingham looks at how in the high and later Middle Ages, the kings of England, and their subjects, perceived their own capacity to transform their neighbouring insular-Celtic societies in their own image. Dauvit Broun, considering the late Rees Davies' idea that a 'loose-limbed' kingdom of Britain might have emerged in the twelfth and thirteenth centuries, examines the notion from the perspective of Scotland's experience of anglicization. Scotland's experience of anglicization was fundamentally different from anglicization in Ireland and Wales, since it took place under the direction of the king of Scots and increased his power, so that, as a result, Britain developed not one 'core', but two: the anglicized inner core of the Scottish kingdom as well as the larger and more wealthy heartlands of England, and was inherently inimical to any notion that a united kingdom of Britain was achievable in the later Middle Ages. In his provocative chapter, he addresses these issues. To what extent did anglicization for some Scots mean self-identification as English? How and when did those who were ethnically English become Scottish? And was it ever conceivable that those who were ethnically Scottish could have become English within an inclusive British kingdom?

This is a subject that also preoccupies Matthew Hammond who, taking the twin themes of Rees Davies' earlier study of English 'domination and conquest', assesses whether the model is sustainable for Scotland. He argues that, while the exercise seems to fit neatly with the steps leading from the establishment of the Welsh March to the capitulation of the independent Welsh principality, and to a lesser extent with Ireland, where the process of conquest eventually ran out of steam, for all the – as he puts it – sweeping grandeur and brilliance of Davies' model, and for all the inherent advantages in taking a cross-border approach to this period, it is to be doubted whether the role of the Scottish kingdom in Davies' paradigm is sustainable. Instead, he argues, while it may be appropriate to talk of Scotland being anglicized in certain well-defined contexts – linguistically, for example – this must be balanced by a consideration of what he terms Scotticization, as the new 'colonial aristocracy' began self-identifying as 'Scottish' by the thirteenth century. Citing one remarkable difference between Scotland and Ireland, the tendency for immigrant knights who married daughters of the native élite to adopt local personal names, either through imitation of the royal family or local magnates, he suggests that the most successful Scottish families of the thirteenth and fourteenth centuries were those that were able to bridge the gap between the Gaelic and Anglo–French cultural orbits. Hammond describes this process as a local form of Europeanization linked closely to a Scottish identity based on the figure of the king. The effects of this process were to maintain the Scottish identity of the acculturated native élites, despite the spread of French and English languages, to redefine the English-speaking parts of the kingdom as Scottish, and to lead to the adoption of Scottish identity among Anglo–French immigrant knights, merchants and clergy. Scotticization was too an expansionist force, using the same techniques as anglicization to spread Scottish power, authority and identity into regions which were seen as barbarous, especially Galloway and the Isles.

The latter area is the theme of Steve Boardman's chapter. Acknowledging that the Hebrides was perhaps the region where the impact of the Davies' 'English empire' was weakest, he argues that many of the same processes of successful or abortive integration are present in the history of the fabled lordship of the Isles. Boardman believes that the Isles represent a region that is especially intriguing to those exploring the growth and decline of polities and identities that do not fit easily into the 'national' narratives around which much modern historiography has been organized. Some see, he argues, the political self-sufficiency enjoyed by the late medieval lords of the Isles as being closely linked to, and partly explained by, a quite deliberate defence of the culture and language of the territories over which they exercised control. Others offer another analysis, which gives full weight to the cultural distinctiveness of the society over which the lords of the Isles presided, without necessarily seeing in this an implicit political challenge to Scottish kingship or a declaration of separatist intent. In his own chapter, Boardman reviews texts which deal with the distinctive structures and institutions said to lie at the heart of the medieval lordship of the Isles, mostly dating from the sixteenth century or later, which have been influential in framing modern understanding of the lordship, but argues that they were produced in a context much altered from that which shaped the actions of fifteenth-century lords, and that our modern inclination to see the historical lordship primarily as a political expression of the cultural distinctiveness of the Western Isles in the medieval period needs to be reconsidered.

It is well-known that English efforts at domination in the Middle Ages were reinforced and often legitimated by a parallel sense of cultural superiority, a sense of superiority which is a notable characteristic of the writings of the great twelfth-century English historians. They painted the English as surrounded by barbarians, and while the Scots and the Welsh felt the wrath of these commentators, it was often the Irish who received the most severe criticism, which had the effect of devaluing Irish cultural and religious stock amongst certain sections of European society. In this volume, Patrick Wadden turns the lens the other way round and investigates the perception of the Norman conquerors of England held by the Irish from the mid-eleventh to the mid-twelfth century. His findings have interesting and in many respects surprisingly astonishing applicability in evaluating Irish attitudes to the invaders who began to arrive on its shores from the late 1160s onwards.

John Reuben Davies examines the impact of cultural transmission, flowing from the Norman Conquest, on saints' cults in the march of Wales. He questions the veracity of the common perception that local cults were insensitively abolished, and churches re-dedicated in honour of more familiar, bona fide universal saints, that, in Wales, the cult of local saints had somehow imbued that nation with a distinctive national character and that the colonizers were in the business of imposing a continental culture upon what they – the colonizers – in their continental sophistication, perceived as a strange, foreign, backward people. His conclusion is that, while we cannot deny that the early Welsh March was the setting for political, cultural, and ecclesiastical conflict, we must do away with anachronistic political and religious judgments in evaluating the nature of that conflict, and that, as regards the cult of saints, conflict was tempered by a cultural transmission which passed as much from conquered to conqueror as the other way around.

Niav Gallagher also considers the experience of the church, exploring the emergence of national identity among the religious of Britain. Beginning with Canterbury's attempts to claim all the British Isles as its primatial right, she shows how the secular church had sought to extend England's spiritual rule into Wales, Scotland and Ireland and in doing so foreshadowed

England's political aspirations. Focusing in particular on the new mendicant orders, she argues that they came to identify closely with the communities, townspeople in particular, upon whom they depended for alms and gifts of property. A possible side-effect of this was a sense of, if not national identity, then native exclusivity that had, she believes, crept into the mendicant orders towards the end of the thirteenth century.

Freya Verstraten Veach, turning on its head the oft-repeated notion that the English settlers in Ireland in the later Middle Ages became 'more Irish than the Irish themselves', examines instead the considerable evidence for anglicization among the native Irish. She argues that this phenomenon was present even in the early stages of the English invasion and was a major influence on many throughout the medieval period: piecing together the various nuggets of information can be a very illuminating exercise which shows, among many other things, that acculturation in one geographical region or within a particular family can, on occasion, be linked with similar findings in another region or family.

Katharine Simms examines the transmission of foreign apologues into the bardic verse of late medieval Ireland. These apologues are summaries or outlines of pre-existing moral or historical tales which the most highly-educated poets were accustomed to insert now and then into their long eulogies, either to draw a flattering comparison between the patron they were addressing and some hero of the past like Cúchulainn or Alexander the Great. She argues that an examination of apologues used by bardic poets can give us some idea of the reading material at their disposal, being a sign of the poet's learning and wide reading. And by analysing surviving verse she demonstrates that, while the bulk of the tales the poets refer to in their apologues are drawn from the Irish saga cycles, and deal with the mythical King Conchobar mac Nessa of Ulster and his warriors of the Red Branch or Finn mac Cumaill and his Fianna warbands, or general 'historical' themes such as the highkingship of Tara, nevertheless there are some 134 poems which contain secular apologues of foreign origins in addition to purely religious anecdotes such as stories from the Bible or the apocrypha or tales of non-Irish saints, which thereby shed light on contemporary Irish engagement with the world beyond its shores. She concludes that that Irish poets may have accessed this material by reading printed English translations by Caxton and others of the medieval Latin anthologies, while their knowledge of classical and Arthurian material went step by step with the translation of various relevant texts into Irish, to be circulated in manuscript form, both in the eleventh and twelfth centuries before the English invasion, and again in the fifteenth and sixteenth centuries in response to the growth of lay literacy among the Irish and Anglo-Irish nobility.

Some views of the Normans in eleventh- and twelfth-century Ireland*

PATRICK WADDEN

The battle of Hastings in 1066 was one of the great turning points in the history of the British Isles. In the estimation of Rees Davies, it was as a result of the Norman conquest that 'the English domination of Britain and, eventually, Ireland resumed a momentum which was not to be exhausted until the early fourteenth century'.[1] Yet, as Davies pointed out, this event made little impact on the contemporary historical record of England's Celtic neighbours; it was not recorded in any of the major Irish annal collections.[2] In fact, the activities of the Normans in Britain were only rarely noted in the annals over the following decades, and then usually only when they affected Welsh or Scottish affairs.[3] It was not until one hundred years after Hastings, when the descendants of the Norman conquerors of England led the invasion of Ireland, that the annalists began to take regular notice of their actions. The goal of this study is to examine, as far as possible, how Irishmen viewed the Normans in the intervening period, before the expansion of the 'first English empire' across the Irish Sea.

That empire was founded on the twin pillars of the Anglo-Normans' military and economic prowess, but was reinforced and often legitimated by a parallel sense of cultural superiority. This sense of superiority is a notable feature of the writings of twelfth-century English historians, such as William of Malmesbury and Henry of Huntingdon, who envisaged 'civilized'

* This contribution is based upon a thesis submitted for the degree of Master of Studies at the University of Oxford in 2007. I am very grateful to my supervisor, Professor Thomas Charles-Edwards, for his guidance and support. I am also very thankful to Professor Huw Pryce, Professor Richard Sharpe and Dr Máire Ní Mhaonaigh for their advice on earlier drafts of what follows and to Professor Seán Duffy and Dr Susan Foran for the invitation to present this work at the 'First English empire?' conference. For all remaining errors, I alone am responsible. 1 R.R. Davies, *The first English empire: power and identities in the British Isles, 1093–1343* (Oxford, 2000), pp 4–5. 2 The Four Masters' record of the battle (*Annála ríoghachta Eirean: Annals of the kingdom of Ireland, by the Four Masters*, ed. J. O'Donovan (Dublin, 1856), 1066) is not from a contemporary source; that in the *Annals of Clonmacnoise* (ed. D. Murphy (Dublin, 1896), 1065) is actually a reference to the battle at Stamford Bridge misinterpreted by the seventeenth-century translator of that text, Conall MacGeoghegan. 3 *The annals of Ulster (to A.D. 1131)*, ed. and trans. S. Mac Airt and G. Mac Niocaill (Dublin, 1983), 1072, 1093; *The annals of Inisfallen*, ed. and trans. S. Mac Airt (Dublin, 1944), 1093; Davies, *The first English empire*, pp 4–5. The Annals of Tigernach (ed. and trans. W. Stokes (*Revue Celtique*, 16–18 (1895–7); repr. Felinfach, 1993, 2 vols)) and *Chronicon Scotorum* (ed. and trans. W.M. Hennessy, Rolls Series 46 (London, 1866)) record the death of Henry I in 1135.

England as being surrounded by countries whose inhabitants were wild barbarians.[4] The most famous expressions of this view, though, were the 'elaborate, interlocking, quasi-anthropological field reports' written by Gerald of Wales.[5] Gerald reserved his most venomous prose for the Irish. Indeed, his writings represent the most influential examples of a contemporary devaluation of Irish cultural and religious stock among a broad section of European society.[6] According to Gerald, the Irish were *gens silvestris, gens inhospita, gens ex bestiis solum et bestialiter vivens; gens a primo pastoralis vitae vivendi modo non recedens* ('a wild and inhospitable people. They live on beasts only and they live like beasts. They have not progressed at all from the primitive habits of pastoral living').[7] In examining contemporary Irish attitudes towards the Normans, we will be attempting to reconstruct the view from the other side of Gerald's lens. Ireland produced no figure comparable to Gerald, however, and there is no Irish equivalent of his ethnographic works that might have provided a focus for such a study. Instead it will be necessary, to paraphrase Ian Short, to scour a wide range of contemporary material in the somewhat hit-and-miss hope of finding incidental references that reveal their authors' attitudes.[8] The result will be no more than a series of patchy images representing the views contemporary Irishmen had of their new neighbours whose impact on British and Irish history was to be so momentous.

NORMANS IN IRISH SOURCES

The first problem encountered in such an investigation is locating the Normans within surviving Irish material. *Nordmanni* was one of several

4 J. Gillingham, 'Conquering the barbarians: war and chivalry in Britain and Ireland' in idem, *The English in the twelfth century: imperialism, national identity and political values* (Woodbridge, 2000), pp 41–58 (first published in the *Haskins Society Journal*, 4 (1992), 67–84); idem, 'Henry of Huntingdon and the twelfth century revival of the English nation' in idem, *The English in the twelfth century*, pp 123–44 (first published in S. Forde, L. Johnson and A. Murray (eds), *Concepts of national identity in the Middle Ages* (Leeds, 1995), pp 75–101). See also Davies, *First English empire*, pp 113–41; D. Bethell, 'English monks and Irish reform in the eleventh and twelfth centuries', *Historical Studies*, 8 (1971), 111–35. 5 Davies, *First English empire*, p. 115; R. Bartlett, *Gerald of Wales, a voice of the Middle Ages* (Stroud, 2006, originally published as *Gerald of Wales, 1146–1223* (Oxford, 1982)), pp 130–71. 6 J. Stewart, '*Topograhia Hiberniae*', *Celtica*, 21 (1990), 642–57; F.X. Martin, 'Gerald of Wales, Norman reporter on Ireland', *Studies*, 58 (1969), 279–92. For further examples of this phenomenon, see Warner of Rouen, *Moriuht, a Norman Latin poem from the early eleventh century*, ed. C. J. McDonough (Toronto, 1995), and D. Scully, 'Ireland and the Irish in Bernard of Clairvaux's Life of Malachy' in D. Bracken and D. Ó Riain-Raedel (eds), *Ireland and Europe in the twelfth century: reform and renewal* (Dublin, 2006), pp 239–56. 7 Gerald of Wales, *Opera*, ed. J.F. Dimmock, 8 vols (London, 1861–91), i, p. 151; *The history and topography of Ireland*, trans. J.J. O'Meara (London, 1951), p. 101. 8 I. Short, '*Tam Angli quam Franci*: self-definition in Anglo-Norman England', *Anglo-Norman Studies*, 18 (1996), 154.

terms used to denote viking raiders in ninth-century annals and in texts derived from them, but it disappeared after the middle of the tenth century as the term *Gaill* (foreigners) came into common use.[9] The old label was revived on a single occasion in the late eleventh century when the Annals of Tigernach recorded the death of *Goffraidh rex Normannorum* in 1095.[10] The subject of this entry was Gofraid Méránach (Godred Crovan), king of Man and one-time king of Dublin. He was described in his obit in the Annals of Ulster as *rí Gall* ('king of the foreigners') and in the Annals of Inisfallen as *ríg Átha Cliath 7 Inse Gall* ('king of Dublin and the islands of the foreigners (that is, the Hebrides)').[11] Contemporary eleventh- and twelfth-century annalists did not use the term *Normanni* to refer to the inhabitants of Normandy or the conquerors of England. Neither, it seems, was a term for Normandy in use in Ireland. Some Irish annals described Henry II as 'duke of Normandy' (*diuic na Normointi / dux Normanniae*) upon his arrival in Ireland, but they are later additions to the record and not contemporary with the events they describe.[12] The twelfth-century literary tale *Cath Ruis na Ríg for Bóinn* ('The battle of Ross na Rí on the Boyne') includes a reference to *Northmannia* alongside *Scithia*, *Dacia* and *Gothia*, but Donnchadh Ó Corráin has argued persuasively that this represents Norway and is listed alongside other Scandinavian countries by an author bent on displaying his broad geographical knowledge.[13]

There is no reason to believe that Normans did not, on occasion, cooperate with viking associates in raids on Ireland. The early eleventh-century Norman Latin poem *Moriuht* by Warner of Rouen claims that Irish slaves were traded in Normandy.[14] We also know that the Norman dukes offered refuge and access to markets to Danish armies raiding in England around the same time.[15] It was long believed that Normans participated in the battle of Clontarf, on the outskirts of Dublin, in 1014,[16] but this belief has recently been undermined. Contemporary Irish records of the battle make no mention of their presence, but a later account in *Cogadh Gaedhel re Gallaibh* ('The war of the Irish with the foreigners') claims that among the

9 AU, 842, 859, 863, 871, 873, 888, etc.; *Cogadh*, pp 16, 228. For the reliance of this section of *Cogadh* on the annals, see M. Ní Mhaonaigh, '*Cogad Gáedel re Gallaib* and the annals: a comparison', *Ériu*, 47 (1996), 101–26. 10 ATig, 1095. 11 AU, AI, 1095. 12 *Miscellaneous Irish annals A.D. 1114–1437*, ed. S. Ó hInnse (Dublin, 1947), pp 46 and 54; *Annála Uladh: Annals of Ulster otherwise Annála Senait, Annals of Senat: a chronicle of Irish affairs from A.D. 431 to A.D. 1540*, ed. and trans. W.M. Hennessy and B. Mac Carthy, 4 vols (Dublin, 1887–1901), 1171. 13 *Cath Ruis na Ríg for Bóinn*, ed. E. Hogan, Todd Lecture Series vol. 4 (Dublin, 1892), p. 10; D. Ó Corráin, 'The Vikings in Scotland and Ireland in the ninth century', *Peritia*, 12 (1998), 315–16. 14 Warner of Rouen, *Moriuht*, pp 90–1. 15 D.C. Douglas, *William the Conqueror: the Norman impact upon England* (London, 1964), p. 160. 16 L. Musset, 'Les relations extérieures de la Normandie du IXme au XIme siècle, d'après quelques trouvailles monétaires récentes', *Annales de Normandie*, 4 (1954), 37; D. Bates, *Normandy before 1066* (Harlow, 1982), p. 7.

foreign forces that fought at Clontarf were *Carlus ocus Ebric, da meic rig Franc* ('Carlus and Ebric, two sons of the king of the *Frainc*'), and others with names of a Norman flavour such as *Simond* (Simon), *Sefraid* (Geoffrey), *Bernard* (Bernard) and *Ricard* (Richard).[17] Another Irish record of the battle preserved in the Annals of Loch Cé also suggests a continental presence in the form of *Grisíne corad Pléimionnaibh, 7 Greisiam á Normannaibh* ('Grisine, a knight of the Flemings, and Greisiam from the Normans').[18] Máire Ní Mhaonaigh has questioned the historicity of these records, however, arguing that accounts of the famous battle became highly fictionalized relatively early. The references to the Norman presence at Clontarf in sources such as the *Cogadh* and the Annals of Loch Cé were late additions, she claimed, 'in the recounting of what was to prove a remarkably elastic affair' and are not reliable records.[19] There is, then, no contemporary evidence to support the belief that there were Normans at Clontarf, only 'late and fanciful reports of the battle'.[20] While it is not impossible that some Normans might have participated in viking raids in the British Isles, if they did they have left no mark on the historical record in Ireland.

So far as I am aware, there is only one contemporary reference to *Normanni* in an Irish source that can be taken with some certainty to refer to the inhabitants of Normandy or their descendants in Britain. Around 1107, Gilbert, bishop of Limerick, wrote to Anselm, archbishop of Canterbury, and congratulated him on having tamed *indomitas Normannorum mentes* ('the untamed minds of the Normans'), so that elections and consecrations of abbots and bishops were being carried out according to canonical rules.[21] This reference is unique in the Irish material and therefore deserves attention. It is a notable feature of all the letters sent by Irishmen to Anselm that they addressed him as *archipraesul Anglorum* ('archbishop of the English') rather than *archiepiscopus* or *servus Cantuariensis*, as Anselm tended to call

---

17 *Cogadh Gaedhel re Gallaibh: the war of the Gaedhil with the Gall*, ed. and trans. J.H. Todd (London, 1867), pp 152, 206–7. The identities of the first mentioned seem to be slightly confused in the mind of the author of the *Cogadh*. Although here listed as sons of the king of the *Frainc*, this designation does not occur again. There is later mention of *Elbric mac ri Lochland* (p. 164) and *Carlus ocus Ciarlus da mac righ Lochlann* (p. 206). 18 *The annals of Loch Cé*, ed. W. Hennessy (Dublin, 1939), 1014. 19 M. Ní Mhaonaigh, *Brian Boru: Ireland's greatest king?* (Stroud, 2007), p. 67; A.J. Goedheer, *Irish and Norse traditions about the battle of Clontarf* (Haarlem, 1938), pp 24–30, 118. 20 C. Downham, *Viking kings of Britain and Ireland: the dynasty of Ívarr to A.D. 1014* (Edinburgh, 2007), p. 134. Lesley Abrams has also recently demonstrated that the *Normanni* said by Adémar of Chabannes to have participated in a great battle in Ireland about this time were not from Normandy but *ex Danamarcha et Iresca regione* ('from Denmark and the Irish region'). Adémar of Chabannes, *Chronique*, ed. J. Chavanon (Pars, 1897), pp 176–7; L. Abrams, 'England, Normandy and Scandinavia' in C. Harper-Bill and E. van Houts (eds), *A companion to the Anglo-Norman world* (Woodbridge, 2003), p. 53. 21 *Sancti Anselmi Cantuariensis Archiepiscopi opera omnia*, ed. F.S. Schmitt (6 vols, Edinburgh, 1951–61), v, p. 374.

himself in his correspondence.[22] If Anselm was archbishop of the English, why then did Gilbert congratulate him on taming the minds of the *Normanni*? There may be a hint in Anselm's reply to Gilbert, which states that the two men had previously encountered each other at Rouen.[23] It may have been his experience in Rouen that caused Gilbert to use the more specific term. While there, Gilbert might have encountered strident assertions of Norman identity, for it was during this period that the Normans' propagandists were creating what has been called the 'Norman myth'.[24] Specifically, there are in Gilbert's phrase echoes of the famous words of the greatest of the Norman myth-makers, Orderic Vitalis. Orderic wrote that *indomita gens Normannorum est et nisi rigido rectore coherceatur ad facinus promptissima est* ('the Normans are an untamed race, and unless they are held in check by a firm ruler they are all too ready to do wrong') and compared them with *indomitus onager* ('an untamed ass').[25] Orderic seems only to have begun writing his *Ecclesiastical history* about 1109, the year of Anselm's death, so Gilbert could not have been drawing upon knowledge of his work.[26] The possibility remains, however, that he was influenced by the image of themselves that the Normans were propagating during this period and that he encountered in Normandy.

From the above examples, however, it is evident that Bishop Gilbert's terminology was not consistent with general Irish usage, probably because most Irish authors were not as well informed as he was. This solitary example aside, it appears that the Irish had no equivalent to the Welsh use of *Normanyeit* or *Normannigeni* to denote the inhabitants of northern France who claimed descent from earlier 'Northmen'.[27] The solution to this problem is not, however, particularly elusive. As mentioned above, the primary Irish annal collections failed to record the battle of Hastings in 1066,

22 Ibid., pp 372, 373, 374, 375, 382 for example. For more discussion on these titles see M.T. Flanagan, 'High-kings with opposition, 1072–1166' in D. Ó Cróinín (ed.), *A new history of Ireland*, i: *prehistoric and early Ireland* (Oxford, 2005), pp 912–13.   23 *Sancti Anselmi opera omnia*, v, p. 375. Denis Bethell has discussed this reference and placed it within the context of the changes occurring both within England and between the Irish and English churches in the aftermath of the Norman conquest of England: 'English monks', 126.   24 R.H.C. Davis, *The Normans and their myth* (London, 1976); M. Chibnall, *The Normans* (2nd ed., Oxford, 2006), pp 107–24; G. A. Loud, 'The *gens Normannorum*: myth or reality?' *ANS*, 4 (1982), 104–16.   25 *The ecclesiastical history of Orderic Vitalis*, ed. and trans. M. Chibnall (6 vols, Oxford, 1969–1990), v, pp 24–5; iv, pp 82–3. See also iii, pp 98–9 and vi, pp 456–7. Orderic was prone to discussions of the Normans' less praiseworthy characteristics: E. Albu, *The Normans in their histories: propaganda, myth and subversion* (Woodbridge, 2001), pp 180–213.   26 *The ecclesiastical history of Orderic Vitalis*, i, p. xiv.   27 *Brut y tywysogyon* ed. T. Jones, *Brut y tywysogyon or the Chronicle of princes: Red book of Hergest version* (Cardiff, 1955), 1066, 1087. The terms are usually only used in titles, the conquerors of England generally being referred to as *Ffreinc*. See W.J. McCann, 'The Welsh view of the Normans in the eleventh and twelfth centuries', *Transactions of the Honourable Society of Cymmrodorion* (1991), 45–7.

but the event did not escape the attention of Irish chroniclers entirely. Marianus Scottus, or Máel Brigte (d. 1083), an Irish monk who wrote his chronicle in Mainz within fifteen years of the conquest, described Duke William's army at Hastings as *Franci*, reserving the use of *Nordmanndi* for the Norwegians who fought at Stamford Bridge earlier in the same year.[28] Marianus' use of these terms is consistent with other European commentators for whom, despite their Norman leadership, the victors at Hastings were *Franci*.[29] The same 'French' terminology was also used by the author of what appears to be the only nearly-contemporary historical source written in Ireland to have recorded the battle. The so-called 'Short annals of Armagh' seem to have been written in the 1130s, and cover the period from the coming of St Patrick to Ireland down to 1134.[30] As Robin Flower noted, this text contains several notices of eleventh-century events that are not found elsewhere in Irish sources, including the following record for the year 1066:

bás Edbaird rig Saxan 7 [...] cath Arailt fri Lochlannaibh dú hi torcair tri mili do Lochlannaibh im in rig 7 noi mile do Shaxanaib 7 [...] cath Arailt iterum fri Francu du i torchair Araltt uadein.[31]

the death of Edward, king of the English, and [...] Harold's battle against the Norwegians, in which three thousand of the men of Norway were killed around the king and nine thousand of the English, and [...] Harold's other battle against the French in which Harold himself was killed.

It was likewise as *Frainc* that the contemporary Irish annals described the Normans active in Scotland and Wales in the 1070s and 1090s, and it had been as *Frainc* ('French') that they described the inhabitants of Rouen in 1045 and as *rí Franc* ('king of the French') that they described the duke of Normandy in 1027.[32]

Similar terminology is found in the Welsh *Brutiau* and the Anglo-Saxon Chronicle, in the latter case in both pre- and post-conquest entries.[33] The account in the chronicle of Marianus, which contrasts the *Nordmanni* of Stamford Bridge with the *Franci* of Hastings, suggests the possibility that the use of the latter term on the part of Irish chroniclers to depict the

28 Marianus Scottus, *Chronicon*, ed. G. Waitz, *MGH, scriptores*, 5 (Hannover, 1844), p. 559. 29 E. van Houts, 'The Norman conquest through European eyes', *English Historical Review*, 110 (1995), 832–53. 30 R. Flower, *Catalogue of Irish manuscripts in the British Museum*, 2 (London, 1926), pp 490–1. 31 G. Mac Niocaill, '*Annála gearra as proibhinse Ard Macha*', *Seanchas Ardmhacha*, 3 (1959), 340. The translation is my own. 32 ATig, AClon, CS 1027; ATig 1045; AU 1072; AU, AI 1093. 33 *Brut y Tywysogyon*, 1072, 1073, 1074, 1109, 1175 are just some examples. See McCann, 'The Welsh view', 45–7. Similarly *The Anglo-Saxon chronicle*, ed. D. Whitelock, with D.C. Douglas and S.I. Tucker (London, 1961), 1051, 1052, 1088, 1107. That the 'Normans' in pre-Conquest England were just as varied in background as were the conquerors themselves has been illustrated by C.P. Lewis, 'The French in England before the Norman conquest', *ANS*, 17 (1994), 123–44.

conquerors of England may have been intended to avoid semantic confusion associated with the use of 'Norman'. Cecily Clark dismissed this argument in her discussion of the use of the terms *France* and *frencisce* in the Anglo-Saxon Chronicle.[34] In the eleventh and twelfth centuries *Francia* was, strictly speaking, the royal demesne of the French king, and the *Franci* were its inhabitants. There was, however, another way in which *Francia* could be used – to denote 'the realm feudally subject to the king of France', as Clark put it, that is, roughly the area of modern France.[35] Both usages are found in the contemporary text of the Anglo-Saxon Chronicle. Just as there existed 'greater' and 'lesser' meanings of *Francia*, so too there could be more and less inclusive uses of *Franci*. Within *Francia*, political, territorial and ethnic divisions were of great importance in defining men's identities, as demonstrated by the Normans' own chroniclers who worked so assiduously to distinguish themselves from the *Franci*.[36] But Duke William's army at Hastings and those he settled in England after the conquest were not just Normans, there were also men from Flanders, the Boulonnais, Picardy and elsewhere.[37] Outside their homeland, especially when under a single political leader, it was shared language and territory that became the key factors in their identity. Hence, for example, one of the earliest of William I's charters, in Old English, is addressed to his subjects as *Frencisce* and *Englisce*, a formula which was later to become standardized in Latin as *Francis et Anglis*.[38] George Garnett has argued that these addresses show that the chancery considered William's subjects to consist 'of two, and only two, races – French and English'.[39] More recently, Richard Sharpe has suggested that the address clauses of eleventh- and twelfth-century English royal charters specifically address language rather than ethnic groups.[40] As Ian Short has argued, the conquerors, 'whether or not they were actually Normans rather than natives of Picardy, Flanders or Brittany, all could identify themselves primarily as speaking the language of the French. *Franci*, in other words, designated those French-speaking incomers originating from the geographical area known as *Francia*.'[41]

For the Irish, it appears that the intricacies of the political and territorial

---

34 C. Clark, '"France" and "French" in the Anglo-Saxon Chronicle', *Leeds Studies in English*, 3 (1969), 40. 35 Ibid., 35–45. 36 Davis, *The Normans and their myth*; Chibnall, *The Normans*, pp 107–24; Loud, 'The *gens Normannorum*', 104–16. 37 D.C. Douglas, *William the conqueror: the Norman impact upon England* (London, 1964), pp 266–7. 38 *Regesta regum Anglorum: The acta of William I*, ed. D. Bates (Oxford, 1998), nos 180 (p. 593), 31 (p. 192), 66 (p. 305), 80 (p. 342), 276 (p. 832) (Old English) and nos 5 (p. 116), 10 (p. 125), 35 (p. 196), 336 (p. 973) (Latin). 39 G. Garnett, '*Franci et Angli*: the legal distinction between peoples after the conquest', *ANS*, 8 (1986), 109–37. 40 R. Sharpe, 'Addressing differed language-groups: the evidence of royal charters from the eleventh and twelfth centuries', delivered at the conference *Multilingualism in medieval Britain, 1100–1400: sources and analysis* (University of Bristol, 11 July 2008). 41 Short, '*Tam Angli quam Franci*', 163.

divisions within *Francia* were either unknown or considered of little importance. In the early eleventh century, for example, the annals record the deaths
of two individuals given the title *rí Franc* ('king of the *Frainc*').[42] One of
these men was actually a duke of Normandy (either Duke Richard II or
Duke Richard III who died only a few months apart) and the other was Odo,
count of Blois. What Lewis says of the English at this time is therefore also
true of the Irish, 'the difference between a Norman and a Boulonnais was
uninteresting: they spoke varieties of what was recognizably the same
language, they shared the same culture, they lived in the same kingdom.'[43]
The linguistic aspect of identity was considered particularly important in
Ireland. The author of the late eleventh-century *Irish sex aetates mundi* set
himself the task explaining why it appeared that there were more nations in
the world than languages, even though there had originally been seventy-two
of each.[44] His inventive solution to this difficulty was to say that although the
number of nations (*cenéla*) had multiplied, those that did not possess their
own languages were considered 'lesser-nations' (*fo-chenéla*). These 'lesser
nations' were not to be enumerated among the true nations of the world but
rather were to be considered part of the greater nations with which they
shared their language.[45] Had the author been trying specifically to explain the
Irish use of *Frainc* he could hardly have put it better.

To Irishmen, all speakers of French were *Frainc* and, Bishop Gilbert
aside, there is no evidence that they recognized the Normans' distinct
identity. This contrasts once again with the situation in Wales where, at least
by the middle of the twelfth century, there was an awareness of the viking
ancestry claimed by the Normans. The text known as *Historia Gruffud vab
Kenan* ('The history of Gruffyd ap Cynan') was probably written during the
reign of Owain Gwynedd (d. 1170).[46] It is a biography of Owain's father,
who was born in Dublin in the late eleventh century to a Welsh father and a
Hiberno-Norse mother. He was raised in the city before returning to Wales

---

42 ATig, 1027, 1038.   43 Lewis, 'The French in England', 130.   44 *The Irish sex aetates
mundi*, ed. and trans. D. Ó Cróinín (Dublin, 1983), pp 67, 111: 'Ocus innat lia na cenéla oldát na
bérlae? Cia lín cenél 7 citni cenéla ná fuillet numir cenél acht a ngabáil i fothechdas na cenél ata
coibniusda dóib?' ('Are the races more numerous than the languages? How many races are there,
and what are the peoples that do not complete the enumeration of the races but which are
included in the races that are related to them?')   45 *The Irish sex aetates mundi*, pp 73–4, 115: 'ar
itát isind Affraic ilchenéla im oénbérla 7 iss ed fot-era sein, ná rabatar acht dá cenél sechtmogat
tall in tan ro-imdaigthe na bérla 7 ciaro-imdaigset na cenéla post ní tharta i n-áirim cenél n-
écsamail acht a lécud hi fothechdas na cenél n-aile ata coibniusta dóib' ('for there are in Africa
many races with the same language and the cause of that was that there were only seventy-two
races there when the languages were multiplied, and though the races multiplied subsequently
they are not listed in the enumeration of the distinct races, but are subordinated to the other races
that are related to them').   46 S. Duffy, 'Ostmen, Irish and Welsh in the eleventh century',
Peritia, 9 (1995), 387–96.

to claim the kingship of Gwynedd.[47] The text claims that Gruffudd, and hence Owain, were descended through Gruffudd's mother and the royal dynasty of Dublin from Haraldr *Haarfager* ('Fairhair') of Norway and, further, that Haraldr was the brother of Rollo, founder of Normandy and ancestor of England's Norman kings.[48] It is highly unlikely that this is an accurate account of Rollo's origins,[49] but was probably constructed to help foster better relations between the Welsh rulers and their Norman neighbours. It is tempting to think that this information came to North Wales from Dublin with Gruffudd and that a tradition existed among the vikings of Dublin that they were related to the Norman dukes, but there is no way to verify this. All we can be sure of is that some people in Wales were aware of the Normans' viking ancestry while there is no evidence that anyone in Ireland was. To the Irish, the conquerors of England were *Frainc* and if we are to discover anything about Irish attitudes toward them it is to depictions of the *Frainc* we must turn. Given the scarcity of references to them in the historical record, however, we must look elsewhere.

THE *FRAINC* IN IRISH LITERATURE

The eleventh and twelfth centuries witnessed great literary activity in Ireland, including the composition of new texts and the redaction of older ones. In recent decades it has become increasingly apparent that these texts were shaped to a very significant degree by the context within which their authors and redactors wrote.[50] It is not surprising, then, to discover that several contemporary works allude to the presence of the Normans in Britain. This becomes apparent when texts of the ninth and tenth centuries are compared with those of the eleventh and twelfth. *Cath Maige Mucrama*, ('The battle of Mag Mucrama') dates from the earlier period.[51] Its plot follows a common structure – the hero, Mac Con, was forced to flee from

---

47 For the date and context of the composition, see S. Duffy, 'Ostmen, Irish and Welsh in the eleventh century', *Peritia*, 9 (1995), 387–96. 48 *Historia Gruffud vab Kenan* (*The history of Gruffyd ap Cynan*), ed. A. Jones, (Manchester, 1910), pp 104–6; *Vita Griffini filii Conani: the medieval Latin life of Gruffudd ap Cynan*, ed. P. Russell (Cardiff, 2005), pp 54–6. See also McCann, 'The Welsh view', 55–8. 49 For more on which see D. Douglas, 'Rollo of Normandy', *English Historical Review*, 57, no. 228 (1942), 417–36. 50 See, for example, M. Herbert, '*Fled Dúin na nGéd*: a reappraisal', *Cambridge Medieval Celtic Studies*, 18 (1989), 75–87; idem, 'The death of Muirchertach Mac Erca: a twelfth-century tale' in F. Josephson (ed.), *Celts and Vikings: proceedings of the fourth symposium of Societas Celtologica Nordica* (Gothenburg, 1997) pp 27–39; idem, '*Caithréim Cellaig*: some historical and literary considerations', *Zeitschrift für celtische Philologie*, 49–50 (1997), 320–32. 51 Máirín O Daly (*Cath Maige Mucrama: The battle of Mag Mucrama* (Dublin, 1975), p. 18) dates the text to the ninth century. Myles Dillon (*The cycles of the kings* (Oxford, 1946, repr. Dublin, 1994), p. 16) places it in the tenth 'at the latest'.

Ireland and sought refuge in Alba before later returning to Ireland with an army to claim the kingship of Tara. That army was provided by the king of Alba, his host while he was in exile:

'Rí Alban atom-chomnaic-se. Ingen ríg Bretan mo máthair. Ingen ríg Saxan mo ben. Nos beir-siu latt uile fri dígail th'osnaide' [...] Dos-n-uc didiu int óenfher for óenslúagad uile in muintir-se. An ro-baí iarum di longaib 7 tibarnaib 7 bárcaib i n-airiur Saxan 7 Bretan tarchomlátha co mbátar i Purt Ríg i nAlbae 7 todlach mór di churachaib leo.

'I am the king of Alba. My mother is the daughter of the king of the Britons. My wife is the daughter of the king of the Saxons. You will take them all with you to avenge your wrong' [...] So the one man took all these people on a single warlike expedition. All the ships and galleys and boats that were on the coast of the Saxons and the Britons were assembled and they were in Port Ríg in Alba and a great concourse of curachs with them.[52]

Similarly, in the tenth-century *Scéla Cano Meic Gartnáin* ('Stories of Cano son of Gartnán'), the hero, Cano, collects forces in Alba for an attack on Ireland and these consist of *Saxain 7 Bretain 7 fir Alban* ('the English, the Britons, the men of Alba').[53]

Implicit in these statements is the understanding that those groups consti-tuted all of the peoples of Britain, listed by the author in order to exaggerate the magnitude of a battle or the achievement of a hero. The authors and scribes who composed or copied texts during the eleventh and twelfth centuries made a notable addition to these lists in recognition of the new presence in Britain. *Fled Dúin na nGéd* ('The feast of Dún na nGéd') is one of a number of texts based on the historical, seventh-century battle of Mag Rath between Domnall mac Áeda, king of Tara, and Congal Cláen, king of the Ulaid. Máire Herbert has argued that this text dates from the early years of the twelfth century in the wake of the battle of Mag Coba in 1103.[54] The story follows a plot very similar to that of *Cath Maige Mucrama* – Congal was forced to flee to Alba before returning with reinforcements:

Tinolaid Congal iar sin sloig Saxan ocus a rig .i. Garb mac Rogairb, ocus sloig na Fraingce ocus a rig .i. Dairbhre mac Dornnmair, ocus sloig Bretan fa Conan Rod mac Echach Aingcis ocus firu Alban fa ceithri macaib Eachach Buide.

Congal assembled hosts of the Saxons with their king, Garb son of Rogarb, and the hosts of the French with their king, Dairbre son of Dornmar, and hosts of the Britons under Conan Rod son of Echu Aingcis, and the men of Alba under the four sons of Eochaid Buide.[55]

---

52 *Cath Maige Mucrama*, pp 46–8. 53 *Scéla Cano Meic Gartnáin*, ed. D.A. Binchy, Medieval and Modern Irish series, 18 (Dublin, 1963), p. 16. 54 Herbert, '*Fled Dúin na nGéd*', 75–87. 55 *The banquet of Dun na n-Gedh and the battle of Magh Rath*, ed. and trans. J. O Donovan (Dublin, 1842), pp 82–3. I have altered the translation to give a more literal sense.

A similar pattern is evident in the recension of *Orcuin Néill Noígíallaig* ('The slaying of Niall of the Nine Hostages') in the twelfth-century manuscript Rawlinson B 502. According to Máire Ní Mhaonaigh, the verse sections of this text can be dated to the ninth century, and the prose to the eleventh.[56] The poem explains Níall's epithet in the following terms:

Ethais gíall cach cói[ci]d	He had a hostage from each province
fo thír nÉrenn ardda,	throughout the land of Ireland,
tuc fri réir cen terbba	he brought against their will, without severance,
cethri géill a hAlba.	four hostages from Alba. [57]

On the other hand, the prose surrounding the poem explains that the appellation was earned because Níall held *cóic géill Hérenn 7 gíall Alban 7 gíall Saxan 7 gíall Bretan 7 gíall Franc* ('five hostages of Ireland and a hostage from Alba and a hostage of the Saxons and a hostage of the Britons and a hostage of the French').[58]

In such examples, as in the earlier literature, the setting is still the British Isles. In *Fled Dúin na nGéd*, Congal left Ireland to find shelter and support in Alba, just as Mac Con had in *Cath Maige Mucrama*. It was here that the heroes met the peoples that accompanied them back to Ireland. The *Frainc* here listed are not continental Franks and the inclusion of the *Frainc* among the participants in the battle of Mag Rath in *Fled Dúin na nGéd* does not, as Moisl and Hamann have argued, suggest the presence of a Frankish noble at the battle.[59] Neither the contemporary sources, nor the earlier, more accurate, literary account of the battle include any reference to such involvement. The inclusion of the *Frainc* in these lists represents, rather, the authors' recognition of the arrival of the 'French' in Britain and a projection into the distant past of the situation as it existed in their own day. The great Welsh scholar Ifor Williams resisted this interpretation, believing that the anachronism of placing Normans in tales set in the distant past would have troubled the authors of these stories.[60] Rather, Williams argued, the use of

56 M. Ní Mhaonaigh, 'Níall Noígíallach's death-tale' in J. Carey, M. Herbert and K. Murray (eds), *Cín Chille Cúile: texts, saints and places. Essays in honour of Pádraig Ó Riain* (Aberystwyth, 2004), pp 178–91.   57 *Orcuin Néill Noígíallaig*, ed. K. Meyer, 'Stories and songs from Irish manuscripts', *Otia Merseiana*, 2 (1900–01), 87, 90. I have altered Meyer's translation slightly. 58 Ibid. I have altered Meyer's translation. See also *Cóir anmann: a late Middle Irish treatise on personal names*, ed. S. Arbuthnot (2 vols, London, 2005–7, ITS 59, 60), 1, p. 113; 2, pp 33–4. 59 H. Moisl and S. Hamann, 'A Frankish aristocrat at the battle of Mag Rath' in M. Richter and J.-M. Picard (eds), *Ogma: essays in Celtic studies in honour of Próinséas Ní Chatháin* (Dublin, 2002), pp 36–47.   60 I. Williams, *Lectures on early Welsh poetry* (Dublin, 1970), pp 28–31. See also, idem, '*franc; francamuis*', *Bulletin of the Board of Celtic Studies*, 7 (1933–5), 366–8; idem, *The beginnings of Welsh poetry*, ed. R. Bromwich (2nd ed., Cambridge, 1980, 1st ed. 1972), pp 95–6. For more on the use of *franc* in Old Welsh see see K. Meyer, *Miscellanea Hibernica*, University of Illinois studies in language and literature, 2 (Urbana, 1917), 35 and J. Rowland, 'Old Welsh

the term *Franc* in Irish literature was related to the use of the term in Old Welsh to denote a mercenary soldier. This does not appear to have been the case. In the first instance, the attestation of the Welsh word dates to the ninth or possibly as early as the seventh century, several hundred years prior to the earliest Irish occurrence.[61] Furthermore, anachronisms such as these are hardly uncommon in Irish literature of the period. Indeed, they were a tool of the trade for some authors, including the composer of the early twelfth-century *Lebor na Cert* ('The book of rights'), who described a meeting between St Patrick and the vikings of Dublin.[62]

DEPICTIONS OF THE *FRAINC*

If, as has been argued above, the presence of the *Frainc* in eleventh- and twelfth-century Irish literary texts reflects their authors' and redactors' cognisance of the presence of the Normans in contemporary Britain, then the depiction of the *Frainc* in these sources offers us our best opportunity to discern Irish attitudes toward the new rulers of England. On the occasions when the *Frainc* appear in Irish texts it is often, as in the above examples, in a list of the peoples of Britain. Nonetheless, there are other instances when we can infer a little more about the authors' feelings toward them from the context in which they appear. In the eleventh-century text of *Orcuin Néill*, for example, the *Frainc* are depicted as enemies of Níall's followers. According to this version of the tale, Níall was killed in Alba (Scotland). After his death, as his followers retreated toward Ireland they were attacked by the *Frainc* and seven battles were fought between them.[63] Níall was the ancestor of the Uí Néill, a group of dynasties spread across the midlands and the north of Ireland. Though this story is set in the early fifth century, I suggest that it might be read as an indication that the Uí Néill, or some portion of them, felt a certain animosity toward the Normans in the eleventh century.

The most powerful of the Uí Néill dynasties during the late eleventh and early twelfth centuries was Cenél Eóghain, whose power extended across what is now northern and central Ulster. The legendary founder of Cenél Eóghain power, and first of the line supposedly to have held the kingship of Tara, was Muirchertach mac Ercae, grandson of the eponymous Eóghan. Muirchertach features in a twelfth-century Irish text in which he is depicted as an enemy of the *Frainc*. *Do fertaib Cairnich* ('Concerning the miracles of

franc: an Old English borrowing?', *Cambrian Medieval Celtic Studies*, 26 (1993), 21–5. 61 Williams, '*franc; francamuis*', 366–8. 62 *Lebor na Cert*, ed. M. Dillon, Irish Texts Society, 46 (Dublin, 1962), pp 114–19. 63 *Orcuin Néill*, pp 87–91.

[Saint] Cairnech') claims that Muirchertach was the son of Erc, daughter of Loarn mac Eirc, king of Scotland, and most of the story is set in Britain.[64] There Muirchertach is said to have fought several battles against the king of the *Frainc* and to have destroyed the lands of the *Fraingc 7 Saxain* ('French and English') before returning to Ireland to take the kingship of that island.[65] *Do fertaib Cairnich* is one of a number of eleventh- and twelfth-century texts that asserts this genealogical relationship between Cenél Eóghain and Cenél Loairn, the descendants of Loarn mac Eirc, a link that Francis John Byrne believed was constructed to reflect the emergence of the rulers of Moray as a political force in the eleventh century.[66] Moray, the territory based around the Moray Firth, was ruled during this period by a dynasty that claimed to belong to Cenél Loairn. Whether it was an independent kingdom or a province of the kingdom of Alba/Scotland is debated, but between the early eleventh and the early twelfth centuries the rulers of Moray attempted to wrest the kingship of Alba from the dynasty that had ruled it since its emergence in the ninth century.[67] The rulers of Alba claimed descent from Fergus mac Eirc, Loarn's brother. These struggles have been portrayed as a conservative reaction by the rulers of Moray, who were more entrenched in the Gaelic world, against the kings of Alba, who had embraced in turn Anglo-Saxon and Norman culture.[68] It is a notable feature of the sources that document these events that while those from England and the southern heartland of Scotland are hostile towards the rulers of Moray, those from Ireland are more willing to recognize the legitimacy of their claims.[69] For example, in 1130 when the last in the line of Cenél Loairn rulers of Moray, Óengus, invaded Alba the Annals of Ulster give him the title *rí* ('king') while Orderic Vitalis calls him *comes* ('earl') of Moray.[70] On that occasion, King David of Scotland was absent at the court of Henry I of England, but the men of Moray were routed and their territory conquered by Edward, son of Siward, one of a group of Anglo-Saxon nobles who sought refuge at the

64 *Do Feartaib Cairnich*, ed. J.H. Todd, *Leabhar Breathnach annso sis: the Irish version of the Historia Britonum of Nennius* (Dublin, 1848), pp 178–81. **65** *Do Feartaib Cairnich*, pp 190–3. **66** F.J. Byrne, 'Ireland and her neighbours, c.1014–1072' in Ó Cróinín (ed.), *NHI* i, pp 896–7. Other texts that attest this version of Muirchertach's genealogy include 'The Ban-shenchus [part 2]', ed. and trans. M. Dobbs, *Revue Celtique*, 48 (1931), 180–1, and Flann Mainistrech, *A ngluind a n-échta a n-orgni batar infir*, ed. and trans. J. MacNeill, 'Poems by Flann Mainistrech on the dynasties of Ailech, Mide and Brega', *Archivium Hibernicum*, 2 (1913), 70, 75. **67** A. Woolf, 'The "Moray question" and the kingship of Alba in the tenth and eleventh centuries', *Scottish Historical Review*, 79, no. 208, part 2 (2000), 145–64; R.A. McDonald, *Outlaws of medieval Scotland: challenges to the Canmore kings, 1058–1266* (East Linton, 2003). **68** G.W.S. Barrow, *Kingship and unity: Scotland 1000–1306*, The New History of Scotland 2 (London, 1981), pp 23–42. **69** S. Duffy, 'Ireland and Scotland, 1014–1169: contacts and caveats' in A.P. Smyth (ed.), *Seanchas: essays presented to Francis J. Byrne* (Dublin, 2000), pp 347–50. **70** AU 1130; *The ecclesiastical history of Orderic Vitalis*, iv, pp 276–7.

Scottish court after the Norman conquest.[71] Alongside the Anglo–Saxons at his court, David was responsible for establishing and promoting the settlement of Normans in Scotland, including Moray, which was, after 1130, under the control of the kings of Scotland.[72]

The sympathy shown by Irish sources toward the rulers of Moray likely reflects the existence of political alliances between some Irish rulers and the 'rebels'.[73] Clear evidence for the existence of such alliances is difficult to find, but at a slightly later date Muirchertach Mac Lochlainn, king of Cenél Eóghain and claimant to the high-kingship of Ireland in the middle of the twelfth century, seems to have had a friendly relationship with Somerled, the semi-independent ruler of Argyll, who backed the claims of another groups of challengers to the Scottish kings in the 1150s and who died during an invasion of Scotland in 1164.[74] Is it possible that the enmity between Muirchertach mac Ercae and the *Frainc* described in *Do Fertaib Cairnich* is related to the fact that Cenél Eóghain was involved in a political dispute in Scotland that pitched it against Normans? This question cannot be answered definitively at present, but it seems a real possibility.

Not all texts that refer to the military activities of the *Frainc* depict them as enemies of the Irish. They are sometimes described as mercenaries in the service of Irish kings. In *Aided Guill maic Carbada ocus aided Gairb Glinne Rige* ('The violent death of Goll son of Carbad and of Garb of Glenn Rige'), which Thurneysen dated to the twelfth century, we find *francamuis* ('French mercenaries') in the service of Conchobar mac Nessa, king of the Ulaid.[75] The soldiers' names are not French, which may be one of the reasons why Williams was loathe to see in this term a reference to the Normans, but this is not the only reference to *Frainc* in the employment of an Irish king. Another example can be found in a metrical tract of the mid-eleventh century in which the following lines occur:

Cuirn maicc Donnchada	The drinking horn of Donnchad's son,
dlegait buidechas	(yellow and bright-peaked),
buide benngela;	deserves thanks:
Francaig fognama	Frenchmen in his service,
fine chuindgeda	an importunate kindred,
sanntaig senmeda.	greedy for old mead.[76]

71 *The ecclesiastical history of Orderic Vitalis*, iv, pp 276–7. Orderic calls Moray a *ducatus* ('duchy'). 72 A.A.M. Duncan, *Scotland, the making of the kingdom*, The Edinburgh History of Scotland 1 (Edinburgh, 1975), pp 133–73, especially 138–9; Barrow, *Kingship and unity*, pp 43–59. 73 Duffy, 'Ireland and Scotland', pp 348–50. 74 McDonald, *Outlaws of medieval Scotland*, pp 77–9, 87–97, 128–30, 160–1. 75 *Aided Guill Meic Carbada ocus Aided Gairb Glinne Rige*, ed. W. Stokes, *Revue Celtique*, 14 (1893), 426–7; R. Thurneysen, *Die irische Helden- und Königsage bis zum siebehnten Jahrhundert* (Halle, 1921), p. 485. 76 Ed. R. Thurneysen, 'Mittelirische Verslehren' in W. Stokes and E. Windisch, *Irische Texte* (3rd series, 2 vols, Leipzig, 1891), i, p.

Thurneysen dated these verses to the 1050s.[77] The son of Donnchad here mentioned is Diarmait mac Máel na mBó, who was king of Leinster during that period, and the poem has been cited as evidence for the presence of Norman soldiers in Ireland during his reign.[78] In 1051–2, Anglo-Saxon England was the scene of conflict between the powerful family of Godwin, earl of Wessex, and the Norman faction in the court of Edward the Confessor. Ultimately, the Normans lost this battle and many of them were forced to flee the kingdom. Some are known to have fled north and found employment in the army of MacBethad mac Findláich, king of Scotland. There they lived for two years until they were killed in a rout of the Scottish king's army by Earl Siward of Northumbria.[79] Those Normans who travelled north to Scotland had previously held castles in Herefordshire on the Welsh border. If these men were willing to make the long overland journey to Scotland, it is quite feasible that others took ship and crossed the Irish Sea to Leinster where they entered Diarmait's service. Byrne thought it possible that Norman mercenaries 'were not unfamiliar at the courts of Irish kings' throughout this period.[80]

Diarmait's *Frainc*, despite being in his service, do not seem to have had a very good reputation. In fact, the short verse just quoted is just one of a number of Irish texts that contain similar depictions of the *Frainc*. The Irish poem beginning *Cumtach na n-Iudaide n-ard* ('The architecture of the noble Jews') is one such example.[81] This poem is a versified translation into Middle Irish, the form of the Gaelic language used between *c*.900 and *c*.1200, of the tract *De proprietatibus gentium* ('On the characteristics of peoples') composed in Oviedo *c*.900.[82] The Irish poem follows its exemplar in listing such stereo-typical national characteristics as the wisdom of the Greeks, pride of the Romans and anger of the Britons. Where most versions of the Latin text refer to *ferocitas Francorum* ('the ferocity of the Franks'), however, the Irish poem has instead *sant hi Frangcaib* ('greed in Frenchmen').[83] Two other

90; ed. K. Meyer, *Bruchstücke der älteren Lyrik Irlands* (Berlin, 1919), p. 18, no. 36; trans. F.J. Byrne, 'The trembling sod: Ireland in 1169' in A. Cosgrove (ed.), *New history of Ireland*, ii: *medieval Ireland, 1169–1534* (Oxford, 1987), p. 22. I have altered Byrne's translation slightly. **77** R. Thurneysen, *Zu irischen Handschriften und Literaturdenkmälern* (Berlin, 1912), p. 89. **78** Byrne, 'The trembling sod', p. 22. **79** *The chronicle of John of Worcester*, vol. ii, ed. R.R. Darlington and P. McGurk, tr. J. Bray and P. McGurk (Oxford, 1995), pp 572–3; F. Barlow, *Edward the Confessor* (London, 1970), pp 124–6; A. Woolf, *From Pictland to Alba, 789–1070*, New Edinburgh History of Scotland 2 (Edinburgh, 2007), p. 261. **80** Byrne, 'The trembling sod', p. 22. **81** K. Meyer, 'Two Middle Irish poems', *Zeitschrift für celtische Philologie*, 1 (1897), 112–13. **82** *De proprietatibus gentium*, ed. T. Mommsen, *MGH, Auctores Antiquissimi*, 11 (Berlin, 1894), p. 389; H. Walther, 'Sherz und Ernst in der Völker- und Stämme-Charakteristik mittelleinischer Verse', *Archiv für Kulturgeschichte*, 41 (1959), 263–301; P. Meyvaert, '"*Rainaldus est malus scriptor Francigenus*"– voicing national antipathy in the Middle Ages', *Speculum*, 66 (1991), 743–6. **83** Meyer, 'Two Middle Irish poems', 112–13. I have altered Meyer's translation slightly. A

eleventh-century poems, *A ngluind a n-échta a n-orgni batar infir* ('Their deeds, their death-dealings, their devastations that were manly'), by Flann Mainistrech, and *Rédig dam a Dé do nim* ('Make easy for me, O God from heaven'), by Dublittir ua hUathgaile, also support the idea that the *Frainc* were associated with a greedy character. The former, dated by MacNeill to between 1047 and 1056, concerns the history of the kingdom of Ailech. Referring to events of 717, Flann wrote *Selaig flaith féic for Bregmaig. Ní franc forbbaig acht is Conall Grant Úa Cernaig* ('Fergal cut down a fierce lord that ruled over the plain of Brega, not an extorting Frank, but Conall Grant grandson of Cernach').[84] *Rédig dam* was written in south Leinster at the end of the eleventh century.[85] It claims that the *Frainc* were descended from Francus and that *ni denaid saint im saebgním* ('[he] was not wont to be greedy in doing wicked deeds').[86] Here the poet defends the *Frainc* against the charge that they are greedy, but the fact that he felt the need to do so speaks to the existence of a belief that they were.[87]

It appears, then, that there existed in eleventh-century Ireland a belief that the *Frainc* were a greedy people. What might have been the origin of this perception? One possibility is that the *Frainc* in the service of Diarmait mac Máel na mBó cultivated such an image, as Normans did in other parts of Europe. See, for example, the work of Geoffrey Malaterra, chronicler of the Normans' conquests in Sicily, who described the Normans as *quippe gens astutissima, iniuriarum ultrix, spe alias plus lucrandi patrios agros vilipendens, quaestus et dominationis avida, cuiuslibet rei simulatrix ac dissimulatrix, inter largitatem et avaritiam quoddam medium haben*s ('a very shrewd people indeed, quick to avenge injury, scorning the fields of their homeland in hope of acquiring something more, avid for profit and domination, ready to feign and conceal anything, maintaining a certain balance between avarice and largess').[88] Geoffrey's chronicle post-dates these Irish sources and there is no evidence that anything comparable had reached Ireland by the 1050s, yet the possibility remains that the Normans in Ireland might have been happy to cultivate such an image of themselves, as they evidently were elsewhere.

---

seventeenth-century version of the poem alters this to read *santaidhe* which fits better with the metre: T. Ó Raithbheartaigh, *Genealogical tracts I* (Dublin, 1932), pp 24–5.   84 Flann Mainistrech, *A ngluind a n-échta a n-orgni batar infir*, 71 and 76.   85 *The Irish sex aetates mundi*, pp 41–8.   86 Ibid., pp 104, 135. I have altered Ó Cróinín's translation slightly.   87 The image died hard. See E. Curtis, 'Murchertach O'Brien, high-king of Ireland and his Norman son-in-law, Arnulf de Montgomery, *circa* 1100', *Journal of the Royal Society of Antiquaries of Ireland*, 51 (1921), 124: 'Ireland, rich, at hand and politically unstable, was in the minds of the restless and greedy Norman race.'   88 Geoffrey Malaterra, *De rebus gestis Rogerii Calabriae et Siciliae comitis et Roberti Guiscardi ducis fratris eius*, ed. E. Pontieri, Rerum Italicarum Scriptores 5, part 1 (2nd ed., Bologna, 1928), p. 4; trans. K.B. Wolf, *The deeds of Count Roger of Calabria and Sicily and of his brother, Duke Robert Guiscard* (Michigan, 2005), p. 53.

It seems more likely, however, that the negative impression of the *Frainc* evident in the above-mentioned sources owes its origin to the political alliances of Diarmait mac Máel na mBó. Diarmait was an ambitious king whose aspirations were not confined to the island of Ireland. Through his conquest of Dublin in 1052 he acquired a claim to authority in the Kingdom of the Isles, a claim his son, Murchad, attempted to realize in 1061 by extracting tribute from the inhabitants of Man.[89] Diarmait also appears to have had Welsh connections, possibly including a claim to overlordship in Gwynedd.[90] The Welsh had experience of dealing with Normans from when Edward the Confessor had established his nephew, Ralph of Vexin, in Hereford in 1049, and had faced them in battle in 1055.[91] It appears, however, that at this stage the Welsh considered Ralph a leader of the English rather than a representative of a different people. The antagonism towards those they termed the *Freinc* or *Normanyeit*, which is so notable in Welsh sources at the end of the eleventh century, did not develop until after the conquest of England, too late to have influenced a poet at Diarmait's court in the 1050s.[92]

Diarmait's political aspirations were given a boost by events in England in 1051. As a result of the conflict between the competing factions at the court of Edward the Confessor, in that year Earl Godwin and his family were proscribed and fled from the kingdom into exile. Godwin himself went to Flanders but a number of his sons, including the future King Harold, sought refuge in Ireland. In Diarmait they found a willing ally who provided them with an army with which they returned to England the following year to reclaim their positions.[93] This alliance between the king of Leinster and the house of Wessex proved resilient. In the aftermath of the battle of Hastings a number of King Harold's sons retraced their father's footsteps to Leinster and once again they found that assistance for their cause was forthcoming. With Diarmait's help, they launched unsuccessful attempts to regain their father's kingdom in 1068 and 1069.[94] The perspective of the family of Earl Godwin on these events can be seen, first, in their actions upon their reinstatement in 1052. At the great council at which they were pardoned,

89 ATig, 1052, 1061; S. Duffy, 'Irishmen and Islesmen in the kingdoms of Dublin and Man, 1052–1171', *Ériu*, 43 (1992), 93–133.   90 Duffy, 'Ostmen, Irish and Welsh', 386–7.   91 *Brut y Tywysogyon, RBH*, p. 24; McCann, 'The Welsh view', 39; R.R. Davies, *The age of conquest: Wales 1063–1415* (Oxford, 1987), pp 25–6; Lewis, 'The French in England', 129.   92 McCann, 'The Welsh view', 39, 49–51.   93 *Vita Ædwardi Regis qui apud Westmonasterium requiescit*, ed. and trans. F. Barlow (London, 1962), pp 24–5; B. Hudson, 'The family of Harold Godwinsson and the Irish Sea province,' *JRSAI*, 109 (1979), 92–100; Byrne, 'Ireland and her neighbours', pp 888–9.   94 *Gesta Normannorum ducum*, ed. E.M.C. van Houts, 2 vols (Oxford, 1992–95), ii, p. 181; *The ecclesiastical history of Orderic Vitalis*, ii, pp 224–5. For an alternative interpretation that sees Tairdelbach Ua Briain as the sponsor of the 1068 and 1069 expeditions, see S. Duffy, '"The western world's tower of honour and dignity": the career of Muirchertach Ua Briain in context' in Bracken and Ó Riain-Raedel (eds), *Ireland and Europe*, pp 58–9.

many of the king's Norman companions were banished from the kingdom.[95] Ironically, some of them may also have ended up in Diarmait's court, as we have seen. The 'Godwinist' E-text of the Anglo–Saxon Chronicle was in no doubt as to who had been to blame for the family's recent difficulties: 'Archbishop Robert was declared utterly an outlaw, and all the Frenchmen too, because they were responsible for the disagreement between Earl Godwine and the king.' [96] Unsurprisingly, this attitude did not soften after the battle of Hastings. *Vita Ædwardi Regis qui apud Westmonasterium requiescit* ('The life of King Edward who rests at Westminster') appears to have been begun before the conquest of England and finished soon afterward at the behest of Edward's widow, Edith, daughter of Godwin and sister of Harold. Although, as its editor put it, 'the anonymous [author of the *Vita*] is not simply "Godwinist", like the E-version of the Anglo–Saxon Chronicle', in tone the narrative is sympathetic to the fate of its patron's family.[97] According to the *Vita*, it was the men of *Francia* who were to blame for the misfortunes suffered by the Godwins.[98] Subtle references to dissatisfaction with the preferential treatment of Edward's French allies can be read in a number of places in the text, including the following comment about Robert of Jumièges, archbishop of Canterbury: *quique potissimum, ut aiunt, regi semper astitit a secretis, eiusque consilio plurima tum digna tum indigna in regno contingebant* ('who, they say, was always the most powerful confidential advisor to the king. By his counsel many things both good and bad were done in the kingdom').[99] Harold's antagonism toward the French in England is acknowledged during the scene which describes Edward's death. On his deathbed, the ailing king is said to have bequeathed his kingdom to his brother-in-law on the condition that Harold protect his sister, Edward's wife, and that he promise not to harm the foreigners who had come to the kingdom out of love for Edward. Instead, he is instructed either to take oaths of allegiance from them or to send them safely home across the Channel.[1] Whether the story is true or not, it reflects the fact that Harold disliked the Norman element Edward had introduced to his court. Paraphrasing a common trope in Irish historiography, Francis John Byrne referred to the resentment felt by the family of Godwin towards the Normans, 'who had now become more French than the French'.[2] It was likely from the family of King Harold, therefore, that the Irish of Leinster gained their negative perception of the *Frainc*.

So far, then, the different images of the *Frainc* we have encountered in

95 Lewis, 'The French in England', 129.   96 *The Anglo–Saxon chronicle*, p. 125.   97 F. Barlow, *The Godwins: the rise and fall of a noble dynasty* (Harlow, 2002), pp 40–1.   98 *Vita Ædwardi*, p. 17.   99 Ibid., pp 11, 17.   1 Ibid., pp 79–80.   2 Byrne, 'Ireland and her neighbours', pp 888–9.

Irish literature have been largely negative. There is another text, however, that offers a much more positive perspective. *Cogadh Gaedhel re Gallaibh* dates from the reign of Muirchertach Ua Briain, most likely between the years 1103 and 1113.[3] It purports to relate the history of the Irish wars against the vikings, especially the activities of Brian Bóruma, Muirchertach's great-grandfather and predecessor as both king of Munster and claimant to the high-kingship of Ireland. In actuality, the author was 'recreating the past ever mindful of the present'.[4] He was probably writing at Muirchertach's behest and the depiction of Brian and his actions in the text are often best understood as references to the career of his great-grandson.[5] The reference in this text to the 'two sons of the king of the *Frainc*' among Brian's opponents at Clontarf has already been mentioned. In a later passage designed to eulogize the Uí Briain, however, the dynasty is described as *Frainc na Fotla fondairdi, ar glicus ocus ar glangaisced .i. meic aibda, ailli, uasli, illbuadacha, Israeil nath Érend illataaigthi, ar cadi, ocus ar cunlacht, ar firinni, ocus ar inracus* ('the French of ancient Ireland, in intelligence and pure valour; the comely, beautiful, noble, ever-victorious sons of Israel of Ireland, for virtue, for generosity, for dignity for truth and for worth').[6] As Benjamin Hudson states, this amounts to a 'definite statement of good feeling towards the Normans' on the part of the Uí Briain.[7] Not only that, but it was also a statement of aspiration, of the Uí Briain's view themselves, and their desire to have others view them as holding the same status in Ireland as the Normans did in Britain. Donnchadh Ó Corráin writes that:

the example of Anglo-Norman England lay close at hand [. . .] We are to understand *Frainc* as Normans and the terms taken literally must mean that the Uí Briain, regarding themselves as the chosen dynasty, intended to extend their rule over all Ireland as the conquering Normans had recently done in England.[8]

After Brian's death at the battle of Clontarf, it took two generations for his descendants to regain the position he had carved out for himself as the most powerful king in Ireland. The first to do so was Tairdelbach Ua Briain (d. 1086), whose accomplishment was matched by his son, Muirchertach (d. 1119). They not only united most of Ireland under their authority, they also extended their authority beyond Irish shores. At the time the *Cogadh* was being written, Muirchertach had a realistic claim to be king of Ireland, had

3 M. Ní Mhaonaigh, '*Cogad Gáedel re Gallaib*: some dating considerations', *Peritia*, 9 (1995), 354–77. 4 Ní Mhaonaigh, *Brian Boru*, p. 46. 5 Ibid., pp 45–6; idem, '*Cogad Gáedel re Gallaib*: some dating considerations', 374–6. 6 *Cogadh*, pp 160–1. I have altered Todd's translation slightly. 7 B. Hudson, 'William the Conqueror and Ireland', *Irish Historical Studies*, 29 (1994), 156 (reprinted in idem, *Irish Sea studies, 900–1200* (Dublin, 2006), pp 109–22). 8 D. Ó Corráin, 'Nationality and kingship in pre-Norman Ireland' in *Nationality and the pursuit of national independence*, Historical Studies 11 (Belfast, 1978), p. 35.

gained authority over the Kingdom of the Isles and even cast himself in the role of king-makers in North Wales.[9] Like Diarmait mac Maíl na mBó, Tairdelbach and Muirchertach Ua Brian sought to bolster their position in Ireland through forging alliances with those they considered their peers in Britain. Although Tairdelbach Ua Briain had been Diarmait mac Maíl na mBó's protégé, after the latter's death in 1072, he did not maintain the policy of assisting the family of King Harold in their struggle to regain their kingdom.[10] Benjamin Hudson has argued that an alliance existed between Tairdelbach and William the Conqueror from as early as the year of Diarmait's death when Tairdelbach took control of Dublin.[11] Within two years of that event, Tairdelbach was corresponding with Archbishop Lanfranc of Canterbury, and letters would continue to flow between Canterbury and the circle of the Uí Briain kings over the following decades.[12] There is no reason to believe that the connections between the Uí Briain and the highest levels of Anglo-Norman society were restricted to the ecclesiastical sphere. As Hudson pointed out, Lanfranc was not just archbishop of Canterbury, but also 'the Conqueror's personal friend, and throughout their association the two men laboured towards similar goals'.[13] Tairdelbach's communication with Lanfranc was probably only one aspect of his relationship with William I. The arrival of a Jewish embassy at Tairdelbach's court in 1079 might lend weight to this argument; Rouen then had the largest Jewish population in north-western Europe and it is very possible that they originated from there and that their mission may have been backed, or at least approved, by William.[14]

Tairdelbach's son, Muirchertach, continued his father's policy of friendship with the highest levels of Anglo-Norman society. Letters continued to flow between Ireland and Canterbury during his reign, and later tradition claimed that he supplied William Rufus with timber to build Westminster Hall.[15] We can be certain, however, that Muirchertach was not always on good

9 J. Ryan, 'The O'Briens in Munster after Clontarf', *North Munster Antiquarian Journal*, 2 (1941), 141–52; 3 (1942), 1–52; Duffy, '"The western world's tower of honour and dignity"', p. 59; idem, 'Ireland, c.1000–c.1100' in P. Stafford (ed.), *A companion to the early middle ages: Britain and Ireland c.500–c.1100* (Oxford, 2009), pp 285–302. The reference in the *Cogadh* (p. 208) to Brian as *ardrí Érenn ocus Alban ocus Saxan ocus Bretan ocus iartair Eorpa* ('high sovereign of Erinn, and Albain, and of the Saxons, and Britons, and of the west of Europe') was probably meant to legitimize the fact that Muirchertach had achieved considerable power outside of Ireland. 10 See note 98 above. 11 Hudson, 'William the Conqueror and Ireland', 145–58. 12 *The letters of Lanfranc, archbishop of Canterbury*, ed. H. Clover and M. Gibson (Oxford, 1979), pp 71–73; M.T. Flanagan, *Irish society, Anglo-Norman settlers, Angevin kingship: interactions in Ireland in the late twelfth century* (Oxford, 1989), pp 7–55; A. Gwynn, *The Irish Church in the eleventh and twelfth centuries*, ed. G. O'Brien (Dublin, 1992), pp 39–40, 46–7, 99–115. 13 Hudson, 'William the Conqueror and Ireland', 151; Duffy, '"The western world's tower"', p. 65. 14 AI, 1079; Hudson, 'William the Conqueror and Ireland', 154; Flanagan, 'High-kings with opposition', p. 903. 15 J.O. Prestwich, 'War and finance in the Anglo-Norman state',

terms with the English king. In 1102, Muirchertach entered into an alliance with the Anglo-Norman lord Arnulf de Montgomery. Arnulf and his more illustrious brother, Robert de Bellême, earl of Shrewsbury, had fallen foul of Henry I because of their participation in a rebellion intended to place Henry's brother, Duke Robert of Normandy, on the English throne.[16] In need of support they turned to Muirchertach, a sign of his increasing importance as a presence on the international scene. To cement their alliance Arnulf was married to Muirchertach's daughter, an event that the Annals of Inisfallen, by this date 'a court chronicle for the descendants of Brian', described as a marriage-alliance between Muirchertach and the *Frainc*.[17] The *Brut y Tywysogion* claims somewhat enigmatically that this event 'made peace' between the 'French' and the Irish, but it did not enamour Muirchertach to Henry I, who imposed trade restrictions on Ireland in response and apparently brought the Irish king to heel with relative ease.[18] After being banished from England, so Orderic Vitalis informs us, Arnulf spent some time with his father-in-law in Ireland before returning to his family lands in Normandy.[19] As well as offering him a temporary safe-haven, Muirchertach may also have tried to use his relationship with Anselm of Canterbury to Arnulf's benefit, he certainly wrote to the archbishop thanking him for intervening on Arnulf's behalf.[20] The intimacy of these relationships between Muirchertach and the Anglo-Normans was perhaps the inspiration for a poem found in the *Cogadh* that claims that *ba hoirderc isin domain toir / imaircor Briain hi Frangcoib* ('Illustrious in the eastern world / was the conduct of Brian among the French').[21]

There is more to the description of the Uí Briain as *Frainc na Fotla* than just a statement of friendship and of the aspirations of Muirchertach to be seen as possessing the same dominance in Ireland as the Normans did in Britain. The *Cogadh* ascribes a certain military, religious and intellectual superiority to the Uí Briain as the basis for their success. Just as the Normans' own propaganda described them as possessing an innate superiority, *Normanitas*, because of which they were predestined to conquer the lands of others, so the *Cogadh* espouses a certain 'Uí Briain-*itas*'. The military might of the Munster dynasty is a constant theme and reaches its hyperbolic peak with the description of Murchad mac Briain at Clontarf:

Royal Historical Society Transactions, 5th series, 6 (1964), p. 31; M. Hanmer, *The chronicle of Ireland*, ed. J. Ware, *Two histories of Ireland* (Dublin, 1633, repr. Amsterdam, 1971), p. 97. 16 Curtis, 'Murchertach O'Brien', 116–34. 17 AI 1102; B. Hudson, *Prophecy of Berchán: Irish and Scottish high-kings in the early Middle Ages* (London, 1996), p. 94. 18 *Brut y Tywysogyon*, 1102; William of Malmesbury, *De gestis regum Anglorum*, ed. W. Stubbs, Rolls Series (2 vols, London, 1887–89), vol. 2, pp 484–5. 19 *The ecclesistical history of Orderic Vitalis*, vi, pp. 31, 48–51. Presumably Orderic meant Normandy when he said that Arnulf 'fled to his own people'. Certainly he would not have been welcome in England and his brother had previously returned to the family lands in Normandy. 20 *Sancti Anselmi opera omnia*, v, p. 372. 21 Ibid., pp 208–9.

Ro gabside a da claidium croda comnerta .i. claidium ina deis, ocus claidium ina cle, uair is
se sin duni dedenach ri ba comdeis imbualta da deis ocus da cli bai in nErind. Isa duni
dedenach irrabi in firgaisced in Erind é. Ise tuc a brethir firaig nach berad oen traig
teighchid reisin ciniud doenna uli, ar coma sa bith, acht minbad cinnti leis can ec tre bithu.
Ise duni dedenach irrabi comlond cet in Erind e. Ise duni dedenach ro marb cet in oen lo e.
[. . .] Robe sin intEctoir intamlaigteach na Erend [. . .] Ro besin intErcoil tanasi ro seris.

He grasped his two valiant strong swords, viz., a sword in his right, and a sword in his left
hand, for he was the last man in Ireland who had equal dexterity in striking with his right
and with his left hand. He was the last man that had true valour in Ireland. It was he that
pledged the word of a true champion, that he would not retreat one foot before the whole
of the human race, for any reason whatsoever but this alone, that he might die of his
wounds. He was the last man in Ireland who was a match for a hundred. He was the last man
who killed a hundred in a single day. [. . .] He was the metaphorical Hector of all-victorious
Ireland [. . .] He was the second powerful Hercules.[22]

Elsewhere Brian is praised highly for promoting learning during his reign: *Ro
cuiritt saoithe, ocus maighistreacha do theaccasscc eccna, ocus eolais, ocus do
chendach leabhar tar muir, ocus tar mórfhairrge* [. . .] *Brian imorro do beiredhsidhe
luach foghlama ocus luach leabhar do gach aon* ('He sent professors and masters
to teach wisdom and knowledge; and to buy books beyond the sea, and the
great ocean; [. . .] and Brian himself gave the price of learning and the price of
books to every one').[23] The statement that the Uí Briain were the *Frainc* of
Ireland for wisdom (*glicus*) and martial skill (*gaisced*) sums up this broad
characterisation and associates it explicitly with the *Frainc*.

'It was', wrote Robert Bartlett recently, 'an axiom of the Middle Ages' that
'scholarship and military power have always flourished in the same place' and
by the twelfth century it was increasingly believed that they were flourishing
in France.[24] In the words of Chrétien de Troyes: 'Our books teach us that
Greece first had the highest reputation for knighthood and learning and then
knighthood and the highest learning came to Rome. Now they have come to
France.'[25] Robert Bartlett has described Paris during this period as 'a
metropolis that drew all to it through an effortless and irresistible cultural
hegemony'.[26] Irishmen may have been among those drawn to the city to
study.[27] The statement that the Uí Briain were the *Frainc* of Ireland there-

---

22 *Cogadh*, pp 186–7. 23 Ibid., pp 138–9. 24 R. Bartlett, 'Heartland and border: the mental
and physical geography of medieval Europe' in H. Pryce and J. Watts (eds), *Power and identity in
the Middle Ages: essays in memory of Rees Davies* (Oxford, 2007), p. 35. 25 Chrétien, *Cligés*, ed.
A. Micha (Paris, 1957), pp 2, 11, 28–34, translation here cited from Bartlett, 'Heartland and
border', p. 35. 26 Bartlett, 'Heartland and border', p. 34. 27 Pádraig Ó Néill (P. Ó Néill, 'An
Irishman at Chartres in the twelfth century – the evidence of Oxford Bodleian Library,
manuscript Auct. F. III. 15', *Ériu*, 48 (1997), 1–35) has shown that there was an Irish scholar at
Chartres in the early twelfth century, and Michael Richter ('The European dimension of Irish
history in the eleventh and twelfth centuries', *Peritia*, 4 (1985), 338) has suggested Domnall Ua
hÉnna, court bishop of both Tairdelbach and Muirchertach Ua Briain, possibly also spent time

fore associated them with both the military and political might of the Normans and with the cultural prestige of France, 'modernity and power' in Bartlett's words.[28] That Muirchertach saw himself as belonging to Europe's cultural and political elite is suggested by his obit in the Annals of Ulster in which he is described as *ri Erenn 7 tuir ordain 7 airechais iarthair in domain* ('king of Ireland and tower of the honour and dignity of the western world').[29] *Cogadh Gaedhel re Gallaib* uses similar terms in eulogizing Brian Bóruma as *airdri Erenn ocus Alban, ocus Saxan ocus Bretan, agus iartair Eorpa* ('high-sovereign of Erinn and Albain, and of the Saxons, and Britons, and the west of Europe'), in describing Brian and his brother Mathgamain as *da tuir croda comnerta comcalma, da laec lonna letarraca luctmara, da comlaid cata, da cleit ugra, da dor didin, da rind aga ocus urlaimi, enig ocus egnuma brota ocus brigi bagi, ocus beodacta iartair Eorpa* ('two stout, able valiant pillars, two gates of battle, two poles of combat, two spreading trees of shelter, two spears of victory and readiness, of hospitality and munificence, of heart and strength, of friendship and liveliness, the most eminent of the west of Europe'), and in calling the Uí Briain *sebuic suarci sairsenga na hEorpa alli* ('graceful, symmetrical hawks of Europe').[30]

Rees Davies argued for a more Anglo-centric model of the process of cultural and political change that Robert Bartlett called 'Europeanization' within the British Isles, suggesting that 'the distinctively insular version of this process' should be termed 'anglicization'.[31] Some of those involved in the early stages of bringing Ireland into close harmony with the politics and culture of Europe's core societies, however, were conscious that the models they aimed to emulate were continental, specifically French. Support for this idea might be sought in a text that has only indirect links with Ireland in that it was not written in Ireland nor by an Irishman. St Bernard of Clairvaux's Life of St Malachy includes much information derived from Malachy's Irish companions on the Continent, but it also contains much that reflects the author's own beliefs. In a story about the building of an oratory in Bangor, the historicity of which is questionable, Bernard puts a speech into the mouth of a local man that contrasts starkly with the sentiments of the *Cogadh*. According to Bernard, Malachy's attempt to build in stone rather than wood met with considerable resistance from locals who disliked the sense of innovation it symbolized, causing one individual to state: *Scoti sumus non Galli*, ('we are Irish not French').[32] If any weight can be placed upon

in a French university. **28** Bartlett, *The making of Europe*, pp 101–5. **29** AU, 1119. **30** *Cogadh*, pp 56–9, 160–1. **31** Davies, *First English empire*, p. 170; Bartlett, *The making of Europe*, pp 269–91. **32** St Bernard of Clairvaux, *Vita Sancti Malachiae*, ed. J. Leclereq, H.M. Rochais, C.H. Talbot, *Sancti Bernardi opera* (8 vols, Rome, 1957–77), iii, 61; Scully, 'Ireland and the Irish in Bernard of Clairvaux's Life of Malachy', pp 239–56. **33** Gillingham, 'Henry of Huntingdon', pp 123–44; Short, '*Tam Angli quam Franci*'; J. Gillingham, 'The English invasion

Bernard's account as an expression of the sentiments of those opposed to the innovations Malachy championed, then we are left with the impression that to both its supporters and its opponents, the Europeanization of Ireland was perceived as being inspired by French examples.

CONCLUSIONS

A little over a century after the Normans conquered England, their descendants were among those who participated in spreading English rule over Ireland. By then the conquerors had begun to embrace their English identity and it was as Englishmen that the invaders were labelled most commonly in both their own and in Irish sources.[33] *Franci* occasionally appear in the address clauses of charters written in Ireland, [34] and are also mentioned in at least one Irish text of the post-invasion period, a fact which likely reflects the continuing presence of Francophones in their midst. In a poem addressed to Cathal Croibdhearg Ó Conchubair, king of Connacht, possibly dating from the 1190s, the *Frainc* appear alongside the Welsh and English as *in ré gránna garb* ('the ugly coarse shoal') that had come to attack the bright salmon of Ireland.[35] Although it is always dangerous to generalize about such issues, one might suspect that during the period of the extension of Anglo–Norman power across Ireland that this poet's sentiments might have reflected those of many of his countrymen towards the invaders. What we have seen above, however, is that there was no single Irish attitude towards the Normans during century that separates the Norman invasion of England from the English invasion of Ireland. The attitudes of Irishmen regarding the Normans, expressed through their depictions of the *Frainc* in literary texts, were contingent upon the immediate political context in which the authors found themselves. The Normans had different relationships with different Irish kings – to some they were rivals, to others allies. Attitudes changed over time as the leading Irish kings embraced the new political reality in Britain, but they also varied from region to region within Ireland. For some Irishmen, the *Frainc* were associated with military successes and cultural prestige they wished to emulate, for others they represented both a political and the cultural threat.

of Ireland' in idem, *The English in the twelfth century*, pp 145–60 (first published in B. Bradshaw, A. Hadfield and W. Maley (eds), *Representing Ireland: literature and the origins of conflict, 1534–1660* (Cambridge, 1993), pp 24–42); M.T. Flanagan, 'The Normans in Ireland' in *Irish history in the classroom: research resources and realization*, Seminar held at Cultra Manor, Holywood, Co. Down from 18th to 21st September 1986 (Belfast, 1987), pp 23–32; S. Duffy, *Ireland in the Middle Ages* (Dublin, 1997), p. 59; Davies, *First English empire*, p. 144. **34** S.J. Brooks, 'An unpublished charter of Raymond le Gros', *JRSAI*, 69, part 3 (1939), 167–9. **35** B. Ó Cuív, 'A poem composed for Cathal Croibhdhearg Ó Conchubair', *Ériu*, 34 (1983), p. 167.

The cult of saints in the early Welsh March: aspects of cultural transmission in a time of political conflict

JOHN REUBEN DAVIES

In 1911, Professor J.E. Lloyd summed up the ecclesiastical consequences of the Norman conquest and settlement in Welsh territories; his readership was informed of '[t]he subjugation of the Welsh church'.[1] This phase of Welsh ecclesiastical history, for Lloyd, could be summed up in the fortunes of church dedications to native Welsh saints:[2]

> The last mark of subjection [...] touched the realm of sentiment merely and yet was none the less keenly felt by a people so imaginative as the Welsh. This was the rededication of churches bearing the names of Welsh founders unknown to the Christian world at large, to saints of wider reputation, commemorated throughout the length and breadth of Christendom [...] it was the substitution of the modern and the civilized for the antique and the grotesque. But in the eyes of the Welshman, it was the displacement of the ancient presiding genius of the place; the new patron [...] was not, like the old, rooted in the soil and endeared by a thousand happy memories [...] In general [...] the effect was [...] to uproot many ancient ecclesiastical landmarks, which told of the heroic days, lying far back in the past, of the church now fallen into weakness and bonds.

Lloyd wrote in this way of the sentimentality of his medieval forebears, it seems, without any sense of irony.

Eight decades after Lloyd's *History* was first published, R.R. Davies, in his own landmark work, *Conquest, coexistence and change*, devoted one of the most substantial chapters to 'Church and religion in an age of change'.[3] Davies' analysis took its lead from Lloyd, although his stylish prose was less emotive. On the question of Normans and the dedications of churches in Wales, he said what follows:[4]

> Towards the native church the Normans showed scant respect [...] its patrons were a motley crowd of unfamiliar 'saints' sporting outlandish names [...] The Welsh saints were treated [...] cavalierly [...] Some were entirely demoted, to be replaced by patrons drawn

1 John Edward Lloyd, *A history of Wales from the earliest times to the Edwardian conquest*, 2 vols (London, 1911), ii, pp 447–61. Sir John Edward Lloyd (1861–1947) was professor of history at the University College of North Wales, Bangor (now known as Bangor University), from 1899 until his retirement in 1930; see R.R. Davies, 'Lloyd, Sir John Edward (1861–1947)' in *Oxford dictionary of national biography*, ed. H.C.G. Matthew and Brian Harrison, 61 vols (Oxford, 2004) [*ODNB*]. 2 Lloyd, *History of Wales*, ii, pp 458–9. 3 R.R. Davies, *Conquest, co-existence, and change: Wales, 1063–1415* (Oxford, 1987), republished in paperback as *The age of conquest: Wales, 1063–1415* (Oxford, 1991), ch. 7 (pp 172–210). 4 Ibid., pp 181–2.

from the international calendar [...] Elsewhere, the native saints were too firmly established and their cults too profitable for such unceremonious demotion; even so, the merits of a local saint might be supplemented by those of an international colleague [...] Most remarkable was the way in which St David was pushed into second place by St Andrew at the cathedral church of Dewi himself [...] just as St Peter naturally took precedence over St Teilo at Llandaf.

Shorn of Lloyd's patriotic sentimentality, Davies' account represented an apparently more reasonable interpretation of events; yet it was fundamentally the same view as Lloyd presented. Davies, like Lloyd, told of the way local cults were insensitively abolished, and churches re-dedicated in honour of more familiar, bona fide universal saints. So at Glasbury, St Cynidr was ousted by St Peter (Prince of the Apostles); at Caerwent, St Tathan was removed in favour of St Stephen (the Protomartyr); at Cilgerran, St Llawddog was displaced by St Lawrence (an early Roman martyr, notoriously roasted alive). In the case of some stubborn local cults, St John the Evangelist joined forces with St Teulyddog at Carmarthen, and St Peter and St Paul bolstered the intercessory powers of St Trinio at Llandrinio.[5]

A view closely similar to Lloyd's also came out in the last book to attempt a serious overview of the ecclesiastical history of early medieval Wales – a work published as long ago as 1977. Siân Victory's *Celtic church in Wales* continued to advance the erroneous idea that Welsh church life before the advent of William the Conqueror was by definition 'Celtic'; this concept was bound up with Victory's implicit acceptance that the active cult of local saints ended in Wales with the arrival of Norman colonizers, who re-dedicated churches to universal saints.[6] Owen Chadwick too, writing two decades earlier, had made a similar assumption in his essay on 'The evidence of dedications in the early history of the Welsh church'.[7]

But this version of history, which J.E. Lloyd made respectable, and which R.R. Davies perpetuated, was flawed. They took for granted that foreign intruders had invaded a nation; and not just a nation, but one where the cult of local saints flourished; where the cult of local saints somehow imbued that nation with a distinctive national character. What is more, they assumed that these colonizers were in the business of imposing a continental culture upon what they – the colonizers – in their continental sophistication, perceived as a strange, foreign, backward people.

This impression, formed and communicated by Lloyd and Davies, was coloured, one suspects, by an outlook that might have accompanied their deep commitment to Welsh language and culture, as well as Welsh

5 Ibid., p. 182.   6 Siân Victory, *The Celtic church in Wales* (London, 1977); pp 35 and 129, illustrate the point nicely.   7 In N.K. Chadwick (ed.), *Studies in early British history* (Cambridge, 1954; rev. imp., 1959), pp 173–88.

Congregationalist and Presbyterian religion.[8] The sincere sentiments of historians concerned for the future of a culture under pressure appears to have leaked into the wash of their narratives, like a scarlet garment in a machine full of whites.

Lloyd's sugary impression of a religious past, 'endeared by a thousand happy memories', was at least blatant in its sentimentality. Davies' premises were not quite so overt, but were there none the less. He presupposed a 'native' church for which the 'Normans' showed 'scant respect'; these Normans were held to have viewed the 'Welsh' saints as a 'motley crowd' who were only so-called 'saints'; and having Welsh names, they were apparently 'outlandish' to the Normans; as such they were treated 'cavalierly'. An examination of the sources, however, exposes Lloyd's and Davies' narrative as a profound misrepresentation of the evidence.

CHURCH DEDICATIONS

The idea that Normans engaged in a general rededication of churches throughout their sphere of influence sprang from a book published in 1836, written by a young Welsh clergyman, Rice Rees (1804–39), professor of Welsh at St David's College, Lampeter.[9] In *An essay on the Welsh saints*, he wrote,[10]

That the Roman Catholics, or, at least, the various conquerors of Wales, all of whom professed that religion, hardly considered the primitive founders in the light of Saints, will further appear from the circumstance that in many instances they gave their churches a new dedication.

Rees went on to give a list of seventeen churches where he thought that a church dedication to a 'Welsh' saint had been changed in favour of a more familiar universal saint (see the appendix to this chapter). Rees, however, was

---

8 Lloyd was chairman of the Union of Welsh Congregationalists ('Lloyd', *ODNB*); Davies was a lifelong Welsh Presbyterian (R.J.W. Evans, 'Davies, Sir (Robert) Rees (1938–2005)', *ODNB*). The present author declares his hand as an English-speaker, brought up in a clerical family of the Church in Wales (a province of the Anglican Communion). As I hope to show, it was in fact nineteenth-century Welsh Anglicans (writing in a patently partisan spirit, typical of the religious climate of that era) who were at the root of the imperfect understanding of the nature of saints' cults in eleventh- and twelfth-century Wales.   9 J.E. Lloyd, 'Rees, Rice (1804–1839)', rev. by N. Banerji, in *ODNB*. Rees was a nephew of W.J. Rees, who took over the editing of the Book of Llandaf upon the former's premature death: *The liber Landavensis: Llyfr Teilo* (Llandovery, 1840). The latter Rees also produced *The lives of the Cambro-British saints* (Llandovery, 1853). 10 *An essay on the Welsh saints: or the primitive Christians usually considered to have been the founders of churches in Wales* (London, 1836), p. 70: this was certainly J.R. Phillips' inspiration (see n. 21, below).

relying, first, on the supposition that the original dedication of churches corresponded to the person who lent his name to a *llan-* toponym; second, that the apparently new dedications were contemporary with the period of Norman settlement; and third, that it was Normans or Anglo-Normans who made any such changes.[11] Let us first consider the examples cited by Lloyd and Davies.

The patron of Glasbury, on the border between Brycheiniog and Herefordshire, was Cynidr, an important local saint of Brycheiniog. In the past, Glasbury had been the seat of a bishop, but there is good reason to think that the community at Glasbury had collapsed in the middle of the eleventh century when the bishopric based there ceased to exist, subsumed as it seems in the diocese of Hereford.[12] In 1088, Bernard de Neufmarché, who was in the course of dominating the minor kingdom of Brycheiniog, made a gift of Glasbury to St Peter's Abbey, Gloucester, together with the 'church of St Cynidr' (*ecclesia sancti Kenedri*).[13] By the nineteenth century, the rebuilt parish church was dedicated to St Peter; yet there is nothing in the cartulary of Gloucester Abbey to suggest such a rededication in the twelfth century.[14] *De situ Brecheniauc*, a text copied around 1200 for an Anglo-Norman patron, associated Cynidr with Glasbury (*sanct[us] Kenider de Glesbyri*);[15] in 1910, A.W. Wade-Evans thought Cynidr was the dedication.[16] Churches associated with Cynidr are clustered in a triangle between Glasbury, Kenderchurch (near Ewyas Harold, on the river Dore in Archenfield; *Lann Cinitr* in the Book of Llandaf),[17] and Llangynidr (near Crickhowell).[18] Indeed, the church of Cynidr at Kenderchurch was consecrated in the reign of William I

---

11 The present author dealt both with Rees' religious prejudices and with the problem of equating Welsh ecclesiastical place names with church dedications in 'The saints of South Wales and the Welsh church' in A.T. Thacker and R. Sharpe (eds), *Local saints and local churches in the early medieval West* (Oxford, 2002), pp 361–95.   12 John Reuben Davies, 'The archbishopric of St David's and the bishops of *Clas Cynidr*' in J. Wyn Evans and Jonathan M. Wooding (eds), *St David of Wales: cult, church and nation*, Studies in Celtic History 24 (Woodbridge, 2007), pp 296–304.   13 William Henry Hart (ed.), *Historia et cartularium monasterii sancti Petri Gloucestriæ*, Rolls Series 33, 3 vols (London, 1863–67), i, p. 314, no. 281. David Walker ('The "honours" of the earls of Hereford in the twelfth century', *Transactions of the Bristol and Gloucestershire Archaeological Society*, 79 (1960), 174–211, at 193, n. 3) thought the date of this gift might have been as late as 1104.   14 In 1868, the parish church was said to be ruinous; the advowson continued in the hands of the bishop of Gloucester after the dissolution.   15 *De situ Brecheniauc*, London, British Library, MS Cotton Vespasian A. xiv, fos. 10v–11v; A.W. Wade-Evans (ed.), 'The Brychan documents', *Y Cymmrodor*, 19 (1906), 18–50, at 26.   16 A.W. Wade-Evans, 'Parochiale Wallicanum', *Y Cymmrodor*, 22 (1910), 22–124, at 43 (also published as a single volume, Stow-on-the-Wold, 1911, p. 23, cited hereafter).   17 J. Gwengovryn Evans (ed.), *The text of the Book of Llan Dâv, reproduced from the Gwysaney manuscript* (Oxford, 1893), pp 275, 277.   18 The church of Llangynidr was dedicated to Cynidr at the time of Pope Nicholas' assessment of 1291 (*Taxatio ecclesiastica Angliae et Walliae auctoritate papae Nicholai IV*, Record Commission (London, 1802) [available online at http://www.hrionline.ac.uk/taxatio/]), where it appears as *Ecclesia de sancto Kened*.

(1066–87).[19] We should also notice that St Cynidr was entered in the *kalendar* that accompanies a collection of saints' lives that we shall encounter later in this chapter; a collection that was put together under the auspices of the same patron for whom *De situ Brecheniauc* was copied, probably Gloucester Abbey.[20]

In the case of Cilgerran, there is also little reason to follow Lloyd's and Davies' assertion that there was a rededication from Llawddog to Lawrence. Davies was following Lloyd, and Lloyd was following J.R. Phillips, who thought that,[21]

foreign conquerors of this neighbourhood, the Normans and the Flemings – who undoubtedly professed the Roman Catholic religion, and who scarcely would consider the original Welsh founder, though honoured with sanctity in his own neighbourhood and by his own countrymen, but not canonized according to the rituals of the Church of Rome – as a saint – was again *re-dedicated* by them to a saint of their own selection, and from their own category.

We find a fair of St Lawrence being held in the seventeenth century, but Llawddog or Lleuddad is still the saint associated with the church in the eighteenth century and at the time Phillips was writing (1867). I have found nothing to connect St Lawrence with the church itself.

At Caerwent, the evidence is muddied, with little that is clear before references to a dedication to St Stephen appears in the nineteenth century, apparently displacing an original dedication to St Tathan. The present dedication is to St Stephen and St Tathan; but the reason for a dedication to St Stephen is almost certainly because the feast day of both saints is 26 December. The feast of St Tathan is recorded in the *kalendar* in BL MS Cotton Vespasian A. xiv (*c.* 1200).[22] *Vita S. Tathei*, the Life of St Tathan (a work of the mid twelfth century), tells us that the holy man founded a collegiate church in Caerwent dedicated to the Holy and Undivided Trinity;[23] but both this life and Lifris' Life of St Cadog make an assumption that the audience knew the church of Caerwent belonged to Tathan.[24] We also know

19 'Tempore Uuillelmi regis consecrauit [Hergualdus episcopus] Lanncinitir' (Evans, *Book of Llan Dâv*, p. 277). 20 Kathleen Hughes, 'British Museum MS Cotton Vespasian A. xiv ('*Vitae Sanctorum Wallensium*'): its purpose and provenance' in Nora K. Chadwick, K. Hughes, C.N.L. Brooke, K. Jackson, *Studies in the early British church* (Cambridge, 1958), pp 183–200. 21 John Roland Phillips, *A history of Cilgerran* (London, 1867), p. 52: this is Lloyd's source for his assertion that St Lawrence displaced Llawddog. Phillips' choice of terms betrays a degree of anti-Roman bias: he assumed that the Welsh did not – by contrast with the Normans and Flemings – profess 'the Roman Catholic religion', and that 'the rituals of the Church of Rome' were not in use in Welsh dioceses. See below. 22 S.M. Harris (ed.), 'The kalendar of the 'Vitae Sanctorum Wallensium' (Vespasian A. 14)', *Journal of the Historical Society of the Church in Wales*, 3 (1953), 3–53. 23 *Vita S. Tathei* (A. W. Wade-Evans (ed. and trans.), *Vitae sanctorum Britanniae et genealogiae* (Cardiff, 1944), pp 270–86), § 6. 24 Lifris, *Vita S. Cadoci* (Wade-

from the Life of St Tathan that there were shrines of St Tathan himself, and of St Machuta, in the church of Caerwent. So the evidence is not there to say that St Tathan was displaced by Stephen as a result of Norman influence.

At Carmarthen, a new Benedictine priory of Battle Abbey was founded by Henry I, around 1110, and was dedicated to St John the Evangelist and St Teulyddog; a few years later it became an Augustinian priory, a dependant of Llanthony.[25] Given the priory at Carmarthen was a new foundation, that it retained a dedication to St Teulyddog is remarkable. The author of the *Chronicle of Battle Abbey*, however, wrote that this church was 'founded there in very ancient times in honour of St Theodore the martyr'; an identification 'quite without warrant', as the chronicle's most recent editor remarked.[26] *Theodorei*, however, could just as easily be a misreading of *Theulacei*.[27] J.E. Lloyd pounced on this as 'a bold endeavour to make respectable the unknown and uncouth Teulyddog'.[28] The idea, however, that there was an attempt to remove Teulyddog from the dedication is contradicted by the cartulary of the Augustinian priory, in which it is called the 'Priory of St John the Evangelist and St Theulacus'.[29] We should also note that the other daughter-house of Battle Abbey founded in Welsh territory around the same time as the earlier foundation at Carmarthen, namely Brecon Priory, was also dedicated to St John the Evangelist.[30]

The evidence for a dedication to anyone other than Trinio at Llandrinio is thin. In 1833, the dedication was said to be St Trinio.[31] In 1309, King Edward II granted to Griffin de la Pole a three-day fair on the eve, day and morrow of the feast of Ss Peter and Paul (29 June) in his manor of Llandrinio.[32] As with St Tathan and St Stephen, we notice that the feast of St Trinio occurred on the same day as Ss Peter and Paul, 29 June.[33] The current dedication to St Trinio, St Peter and St Paul, may date from that period.

Evans, *Vitae*, pp 24–140), §§ 1–8.   **25** See Alison Binns, *Dedications of monastic houses in England and Wales, 1066–1216*, Studies in the History of Medieval Religion 1 (Woodbridge, 1989), p. 127. **26** 'ecclesiam antiquiiisimis temporibus in honore sancti Theodorei martiris ibidem fundatam': *The Chronicle of Battle Abbey*, ed. and trans. Eleanor Searle (Oxford, 1980), pp 124–5; see n. 2. **27** As Alcwyn C. Evans pointed out as early as 1876: 'St John's priory, Carmarthen', *Archaeologia Cambrensis*, 31 (1876), 96–102, at 97.   **28** Lloyd, *History of Wales*, ii, p. 432, n. 108; also quoted by Searle, *Chronicle of Battle*, p. 125, n. 2.   **29** Thomas Phillips (ed.), *Cartularium S. Johannis Baptistae de Carmarthen* (Cheltenham, 1865). We should also notice some apparent confusion in the dedication to St John: is it St John the Baptist or Evangelist? One explanation might be that it is to both, in imitation of the pope's cathedral at the Lateran, dedicated to the Holy Saviour and St John the Baptist and St John the Evangelist. The instances are laid out by Evans, 'St John's priory', 101–2.   **30** *Chronicle of Battle*, pp 86–7; F.G. Cowley, *The monastic order in South Wales, 1066–1349* (Cardiff, 1977), pp 13–14.   **31** Samuel Lewis, *A topographical dictionary of Wales*, 2 vols (London, 1833; 3rd ed., 1845), i, p. 537.   **32** London, TNA, MS C 143/71/3.   **33** 'His festival seems only to occur in the calendar in the autograph of Gutyn Owain in *Peniarth MS 186* (late fifteenth century), where it is given on June 29, but in a later hand': S. Baring-Gould and John Fisher, *The lives of the British saints: the saints of Wales and Cornwall and such Irish saints*

R.R. Davies' sole source for his account of church dedications in the 'post-Conquest' dioceses of Wales appears to have been Lloyd's *History of Wales*; and the basis for Lloyd's assertions were, in the main, a mixture of assumption and the anti-papal prejudices of early nineteenth-century Anglican clergymen.[34]

THE CATHEDRALS OF WALES

Lloyd and Davies queered the pitch when it came to the cathedrals of Wales too. Both the cathedrals of the two southern medieval dioceses, Llandaf in the South East, and St David's, in the South West, were rebuilt in the first half of the twelfth century. At St David's, the principal cult was of the founding bishop, David, known locally as Dewi Sant. But Dewi's co-patron, who first appears in the twelfth century, was St Andrew the Apostle.

Sometime during his pontificate, the *conuentus* of the 'church of St Andrew and St David' had written to Pope Honorius II (1124–1130), arguing in support of the claims of Bishop Bernard (1115–48) to metropolitan authority over the other Welsh bishoprics.[35] Now, the corporeal relics of St David had almost certainly been lost in about 1090, when the shrine was despoiled by vikings.[36] Bishop Bernard, aware of the value of the cult of Dewi Sant to his cathedral church, moved to obtain a signal of papal recognition, and it is William of Malmesbury who tells us that Pope Calixtus II (1119–24) encouraged English pilgrims to go to St David's rather than Rome, because of the length of the journey, and that those who went twice to St David's should have the same privileges in the way of blessing as those who went once to Rome.[37] The acquisition of such an indulgence from Pope Calixtus was an additional outcome of Bishop Bernard's visit to the papal court in 1123.

as have dedications in Britain, 4 vols (London, 1907–13), iv, p. 265.   **34** It is nevertheless a credit to Lloyd's scholarship that his sources are more or less transparent; Davies was restricted in his references by the format of the series in which his book was published (*Age of conquest*, p. vi). **35** Gerald of Wales, *Libellus inuectionum*, ii, 9; ed. W.S. Davies, 'The Book of Invectives of Giraldus Cambrensis', *Y Cymmrodor*, 30 (1920), 1–248, at 143. Parts of the letter, however, appear to rely on material that is to be found in Geoffrey of Monmouth's *Historia regum Britanniae*, which was not published until 1136, six years after Pope Honorius' death. **36** 'Scrinium sancti Dauid de ecclesia sua furatur et iuxta ciuitatem ex toto spoliatur' ('The reliquary of St David is stolen from his church and, near the city, is wholly stripped bare'): *Annales Cambriae* 'C'-text: Williams ab Ithel (ed.), *Annales Cambriæ* (London, 1860), pp 28–9. Cf. Thomas Jones (ed.), *Brut y Tywysogion, or Chronicle of Princes: Peniarth MS 20 Version* (Cardiff, 1940), p. 18.   **37** *Gesta regum Anglorum*, v, 435 (R.A.B. Mynors, M. Winterbotton, R.M. Thomson (ed. and trans.), *William of Malmesbury: Gesta regum Anglorum: The history of the English kings*, 2 vols (Oxford, 1998), i, p. 778–81).

The addition of St Andrew as a patron of the cathedral church of St David's is intriguing. Likewise, at Llandaf, the new cathedral was dedicated not just to St Dyfrig, St Teilo, and St Euddogwy, the founding episcopal saints, but also to St Peter. We may note that the pairing of dedications to St Peter and St Andrew (his brother) may be found elsewhere in Britain in the early Middle Ages, most notably at the monastery of St Peter and St Paul at Canterbury and the cathedral of St Andrew at Rochester.[38] There is no evidence, however, to support a view that respective dedications to St Peter and St Andrew existed at Llandaf and St David's before the rebuilding of the cathedral churches in the twelfth century. We may suppose, however, that the dedications are to some extent a result of rivalry between the sees of Llandaf and St David's, and not of embarrassment over the prestige of the local cult on the part of a reformed church hierarchy. Urban of Llandaf had been courting Canterbury and the pope, and to emphasize his loyalty to both, was producing pseudo-historical accounts of early links with Rome, and immediate acceptance by the 'archbishops of Llandaf' of St Augustine's authority when he arrived in Britain. A Petrine dedication for the new cathedral at Llandaf demonstrated where Bishop Urban's allegiance lay.

As for St Andrew at St David's, the new additional dedication would make sense too, for St Andrew was associated with the foundation of the earliest church at Byzantium – a kind of counterweight to Rome's association with St Peter and St Paul.[39] As the brother of Peter, Andrew was the obvious choice for this role as his counterbalance. The author of the St Andrew's foundation legend wrote of St Andrew's that, 'in relation to the first Rome, this is the second'.[40] Like St Andrew's, then, St David's was developing a view of itself as being like a second Rome. Of course, Bishop Bernard would have been familiar with the historical tradition of St Andrew's. Immediately before his election to St David's, Bernard had for many years been chaplain to Henry I's consort, Queen Matilda, daughter of the Scottish monarch King Malcolm III and his queen, Margaret.[41] Through Matilda, Bernard must have known Turgot, bishop of St Andrew's (1107–15), author of the

38 See James E. Fraser, 'Rochester, Hexham and Cennrígmonaid: the movements of St Andrew in Britain, 604–747' in Steve Boardman, E. Williamson, and J.R. Davies (eds), *Saints' cults in the Celtic world*, Studies in Celtic History 25 (Woodbridge, 2009), pp 1–17.   39 Fraser, 'Rochester', p. 8; citing D.H. Farmer, *The Oxford dictionary of saints*, 4th ed. (Oxford, 1997), p. 21. 40 Fraser, 'Rochester', p. 8; citing D. Broun, 'Church of St Andrew's and its foundation legend in the early twelfth century: recovering the full text of Version A of the Foundation Legend' in S. Taylor (ed.), *Kings, clerics and chronicles in Scotland, 500–1297* (Dublin, 2000), pp 108–14, at p. 111.   41 For a summary of Bernard's career prior to his election to St David's, see my 'Aspects of church reform in Wales, c.1093–c.1223' in C.P. Lewis (ed.), *Anglo-Norman studies: proceedings of the Battle Conference 2007*, Anglo-Norman Studies, 30 (Woodbridge, 2008), pp 85–99, at p. 88; Julia Barrow (ed.), *St David's Episcopal Acta, 1085–1280* (Cardiff, 1998), pp 2–4, gives a more detailed account of Bernard's episcopate.

Life of St Margaret the Queen (Queen Matilda's mother). From a point sometime in the 1130s, until 1174, there was also a direct link between the Scottish crown and the see of St David's; for the stewardship of the lands of the bishopric of St David's was given by Bishop Bernard to Earl Henry, son of King David I (and Queen Matilda's nephew). Bernard had also appointed as one of his archdeacons Jordan, one of Earl Henry's chaplains, and chancellor to David I. We might also notice the neat association between David and Andrew at Mynyw, which would have reflected the association between King David (brother of Bishop Bernard's former patron) and Scotland's patron.[42] We can, therefore, identify several motives for making St Andrew a patron of St Davids cathedral – motives other than the rather unimaginative and prejudiced idea, favoured by a former generation of Welsh historians of Wales, that St Andrew was needed because Anglo-Normans would not have recognized Dewi as a 'proper saint'.

We should also be aware that there were the newly enshrined relics of a recently deceased local saint, Caradog Fynach. A miracle-working hermit, Caradog had died in 1124, and an unofficial cult had grown up among the local Welsh, Flemish and Anglo-Norman inhabitants.[43] From Gerald of Wales we learn that the church also claimed relics of St Stephen the Protomartyr.[44] Bishop Bernard, a prelate with close ties to the Scottish court, was developing an identity for his see as a second Rome – another Constantinople – a counterpart to St Andrews in Fife, and a counterbalance to the neighbouring cathedral church of St Peter at Llandaf: we need not be startled, disturbed, or perplexed, therefore, by the appearance of St Andrew in the dedication of Bernard's new cathedral.

Now, in June 1120, the bishop of Llandaf (a Welshman, trained at Worcester, who had taken the name Urban), arranged for the bones of St Dyfrig to be solemnly translated from Bardsey Island and interred in a tomb at the new cathedral church of Llandaf. So too were the teeth of Ælfgar (*Elgarus*), a recently deceased hermit of Bardsey Island, and a native of Devon. Llandaf Cathedral now housed, therefore, the relics of the most venerable saint of the southern Britons, and the most recent.

The translation of Ælfgar's teeth, like the later translation of St Caradog Fynach's bodily relics, is a demonstration of how saint-making went on in reforming dioceses of twelfth-century Britain – and there can be no doubt

42 For all this, see Barrow, *St David's*, p. 28.   43 The account of the translation is to be found in *De sancto Caradoco heremita* (Carl Horstman (ed.), *Nova Legenda Anglie*, 2 vols (Oxford, 1901), i, p. 176) and by Gerald of Wales, *Itinerarium Kambriae*, i, 11 (J.F. Dimock (ed.), *Giraldi Cambrensis Opera*, vol. 6, Rolls Series 21 (London, 1868), pp 86–7); see F.G. Cowley, 'The relics of St David: the historical evidence' in Evans and Wooding (eds), *St David of Wales*, pp 274–81, at p. 275.   44 *Itinerarium Kambriae*, i, 11 (ed. Dimock, p. 87).

that Bishop Urban was a reforming bishop who looked to Canterbury and Rome.[45] Relics of this recently dead holy man were sought, and obtained by a bishop who enshrined them in his cathedral church, and commissioned a hagiography to accompany the translation. The idea of official canonization at Rome is anachronistic at this date.

The two northern cathedral churches are dedicated in honour of founding bishops. The dedication of Bangor cathedral is St Deiniol (that is, Daniel). The antiquity of this dedication is not disputed.[46] Although the diocese of Bangor was the first to come under direct Anglo–Norman control in the early 1070s, it quickly reverted to native royal control, and fell out of the orbit of the Welsh March.

In the north-east, two or three decades after the activities of Bishop Urban and Bishop Bernard in the south, Geoffrey of Monmouth became perhaps the third bishop of Llanelwy since its foundation in 1141. Geoffrey professed canonical obedience and subjection to Canterbury in February 1152. He is the first bishop of that diocese to style himself 'Bishop of St Asaph' rather than 'Bishop of Llanelwy'; and this was surely no coincidence. There appears to have been a translation of St Asaph's relics, and there are the remnants of a life, and possibly a charter of the type found in the Book of Llandaf.[47] There is no direct evidence that either Kentigern or Asaph was connected with the see of Llanelwy before Geoffrey of Monmouth's appearance on the scene.

---

45 See John Reuben Davies, *Book of Llandaf and the Norman church in Wales*, Studies in Celtic History 21 (Woodbridge, 2003); idem, 'Aspects of church reform'. Bishop Urban had spent half of his episcopate engaged in appeals to Canterbury and the papal curia, and his literary legacy, the Book of Llandaf, records these in detail, preserving the texts of forty-six papal bulls in the process: see Davies, *Book of Llandaf*, pp 32–45, 153–9.   46 Deiniol is first recorded in the early ninth-century Irish Martyrology of Tallaght, where his feast day is given as 11 September; this agrees with almost all the later Welsh *kalendars*. In the Martyrology of Tallaght, he is given as 'Deiniol, bishop of Bangor', but in his obit in *Annales Cambriae*, s.a. 584, he is 'Daniel of the Bangors'. This suggests that he was already known as the patron saint of his foundation, Bangor Is-coed, the monastery mentioned in a famous story in Bede's *Historia ecclesiastica*, about the battle of Chester, assigned by *Annales Cambriae* to 613, nearly thirty years after Deiniol's death. Entries in Irish annals referring to Bangor in Britain and the fact that he was one of only three Welsh saints to be included in the Martyrology of Tallaght also indicate the importance of his foundations in the pre-viking period.   47 Jocelin of Furness, in *Vita S. Kentegerni*, § 25, alludes to a 'little book' of the life of St Asaph, which we may suppose him to have used as a source for the episodes relating to Llanelwy in that Life (Alexander Penrose Forbers (ed. and trans.), *Lives of S. Ninian and S. Kentigern* (Edinburgh, 1874), p. 205). The lost thirteenth- or fourteenth-century manuscript called the Red book of St Asaph (*Llyfr Coch Asaph*) is known to have contained a *Vita Sancti Assaph*: 'Index to "Llyfr Coch Asaph"', *Archaeologia Cambrensis*, 14, 3rd series (1868), 151–66 and 433–42, at 442; for the subsequent history of the manuscript, see D.L. Evans, 'Llyfr Coch Asaph', *National Library of Wales Journal*, 4 (1945–6), 177–83, and O.E. Jones, 'Llyfr Coch Asaph: a textual and historical study', 2 vols (MA, University of Wales, Aberystwyth, 1968).

The relics of native Welsh saints, one may therefore argue, were called into service by a reformed episcopate, to establish and dig-in the redefined or re-founded Welsh bishoprics of the early twelfth century. This was a self-conscious enterprise, which sought to give a grounding in historical tradition to a reformed ecclesiastical structure, both justifying its new appearance and providing itself with historical and cultural reference points. An important aspect of this endeavour was the production of a corpus of hagiography – the lives of Welsh saints.

THE LIVES OF THE WELSH SAINTS

Lloyd's view of the Norman impact on 'the Welsh Church' gave rise to the idea that the composition of a new body of hagiography around this time, with the lives of local Welsh saints as the subject matter, was a reaction against the appropriation of ecclesiastical property by marcher lords, most of whom donated church lands in Wales to their own monastic foundations. The property rights of the native saints were a prominent feature in the new saints' lives that began to appear at the end of the eleventh century; and the saints were jealous in the defence of their churches' lands. Gerald of Wales was certainly aware of the vengeful character of Irish and Welsh saints, which he would have discovered from their *uitae*.[48]

As I have made clear in my *Topography of Ireland*, both the Irish and the Welsh are more prone to anger and revenge in this life than other nations, and similarly their saints in the next world seem much more vindictive.[49]

The phenomenon is especially visible in Lifris of Llancarfan's Life of St Cadog, which, hardly begun, has the saint, as a boy, calling down fire on one of his father's servants who has refused to give him coals.[50] Lifris' Life of St Cadog has attached to it a kind of cartulary, recording gifts of land to the church of Llancarfan; and the Book of Llandaf is really a series of saints' lives incorporating a substantial corpus of pseudo-charters. The assumption again was that the reformed ecclesiastical order in Wales was inimical to the cult of Welsh saints. A comparable view had persisted for the English situation, where scholarship perceived a general disapproval of Anglo-Saxon

48 That Gerald read the lives of the saints is shown, for example, in *The topography of Ireland*, i, 29 (James F. Dimock (ed.), *Giraldi Cambrensis opera*, vol. 5, Rolls Series 61 (Oxford, 1867), p. 62), where he remarks, 'One reads in the ancient writings of the saints of that land [...]'.
49 Lewis Thorpe (trans.), *Gerald of Wales: The journey through Wales and the description of Wales* (London, 1978), p. 189 (Gerald of Wales, *Itinerarium Kambriae*, ii, 7; ed. Dimock, p. 130).
50 §7; see also §§8, 15, 16, 19, 23, 24, 36, 40, 69, for further stories of the saint's vengeance.

saints in England in the early Norman period. This perception, however, has been definitively offset, now that we have come to see how the translation of saints' relics in England had been revived in the 1090s, reflecting a desire of major churches to renew particular local cults. Professional hagiographers – Goscelin of Canterbury, Osberne of St Augustine's, Eadmer – made a career out of promoting the cult of local saints for both English and Norman patrons.[51] A phenomenon of similar type can be observed in Wales, where the hagiographers, whose names we know, were all home-grown: that is, Rhygyfarch ap Sulien of Llanbadarn Fawr, Lifris of Llancarfan, and Caradog of Llancarfan.[52]

As one reads through the dossier of the lives of Welsh saints (there are about eighteen of them) written in the period from the last decade of the eleventh century to the middle of the twelfth, criticism of the new political regime is not forthcoming. On the contrary, it is the native rulers of the Welsh territories (although usually of the distant past) who come in for unsympathetic treatment.

The most striking example of a Welsh ruler as villain occurs in the Life of St Gwynllyw – one of the lives that looks as though it was written by Caradog of Llancarfan, the *contemporaneus* of Geoffrey of Monmouth.[53] In §12 we read of a piratical raid against St Gwynllyw's church, undertaken by Gruffudd ap Cynan (d. 1137), the exiled ruler of Gwynedd. In another story (§14), Ednywain of Gwynedd, a friend of Caradog of Glamorgan (d. 1081), broke into St Gwynllyw's church. In §15, King Caradog takes into his protection a number of Norman knights who had rebelled against William the Conqueror. In the last chapter of the Life of St Illtud, there is an episode in which the army of Gwynedd is put to flight by the power of St Illtud, and the English-born and Norman-born are referred to as *ciues*, 'fellow citizens'.

The Life of St Cybi (*Vita I S. Kebii*, §§17–19), patron of Caergybi (Holyhead), tells of a dispute between Maelgwn Gwynedd (the progenitor of the kings of Gwynedd, and a famous addressee of Gildas' polemic) and Cybi.[54] In the Life of St Padarn (patron of Llanbadarn Fawr), Maelgwn is again the villain, being 'ever the tempter of the saints', *semper temptator sanctorum* (§15).[55] The Life of St Cadog by Lifris also offers several unfavourable tales of native Welsh rulers.[56]

---

51 See Davies, *Book of Llandaf*, pp 96–7.   52 But one suspects that Caradog had been educated in a continental school: this is what I take from Geoffrey of Monmouth's reference to him as his 'contemporary' in the Bern manuscript of *Historia regum Britannie* (Neil Wright (ed.), *The Historia regum Britannie of Geoffrey Monmouth I. Bern, Burgerbibliothek MS 568* (Cambridge, 1984), p. 147). See next paragraph but one.   53 Davies, *Book of Llandaf*, pp 133–6; *Vita S. Gundlei*: Wade-Evans, *Vitae*, pp 172–92.   54 Wade-Evans, *Vitae*, pp 234–50.   55 *Vita S. Paterni*: Wade-Evans, *Vitae*, pp 252–68.   56 §22, The dispute between St Cadog and King Arthur; §23, Vengeance on the king of the men of Gwynedd for injury done to the man of God;

An interesting example of a saint's life that works in the other direction is that of St Winifred. Gwenfrewi (as Winifred is known in Welsh) is the patron of Holywell (Flintshire) and Gwytherin (Denbighshire). Her relics were translated to Shrewsbury in 1138, but even before that date she had an English as well as a Welsh cult. Tegeingl, an area of north-east Flintshire, where she is said to have been born, was under Mercian control in the tenth century; it was re-conquered by the men of Gwynedd shortly before the appearance of the Normans in Britain, but afterwards came under the control of the earls of Chester. Gwenfrewi's English name, Winifred, and her English cult probably originate in the period of Mercian rule. The origin of *Ffynnon Wenfrewi* (Winifred's Well) at Holywell – the most famous of local Welsh cults centred on wells – is explained in her *uitae*. The earlier of two lives of St Winifred tells how a local prince, Caradog ab Alog, decapitated Winifred when she refused him sexual favours. On the spot where her blood stained the ground, a spring gushed forth. Winifred's uncle, a holy man called Beuno, cursed the murderer, causing him to melt like wax. Beuno then fitted the head back to the body, and by the holy man's prayers, God brought Winifred back to life. Beuno's response to this miracle was to order a priestly vestment from his resuscitated niece: one chasuble was to be sent to him every year.[57]

Soror mi, hunc Deus tibi destinauit locum; meque oportet alias tendere, ubi Deus mihi prouiderit perendinare. Mihi autem circa hunc diem unoquoque anno hoc facito: casulam mihi dirige de uestro opere proprio.

My sister, God has chosen this place for you; and it is fitting for me to go on to another place, where God will make provision for me to dwell. But every year, about this day, do this for me: send me a chasuble made by your own labour.

The vestments must have gone to Beuno's principal church at Clynnog Fawr, and one might speculate that the story justified an arrangement whereby the community at Holywell supplied sacramental vestments for Clynnog Fawr. (All previous translators appear to have had scruples about rendering *casula* as 'chasuble', preferring the less priestly 'cloak', lest we might suspect that St Beuno might ever have celebrated the mass.) In this way, Gwenfrewi's church at Holywell, the most significant cult-centre of Tegeingl, was linked with one of the principal churches of the Gwynedd heartlands, whose ruler, Gruffudd ap Cynan, at the date of the life's composition, had recently taken back control of Tegeingl from the Normans.

---

§24, The blinding of King Rhun for the injury inflicted on saint Cadog; §44, Another king of Rheinwg attempts to invade Glamorgan; § 69, The blinding of King Maelgwn.   **57** London, British Library, MS Cotton Claudius A. v; Wade-Evans, *Vitae*, pp 288–308, p. 293.

A noteworthy feature of the Life of Gwenfrewi is that the post-mortem miracles recorded there had occurred lately, *tempore Francorum*, that is, when Tegeingl was under the control of the Norman earls of Chester. One miracle (§ 26) suggests Gwenfrewi's posthumous approval of the expulsion of the French from Gwynedd: after this event, for three days, her well was seen to flow with a milky liquid, sweet to the taste. This earlier, anonymous, Life of Gwenfrewi was written for a native audience of Gwynedd; a second life was written by Robert, prior of Shrewsbury, to accompany the translation of St Winifred's relics to Shrewsbury in 1138, and was therefore addressed to an Anglo–Norman audience.

Here, then, is the case of a local cult which becomes important for the native inhabitants of Gwynedd, the Mercian English, and the Anglo–Normans, crossing those cultural boundaries. The most important factor to recognize in the cross-cultural popularity of this cult is its perceived efficacy. If a cult was efficacious, Anglo–Norman churchmen were as keen as the next man to apply themselves to it. Gerald of Wales demonstrated this phenomenon in *The topography of Ireland*:

Just as the marvels of the east have through the work of certain authors come to the light of public notice, so the marvels of the west, which, so far, have remained hidden away and almost unknown, may eventually find in me one to make them known even in these later days.[58]

Most of the foregoing lives of Welsh saints are preserved in London, British Library, MS Cotton Vespasian A.xiv (to fol. 107). The manuscript demonstrates the interest that Anglo–Norman settlers developed in the historical materials of British Christianity. It is, as Kathleen Hughes described it,

an industrious record of texts mainly written or rewritten in the twelfth century. It reflects the restless enterprise of this period of Norman–Welsh history – the expansion of Gloucester, the rise of Llandaf, and the preservation, though abbreviated, enfeebled and but half-understood, of the traditions of the pre-Norman Welsh Church.[59]

Although it may be an obvious point to make, the most striking feature of the Vespasian collection is that it was the product of an Anglo–Norman monastic house. This, one of the two most important manuscripts relating to the churches of the Welsh March, came either from Gloucester Abbey or Monmouth Priory.

The other important repository of lives of Welsh saints written in a context of Anglo–Norman colonization is the Book of Llandaf, a history of

---

58 *Topographia Hibernica*, ii, preface (Dimock, p. 74); John O'Meara (ed.), *Gerald of Wales: The history and topography of Ireland* (rev. ed., London, 1982), p. 57 (§ 33).   59 'British Museum MS. Cotton Vespasian A. xiv', p. 200.

the bishops of Llandaf through seven centuries – copied into a gospel book.[60] One of the most noticeable features of the sources for the Llandaf lives is the prevalence of material from Brittany: the Life of St Samson of Dôl, the Life of St Paul Aurelian (by Wrmonoc of Landévennec), the Life of St Turiau, and the charters of Landévennec have all been used as sources for the hagiographies contained between the boards of *Liber Landauensis*.[61] The monks of Monmouth, who contributed in some important way to the Vespasian collection, had probably acted as a conduit for hagiographical materials for Llandaf at some earlier stage. Monmouth priory, we should remember, was a daughter-house of the Benedictine abbey of St Florent, Saumur, and had been founded by a Breton noble, Wihenoc, lord of Monmouth, in 1074–86.[62] Again, we can only draw the inference that reformed churchmen of continental origin – monks with martial patrons – were contributing to, rather than detracting from, the hagiology and *cultus* of local saints in the early Welsh March.

CULTURAL TRANSMISSION IN THE EARLY WELSH MARCH

The historiography of the Church in the early Welsh March has been dominated by readings that have led to – what appears to be – a considerable overestimation of Anglo-Norman imperialism in the spheres of religious and ecclesiastical culture. A particular nationalistic and religious predisposition – whether conscious or not – has distorted our view of the period for generations. A scene in which ecclesiastical colonizers replaced dedications of churches to local Welsh saints with dedications to universal saints now appears as the invention of outmoded prejudices (which have gone into retirement, even if they stubbornly refuse to die). One should more readily take notice of an ecclesiastical landscape in which each of the four Welsh cathedrals was founded upon the cult of a local episcopal saint. And in the truly 'Marcher' sees of Llandaf and St Asaph, these local cults were given definitive affirmation with the building of new cathedral churches and the complete re-foundation of the bishopric in the twelfth century. And this was only part of a renewal of indigenous cults, which also saw the inauguration

60 *Liber Landauensis*, Aberystwyth, National Library of Wales, MS NLW 17110E; for the codicology, see Daniel Huws, 'The making of *Liber Landavensis*', *National Library of Wales Journal*, 25 (1987–8), 133–6 (reprinted in idem, *Medieval Welsh manuscripts* (Cardiff, 2000), pp 123–57); in general, see Davies, *The Book of Llandaf*. 61 *Vita S. Turiani* (ninth-century Brittany) was a source for the Life of St Teilo. Other Breton elements in the Book of Llandaf include the Life of St Samson, based on *Vita I*; there are also references to Armorican cavalry and Breton counts. See Davies, *Book of Llandaf*, pp 129–31. 62 Cowley, *Monastic Order*, pp 14–15, 271.

and evolution of new cults of local holy men, such as Ælfgar at Llandaf, and Caradog Fynach at St David's. All these cults were furnished with shrines, and equipped with hagiographies.

The new hagiographical corpus produced in this period, moreover, emphasizes the distortion produced by the looking-glass into which the heirs of Rice Rees gazed while fashioning their version of Welsh ecclesiastical history. Far from the supposed propaganda of quasi-protestant Welsh churchmen resisting the incursion of 'Roman Catholic' Normans, the lives of the Welsh saints were written, in the main, by reformed churchmen for a largely Anglo-Norman audience. Indeed, the two principal collections of Latin hagiography, Vespasian A.xiv and the Book of Llandaf, were created respectively by the patronage of Gloucester Abbey, and the Anglo-Norman marcher lords upon whom the bishopric and cathedral church of Llandaf depended for their existence.

We cannot deny that the early Welsh March was the setting for political, cultural, and ecclesiastical conflict; yet we must do away with anachronistic political and religious judgments in evaluating the nature of that conflict. For in contemplating the cult of saints, it has become difficult to avoid the impression that conflict was tempered by a cultural transmission which passed as much from conquered to conqueror as the other way around.

APPENDIX

Churches claimed by Rice Rees to have had their dedications to local saints changed to universal saints as a consequence of Norman settlement.[63]

STEYNTON (PEMBS) 'St Kewill' [Cewydd] > St Peter

An *inspeximus* of 1297/8 (25 Edward I) to Pill Priory, includes *ecclesiam Sancti Kewit de Steintona*, i.e. the church of St Cewydd.[64]

CHERITON / STACKPOLE ELIDOR (PEMBS) St Elider > St James

Baring-Gould and Fisher doubted that Elidor was a saint's name at all.[65]

LLANTHONY (MONM) St David > St John Baptist

Llanthony is properly Llanddewi Nant Honddu: a dedication to Dewi (St David) is implied in the placename; but place-name elements should not be confused with church dedications. Gerald of Wales tells of a chapel of St David the archbishop

---

63 *An essay on the Welsh saints*, pp 70–1. Those churches already mentioned in the foregoing text have been omitted from this list.   64 Baring-Gould and Fisher, *Lives*, iv, p. 442, citing William Dugdale, *Monasticon Anglicanum*, 6 vols (London, 1817–30), iv, p. 503.   65 Baring-Gould and Fisher, *Lives*, ii, p. 446.

which had formerly been there.[66] Whether or not there had been a chapel dedicated to St David on the site, the Augustinian house founded at Llanthony was a new church, dedicated in 1108 by the bishops of Llandaf and Hereford: this was not the re-dedication of an existing church, but the dedication of a completely new house of Augustinian canons.[67]

LLANFEUNO / LLANVEYNOE (HEREFORDSHIRE) St Beuno > St Peter

The earliest evidence for a dedication to St Peter comes from 1868.[68] Browne-Willis, in the eighteenth century, probably influenced by the place-name (*Llan* + *Beuno*) thought the dedication was to Beuno; but Frances Arnold-Forster (although without providing the evidence) considered the pre-Reformation dedication to be St Peter.[69] We can neither be sure that there ever was a church dedication (rather than just an ecclesiastical place-name) to Beuno, not that a dedication to St Beuno was overturned in the twelfth century for one to St Peter.

LLANSILLOE / LLANCILLO (HEREFORDSHIRE) St Tyssilio > St Peter

This is *Lann Sulbiu* or *ecclesia sancti Sulbiu* of the Book of Llandaf.[70] The ascription of Tyssilio as the earliest dedication of this church is wrong, as the name is properly Sulfyw; but there can be no doubt that the church was dedicated to Sulfyw as the Book of Llandaf unequivocally refers to 'the church of St Sulfyw'. I have found no medieval references to a church of St Peter, but this is the only dedication known by the time Rees was writing.[71]

LLANGATHAN (CARMARTHENSHIRE) St Cathen > St Michael and All Saints

There appears to be no suggestion that the church of Llangathen had any other dedication than St Cathen; the dedication to Michael belongs to another nearby church in the parish of Llandeilo Fawr, that of Llanfihangel Cilfargen.[72]

ST DOGMAEL'S / LLANDUDOCH (PEMBROKESHIRE) St Dogmael > St Mary

The Tironensian priory at St Dogmael's was established *c.*1113 × 15 and became an abbey in 1120.[73] The house was founded *in honore sanctae Dei genetricis semper Virginis Mariae* ('in honour of the holy Mother of God, Mary ever virgin') from Robert FitzMartin's gift of *ecclesiam sancti Dogmaelis* ('church of St Dogmael').[74]

66 *Itinerarium Kambriae*, i, 3 (Dimock, p. 37; Thorpe, p. 97). 67 *Historia prioratus Lanthoniae in com. Glocest.* (London, BL, Cotton Julius D.x, fos. 31–51, at 36r), translated in James Conway Davies, *Episcopal acts relating to Welsh dioceses, 1066–1272*, 2 vols (Cardiff, 1946–8), ii, p. 615 (no. L. 26). 68 N.E.S.A. Hamilton (ed.), *The national gazetteer: a topographical dictionary of the British islands*, 3 vols (London, 1868). 69 Wade-Evans, *Parochiale Wallicanum*, p. 21; Frances Arnold-Forster, *Studies in church dedications: or, England's patron saints*, 3 vols (London, 1899), iii, p. 185. 70 Evans, *Book of Llan Dâv*, p. 160, and pp 31, 43, 90. 71 Arnold-Forster (*Studies*, iii, p. 184) considered the pre-Reformation dedication to be to St Peter, but again without providing the evidence. 72 Samuel Lewis, *A topographical dictionary of Wales*, 2 vols (London, 1844), ii, pp 29, 141. 73 Cowley, *Monastic order*, p. 20; Binns, *Dedications*, p. 104. 74 From the foundation charter of Robert FitzMartin in *Monasticon*, iv, p. 130, quoted in Binns, *Dedications*, p. 140.

The dedication later appears in several forms: St Mary, St Dogmael, Ss Mary and Dogmael.[75] A dedication to Mary was common in Tironensian houses; the retention of St Dogmael is significant in a new foundation.

NORTHOP / LLANEURGAIN (FLINTSHIRE) St Eurgain > St Peter

The dedication to Peter is probably late, and most likely arises from the occurrence of the feast of St Eurgain on 29 June, the feast also of St Peter.[76]

LLANGYNYW (MONTGOMERYSHIRE) St Cynyw > All Saints

That Cynyw was still the dedication at the end of the thirteenth century is attested by the *Taxatio* of Pope Nicholas IV.[77]

LLANEGRYN (MERIONETHSHIRE) St Egryn > St Mary

An association of Egryn with the church of Llanegryn and the surrounding area seems to have persisted through the sixteenth century and beyond, but positive evidence for a dedication to Egryn is lacking. The church eventually came to be dedicated to the Blessed Virgin Mary on the Feast of the Assumption: we may safely assume that this occurred before the break with Rome.[78]

LLANBLEDDIAN (GLAMORGANSHIRE) St Bleddian > St John Baptist

Baring-Gould and Fisher dismissed the notion that Llanbleddian was dedicated to a St Bleddian. The person in question may have been an Elyddon or Lythan, but there is no evidence of a church dedication – only a place-name element, which is not the same thing.[79]

LLANFABON (GLAMORGANSHIRE) St Mabon > St Constantine

There is no direct medieval evidence for a dedication to Mabon; but this is the dedication reported in the eighteenth century, and the attribution of a dedication to St Constantine appears to have been erroneous.[80]

DYNSTOW / DYNGESTOW (MONMOUTHSHIRE) St Dingad > St Mary

A cult of Dingad existed here at an early date, and certainly before the twelfth century, when the tell-tale designation *Merthir Dingat* is found in the Book of Llandaf – *merthyr* being a sign that the church housed corporeal relics.[81] There is no evidence of a dedication to the Blessed Virgin Mary before the nineteenth century.[82]

---

75 Ibid.   76 Baring-Gould and Fisher, *Lives*, ii, p. 474.   77 *Taxatio ecclesiastica*, p. 287. 78 Baring-Gould and Fisher, *Lives*, ii, p. 415.   79 Ibid., iii, pp 365–6.   80 Ibid., iii, p. 391, citing Browne-Willis, who gave both Mabon and St Constantine.   81 Evans, *Book of Llan Dâv*, 31, 43, 90, 227 (Merthir Dincat); 284 (Lann Dinegat); on the significance of *merthyr* as an element in Welsh place-names, see Richard Sharpe, 'Martyrs and local saints in late antique Britain' in *Local Saints*, ed. Thacker and Sharpe, pp 75–154, at pp 130–54.   82 Arnold-Forster (*Studies*, iii, p. 106) thought the pre-Reformation dedication was to St Dingad and St Mary.

LLANGYNIOW (LLANGEVIEW / LLANGYFYW) (MONMOUTHSHIRE) St Cynyw [for Cynfyw] > St David

The dedication by the early nineteenth century was to St David, as Rees attests. Again there is only the toponymic suggestion for a dedication to Cynfyw – which is not evidence for a dedication.[83]

---

83 Arnold-Forster (ibid., p. 185) gave David as the pre-Reformation dedication.

Expectations of empire: some twelfth- and early thirteenth-century English views of what their kings could do

JOHN GILLINGHAM

That those who invaded Ireland in the late twelfth century were encouraged to think that they were engaged in a civilizing mission is well known. But did they also believe that a deliberate policy of civilizing could have been devised and implemented? In his book on *The governance of Norman and Angevin England* (1987), Lewis Warren wrote that for much of the period 1086–1272, 'the means for the direct exercise of royal authority were restricted in scope. The essence of the matter is that early medieval societies were in practice fashioned and controlled more by social, economic and religious factors than by institutionalized government and the will of rulers'.[1] He – and the many others who say similar things – may be right, but is this what people at the time thought? Did they imagine that the means for the exercise of royal authority were indeed restricted in scope? Or did they assume that societies could be fashioned by the will of rulers and institutionalized governments? The answers to these questions matter because, as Rees Davies wrote, 'how men see the world – how it is and how it should be – very considerably shapes how they act and their reasons for doing so'.[2] No one wrote more illuminatingly about perceptions and expectations than Rees Davies did and it is with this virtual world of perceptions and expectations that I shall be concerned. Did many of the English imagine that their kings could set out to 'civilize' Celtic societies as a matter of conscious policy? And if they did, then by what means did they expect such a policy to be promoted? Did they think that the twelfth- and early thirteenth-century kings of England had sufficient power to be able to implement such a policy?

It is well known, of course, that in his *Topographia Hibernica*, Gerald de Barri expressed a maximal view of Henry II's power.[3] In the *Expugnatio Hibernica*, he claimed not only that the king's ecclesiastical policy was intended to anglicize and improve the Irish, but that it was already beginning

1 W.L. Warren, *The governance of Norman and Angevin England* (London, 1987), pp xiv–xv.
2 R.R. Davies, *Domination and conquest* (Cambridge, 1990), pp 64, 113–14.   3 *Giraldi Cambrensis Opera*, 8 vols, ed. J.S. Brewer, J.F. Dimock and G.F. Warner, Rolls Series (London, 1861–91), v, pp 189–90.

to have some effect.[4] No doubt it would be rash to assume that Gerald's English contemporaries shared his views about what their kings could and could not do. He, after all, was a remarkably creative writer with axes of his own to grind. He and his family were deeply involved in the conquest and settlement of Ireland, just as they had been in Wales.[5] In the first version of his *Descriptio Kambriae*, he proposed some radical solutions to the 'problem of Wales'. 'After the king has expelled the old inhabitants and deported them to other kingdoms, he will be able to make Wales a colony – though whether so rough and trackless a country could ever have biddable inhabitants, I'm not sure, and there are some who think that for a prudent prince it might be much safer and more sensible to leave Wales as wasteland for animals, turning it into forest.'[6] When he wrote this he still hoped for the kind of career in government service that would land him a plum bishopric. Hence he dedicated the work to Hubert Walter, one of the most efficient and toughest of government ministers – an archbishop of Canterbury, who used ruthless violence to dispose of the threat that William FitzOsbert was believed to pose to civil order in London.[7] There is some evidence that the Welsh took such threats seriously – or at least found it convenient to do so – thus the report in the *Brut* that Henry I and his allies (including Alexander of Scotland) planned either to exterminate the Welsh or drive them into the sea 'so that the Britannic name should never more be mentioned'.[8] But that is one thing. Whether the English could ever have contemplated anything so drastic is another.

In this essay, I shall try to see what the ways in which a number of twelfth- and early thirteenth-century English authors interpreted the past might reveal about their assumptions about the reach of the king's government.

---

4 Giraldus Cambrensis: *Expugnatio Hibernica,* ed. A.B. Scott and F.X. Martin (Dublin, 1978), pp 98–100.   5 Through his father, Gerald claimed kinship with the English barons who held the incastellated coast lands of Wales, Giraldus Cambrensis: *De invectionibus,* ed. W.S. Davies, *Y Cymmrodor* 30 (1920), p. 86; translated in *The autobiography of Gerald of Wales,* ed. and trans. H.E. Butler (Woodbridge, 2005), p. 172. On Gerald's allegiances, see John Gillingham, 'Slaves of the Normans? Gerald de Barri and regnal solidarity in early thirteenth-century England' in *Law, laity and solidarities. Essays in honour of Susan Reynolds,* ed. Pauline Stafford, Janet L. Nelson and Jane Martindale (Manchester, 2001), pp 160–71.   6 'Unde et expulso prorsus veteri colono, aliaque ad regna translato, de Cambria coloniam princeps efficere praevalebit. Porro terram tam hispidam et tam inviam, tamque colonos domabiles habere nesciam, quasi desertum penitus bestiis relinquere, atque forestam inde facere, provido principi longe tutius et consultius fore, nonnulli sunt qui arbitrentur,' *Descriptio Kambriae,* Bk II, ch. 9. The Rolls Series editor relegated this passage to a footnote (*Giraldi Opera,* vi, p. 225 n. 4), while Lewis Thorpe in his translation for Penguin Classics made it easy to miss altogether by having it printed separately from the rest of the text, Gerald of Wales, *The journey through Wales/ The description of Wales* (London, 1978), pp 51–2.   7 And who in the process was alleged to have shown scant regard for the rights of churches. See John Gillingham, 'The historian as judge: William of Newburgh and Hubert Walter', *English Historical Review,* 119 (2004), 1275–87.

Among these authors are two whose historical views have, in one way or another, been seriously neglected – an oversight I hope to remedy. These two are the witty Winchester monk, Richard of Devizes, and the anonymous Londoner known as the London Collector. But I begin with one of the acknowledged masters of twelfth-century historical writing, Henry of Huntingdon, and with one of his reminiscences. 'In my childhood I heard very old men say that the king (Æthelred) sent secret letters to every town, ordering a simultaneous action against the Danes. They were all to be taken by surprise at exactly the same time on the same day and either put to the sword or taken prisoner and burned alive'. This was, of course, how he imagined the St Brice's Day massacre (13 November 1002) being organized.[9] Similarly, the earlier Norman version by William of Jumièges not only gave gory details – women being buried up to their waists and having their nipples torn off by ferocious dogs, children having their brains dashed out against door posts – it also emphasized that this was all done on one and the same day.[10] As Len Scales has recently observed, Henry's reminiscence shows 'how ambitious was his view of the capabilities of English royal government that he judged such a co-ordinated pogrom conceivable'.[11] Like Gerald's proposal for the ethnic cleansing of Wales, these reports of the St Brice's Day massacre suggest that governments were believed to be capable of deploying great power for sinister ends.[12] Very different, but equally suggestive of the power of government to transform society is William of Malmesbury's report that William I 'had broken the schemes of those villains who in the customary fashion (*consueto more*) had been selling slaves to Ireland'. In William of Malmesbury's book, both Archbishop Lanfranc and Bishop Wulfstan of Worcester deserved credit for persuading the king to take this course of action, but it was the king who broke the trade and who sacrificed his own share of the profits in consequence.[13] *We* may think that underlying demographic and economic change had more to do with the end of the slave export trade than royal policy did – but that is not how the greatest historian of the time saw it.[14]

8 *Brut Y Tywysogyon, Red book of Hergest version*, ed. and trans. Thomas Jones (Cardiff, 1952), pp 78–81. 9 Henry Archdeacon of Huntingdon: *Historia Anglorum*, ed. and trans. D. Greenway (Oxford, 1996), p. 340. 10 The *Gesta Normannorum ducum* of William of Jumièges, Orderic Vitalis and Robert of Torigni, ed. and trans. Elisabeth M. C. Van Houts, 2 vols (Oxford, 1992–5), ii, p. 16. 11 Len Scales, 'Bread, cheese and genocide: imagining the destruction of peoples in medieval western Europe', *History*, 92 (2007), 284–300, 297. 'The capacity of medieval governments violently to re-fashion peoplehood may have been greater than such (i.e. modernist) perspectives allow', ibid., 288. 12 'Images of ethnic purge and replacement were written into the very DNA of medieval religious and political assumption', ibid., 300. 13 William of Malmesbury: *Gesta regum Anglorum*, ed. and trans. R.A.B. Mynors, R.M. Thomson and M. Winterbottom (Oxford, 1998), ch. 269. 14 Though he understood economic and commercial forces well enough. 'Whenever poor harvests mean that food prices are high all

Historians such as William of Malmesbury and Henry of Huntingdon were, of course, acutely aware of the divisions in post-Conquest England. In Henry of Huntingdon's interpretation, 'God had chosen the Normans to wipe out the English nation (*ad Anglorum gentem exterminandam*) and in consequence, because all the English had been reduced to servitude and lamentation (*omnes ad servitutem et moererem redacti essent*), it became shameful even to be called English (*ita etiam ut Anglicum vocari esset, opprobrio*).' As late as 1125, William of Malmesbury could observe that 'today no Englishman is an earl, a bishop or an abbot; everywhere newcomers enjoy England's riches and gnaw at her vitals (*Nullus hodie Anglus vel dux, vel pontifex vel abbas; advenae quique divitias et viscera corrodunt Angliae*). Nor is there any hope of ending this miserable state of affairs.'[15] Since these two were the most widely read of twelfth-century English historians, it is no surprise that later authors thought of the post-Conquest decades as a period characterized by ethnic violence. As Richard FitzNigel put it, 'In the period immediately following the conquest, the defeated survivors set ambushes for the hated Normans and murdered them in woods and unfrequented places as opportunity offered'.[16] According to Gerald's fellow royal servant, Walter Map, the reigns of William I (1066–87) and William II (1087–1100) had witnessed *per universum sevissima regnum sedicio*; the first Norman kings had not been able to rule over a land *compositam ad pacem*, because its old inhabitants (*veteres incole*) had continued to offer violent resistance to the incomers. But the present king's grandfather, Henry I, had managed to overcome these problems. 'He brought the two peoples together in firm friendship (*ad firmam populos utrosque federavit concordiam*) and reigned long and happily to the honour of God and the great wealth and enduring gladness of his subjects'. Henry I had achieved this, in Map's view, 'by arranging marriages between newcomers and old inhabitants and by all other means he could contrive'.[17] Other authors such as Aelred of Rievaulx and Richard FitzNigel also believed that thanks to intermarriage the old divisions were being or had been overcome. According to Aelred, 'England now has a king of English

over England, essential foodstuffs can be bought and sold in London more cheaply than anywhere else; buyers spend less and sellers make lower profits owing to the presence there of traders from every land', William of Malmesbury, *Gesta pontificum Anglorum*, ed. and trans. M. Winterbottom (Oxford, 2007), ch. 73. **15** *Henry Archdeacon of Huntingdon, Historia Anglorum*, ed. Diana Greenway (Oxford, 1996), Book VI ch. 38 (pp 402, 412); William of Malmesbury: *Gesta regum*, ch. 227. Yet William had in fact written of the birth of Henry I's and Matilda's son William as a sign of hope. **16** Richard FitzNigel, *Dialogus de Scaccario*, ed. Charles Johnson, F.E.L. Carter and Diana Greenway (Oxford, 1983), p. 52. John Hudson, 'Administration, family and perceptions of the past in twelfth-century England: Richard FitzNigel and the dialogue of the exchequer' in Paul Magdalino (ed.), *The perception of the past in twelfth-century Europe* (London, 1992), pp 75–98. **17** Walter Map, *De nugis curialium*, eds Montague R. James, Christopher N.L. Brooke and R.A.B. Mynors (Oxford, 1983), p. 436.

descent, and bishops, abbots, magnates and knights born from the seed of both peoples'.[18] Richard too saw intermarriage between English and Normans as the key.[19] Neither Aelred nor Richard, however, attributed this, as Walter Map did, to deliberate royal policy. The historiography of both English and Normans may have made it easy to think of the integration of peoples as a natural process. This, after all, was the way in which Bede's authoritative history had been structured – the emergence of the 'gens Anglorum [. . .] de tribus Germaniae populis fortioribus, id est Saxonibus, Anglis, Iutis'. In Normandy a passage in the *Inventio et miracula Sancti Vulfranni*, a mid eleventh-century history of the relics and monastery of St Wandrille, speaks of the making of one people out of many different peoples: *atque unum ex diversibus gentibus populum effecit.*[20]

But Walter Map was not alone in attributing this piece of social engineering to royal initiative. An anonymous author writing in London during King John's reign also credited a great king with a marriage policy intended to bring about harmony between different peoples living in a single kingdom. This writer, whose name is still unknown and whose very existence was unsuspected until deduced by some brilliant detective work by Felix Liebermann, is the compiler of what has become known as the London Collection.[21] He not only assembled a collection of codes of law and administrative documents, many – but not all – relating to London, but was also the first to put the law codes into chronological order beginning with the laws of King Ine of Wessex (reigned 688–726?) and ending with Henry II's 'Glanvill'. He further signaled his interest in royal achievements by composing short linking passages about the kings in whose names those laws were issued.[22] He selected, manipulated and fabricated his material in order

---

18 'Habet nunc certe de genere Anglorum Anglia regem, habet de eadem gente episcopos et abbates, habet et principes, milites etiam optimos qui ex utriusque seminis conjunctione procreati.' These phrases from Aelred's *Vita Sancti Edwardi* are taken from the improved text passages printed in Ian Short, *'Tam Angli quam Franci*: self-definition in Anglo-Norman England,' *Anglo-Norman Studies*, 18 (1995) 170–2. Cf. Aelred of Rievaulx: *The historical works*, trans. J.P. Freeland, ed. M. Dutton (Kalamazoo, 2005), pp 208–9.   19 'sed iam cohabitantibus Anglicis et Normannis et alterutrum uxores ducentibus vel nubentibus, sic permixte sunt nationes ut vix decerni possit hodie, de liberis loquor, quis Anglicus quis Normannus sit genere.' FitzNigel, *Dialogus de Scaccario*, p. 53.   20 Discussed by Cassandra Potts, *'Atque unum ex diversibus gentibus populim effecit*: historical tradition and the Norman identity,' *Anglo-Norman Studies*, 18 (1995) 139–52, 142–5.   21 Felix Liebermann, *Über die Leges Anglorum Saeculo XIII ineunte Londoniis collectae* (Halle, 1894). So fierce and frequent are Liebermann's denunciations of the London Collector as a bare-faced liar and forger that it rather looks as though it was moral outrage which drove Liebermann to identify him by uncovering his misdeeds, his modus operandi.   22 On this aspect of his work, John Gillingham, *'Stupor mundi*: 1204 et un obituaire de Richard Coeur de Lion depuis longtemps tombé dans l'oubli' in M. Aurell and N-Y. Tonnerre (eds), *Plantagenêts et Capétiens: confrontations et héritages. Actes du colloque de Poitiers et Fontevraud, May 2004* (Turnhout, 2006), pp 397–411.

to promote his own interests and those of the London mercantile groups to which he presumably belonged.[23] Some of his ideas, notably those contained in his interpolations into the 'Laws of Edward the Confessor', have been seen as part of the intellectual background to Magna Carta and in consequence attracted the attention of twentieth-century historians of English law and constitution.[24]

Other ideas of the London Collector's struck Liebermann very forcibly; he called them 'sein Programm eines Grossbritannischen Kaiserthums'.[25] Apart from some paragraphs by Walter Ullmann on the English claim to lordship over Scotland, these ideas were, however, very largely ignored until Rees Davies remarked on them in *The first English empire*.[26] As Davies pointed out, the collector 'thought in extravagant pan-British terms: he peppered his text with references to the kingdom of Britain and to the monarchy and crown of the same; he even proclaimed that empire (*imperium*) was a more appropriate word than kingdom (*regnum*) for such an assemblage of power'.[27] In the collector's view, the first king to obtain the monarchy of the whole kingdom of Britain after the arrival of the English was Ine of Wessex.[28] During his victorious reign, 'a single folk and a single people (*gens una et populus unus*) had been created throughout the whole kingdom of Britain. As result everyone substituted the name "kingdom of the English" for what had hitherto been called "the kingdom of Britain."'[29] This name change particularly engaged Davies' attention. He saw it as a typically English solution to what he called the 'British problem', i.e., the fact that 'it was the Welsh who claimed to be the true descendants of the Britons and who were the begetters of the mythology and prophecy of Britain'. One

---

23 Much the best introduction to his thought is Derek Keene, 'Text, visualization and politics: London, 1150–1250', *TRHS*, 6th ser., 18 (2008), 80–99. 24 F.M. Powicke, *Stephen Langton* (Oxford, 1928), pp 114–15; J.E.A. Jolliffe, *Angevin kingship* (2nd ed., London, 1963), pp 6, 15, 18, 322–3; Walter Ullmann, 'On the influence of Geoffrey of Monmouth in English history' in *Speculum historiale*, eds Clemens Bauer, Laetitia Boehm and M. Müller (Freiburg, 1965), pp 257–76; James C. Holt, 'The origins of the constitutional tradition in England' in idem, *Magna Carta and medieval government* (London, 1985), pp 1–22; idem, *Magna Carta* (Cambridge, 1992), pp 56, 93–94; Patrick Wormald, *The making of English law: King Alfred to the twelfth century* (Oxford, 1999), pp 237–42; idem, '*Quadripartitus*' in *Law and government in medieval England and Normandy*, ed. George Garnett and John Hudson (Cambridge, 1994), pp 112, 119–20; Bruce O' Brien, *God's peace and king's peace: the laws of Edward the Confessor* (Philadelphia, 1999), pp 118–19. 25 Liebermann, *Über die Leges*, p. 6. 26 Ullmann, 'On the influence of Geoffrey', pp 264–5. 27 'de iure potius appellari debet excellentia corone imperium quam regnum.' See R.R. Davies, *The first English empire* (Oxford, 2000), pp 16–17. 28 Liebermann, *Über die Leges*, p. 14. 29 'effecti fuerunt gens una et populus unus per universum regnum Britannie […] Deinde universi vocaverunt regnum Anglorum, quod ante vocatum fuit regnum Britannie.' *Die Gesetze der Angelsachsen*, ed. Felix Liebermann, 3 vols (Halle, 1903–16), i, p. 659. When he reached Cnut's reign, the collector gave this people a name: Angli-Britones, ibid., 664; cf. Liebermann, *Über die Leges*, pp 24, 26.

English solution was to hijack the Matter of Britain and turn Arthur into a king of England.[30] Another solution was that adopted by the collector. He was not being original. Rees Davies traced the idea of name change from Britain to England back to the late tenth century and to Ealdorman Aethelweard's assertion that 'Britain is now called England (*Anglia*), thereby assuming the name of the victors. He noted similar words used by Henry of Huntingdon, Chrétien of Troyes and William of Newburgh, coming to a climax with Gervase of Canterbury's '[a]nd so the name of Britain was deleted'. This Rees Davies interpreted as the English 'final solution to the British problem. It solved it by eliminating it'.[31]

What has not been highlighted since Liebermann's day, however, is the London Collector's explanation for the intermarriage between Britons and English. It was, according to the collector, on King Ine's orders (*per preceptum regis Ine*) and by the common counsel and assent (*per commune consilium et assensum*) of all magnates and wise men of whole kingdom that the English took British wives and the Britons took English wives.[32] This was, in other words, carefully considered government policy. King Ine's policy on inter-marriage, the making of 'one people', can be seen as his deliberate implementation of the ruler's duty to bring divided peoples together as one in harmony and peace. This was the obligation imposed upon kings of Britain by the papacy, the instruction they received in a letter sent by Pope Eleutherius to King Lucius of Britain in 169 AD.[33] Historians long before the collector had known that such a papal letter must have existed, a reply to the one which, according to Bede (*Historia Ecclesiastica*, I. c. 4), King Lucius had sent to the pope, but its text had remained unknown for four hundred years until the London Collector, forging where even Geoffrey of Monmouth had feared to forge, helpfully provided it.[34] Whatever the reality might have been, Ine of Wessex, the king responsible for the earliest law code in his collection, loomed large in our Londoner's imagination. He not only actively promoted inter-marriage, he also intervened directly in economic

---

30 As was first recorded by Roger of Howden who, writing *c.*1190, referred to Arthur as 'rex Britonum' and then a few years later as 'rex Anglie'. Noted in John Gillingham,'The context and purposes of Geoffrey of Monmouth's *History of the kings of Britain*', *Anglo-Norman Studies*, 13 (1991–2), 99–118, repr. in John Gillingham, *The English in the twelfth century* (Woodbridge, 2000), pp 19–39, 23 n. 23. 31 Davies, *First English empire*, pp 48–9, citing Huntingdon, *Historia*, pp 12–13; William of Newburgh, *Historian rerum Anglicarum*, ed. R. Howlett, 2 vols. (RS, 1884–5), i, p. 132; Gervase of Canterbury: *Historical works*, ed. William Stubbs (RS, 1879–80), ii, p. 21. 32 Liebermann, *Gesetze*, p. 658. For the mistaken understanding of Old English which led the collector to this important conclusion, Liebermann, *Über die Leges*, pp 44–5. 33 'Gentes vero regni Britannie et populi vestri sunt, quos divisos debetis in unum ad concordiam et pacem [. . .] congregare', Liebermann, *Gesetze*, p. 637. 34 Liebermann, *Über die Leges*, pp 40–3. Ullmann called the pope's letter 'the pivotal point of the whole section he had entitled *De jure et appendiciis coronae regni Britanniae*', Ullmann, 'On the influence', p. 260.

affairs. His was the command that there should be only one currency and that an assize of weights and measures should apply throughout the whole kingdom of Britain. The collector attributed to him a law prohibiting the export of raw wool and allowing only the export of manufactured woollen cloth, evidently a forgery reflecting his own preferred commercial policy to which he was giving the authority of antiquity.[35] The range of interventions attributed to King Ine shows that in this early thirteenth-century observer's mind, the potential scope of royal policy was very wide.

It was also widely assumed that a king might be well advised to insist that all inhabitants of a single kingdom should obey a single common law. This is how Aelred of Rievaulx had conceived of a key development in England's tenth-century past and the work of King Edgar. Aelred presented him as a model ruler: 'no less memorable to the English than Cyrus to the Persians, Charles to the Franks, and Romulus to the Romans. He united the kingdom of the English in a kind of heavenly peace, and joined peoples of different languages by the pact of one law (*regnum Anglorum celesti quadam pace composuit, et multarum linguarum gentes, unius foedere legis conjunxit)*'.[36]

Richard of Devizes made some similar points about law. Not the familiar Richard of Devizes, author of a well-known narrative of the early years of Richard I's reign, but an unfamiliar Richard, author of the Winchester annals from 519 to 1139.[37] As author of a *Gesta Ricardi*, Richard of Devizes has long been portrayed as one of the most remarkable authors of the time, witty, sardonic and urbane.[38] Yet despite their potential interest as evidence for the outlook of so remarkable an author, these annals has been almost totally ignored; indeed his text for the period from 1066 to 1139 have not even been printed in full, only 'the more interesting entries'.[39] Although the annals from 539 to the Conquest were printed in the Rolls Series, not even his observation that 'while Arthur was occupied in Gaul, the Saxons built those forts on all the hills and high points, of which remains can still be seen today'

---

35 Liebermann, *Über die Leges*, pp 12–13.   36 Aelred, *Genealogia regum Anglorum*, Migne PL 195, col. 726, composed in the 1150s. 'hic enim regnum Anglorum celesti quadem pace composuit, et multarum linguarum gentes, unius foedere legis conjunxit [...] tota ei insula sine sanguine manus daret, et ad subdendum se ei Scotia, Cumbria, Wallia libens accurreret [...] terra fecundior et totius regni facies abundiatori decore venustior.' Translated in Aelred, *Historical works*, pp 95–6.   37 Although it did not win Gransden's wholehearted support, the case for Richard's authorship of the annals up to 1139, thought quite likely by H.R. Luard, the Roll Series editor of the Winchester Annals, was fully made in J.T. Appleby, 'Richard of Devizes and the Annals of Winchester', *Bulletin of the Institute of Historical Research*, 93 (1963), 70–7. On the other hand, his authorship of the annals for 1196–1202 seems unlikely. Antonia Gransden, *Historical writing in England c.550 to c.1307* (London, 1974), p. 252. See the entry on Richard of Devizes by G.H. Martin in the *Oxford dictionary of national biography*.   38 Nancy Partner, *Serious entertainments: the writing of history in twelfth-century England* (Chicago, 1977), pp 143–79.   39 Appleby, 'Richard of Devizes', 75.

has attracted much interest.[40] For as long as modern historians saw chroniclers almost exclusively as purveyors of facts, to be judged as either reliable or unreliable, there was little interest in what they wrote about centuries long before their own.

Here I wish only to draw attention to some aspects of Richard's view of the Anglo-Saxon past. In it, he too expressed the view that the names of territories and peoples could be changed, indeed he explicitly attributed the change to royal command. In his entry for 828, he wrote that on the day that Egbert, in the presence of the leaders of all the kingdoms he had conquered, was crowned 'king of all Britain' at Winchester, 'he ordered that in future the island should be called England, and that those who had been called Jutes and Saxons, should all in common bear the name English.' Under 1017, he described Cnut ordering the Danes to abide by the laws and rights of King Alfred. English and Danes were to be one people ('sed essent Angli et Daci populus unus, et omnes Eluredi regis Anglorum leges et jura tenerent'). What were these laws? In his entry for the year 872, he wrote: 'King Alfred translated the laws of the Britons into English, which were from then on called the laws of King Alfred.'[41] Richard, it seems, accepted Geoffrey of Monmouth's tall tale of Alfred as translator of the *Lex Martiana*, the code composed by Marcia, noble wife of the British king Guithelinus.[42] We may recognize this as fiction, but the point here is that Richard of Devizes saw a process by which, as a consequence of royal translation and command, different peoples, first Britons and English, then Britons, English and Danes, all came to share a common law.

Another of Alfred's achievements, Richard of Devizes noted laconically, was the institution of hundreds and tithings.[43] This Richard clearly borrowed from William of Malmesbury's *Gesta regum*. According to William, 'The barbarian invasions had given the English too an appetite for thieving such that no man's journey was safe without armed protection; and so he instituted the centuries which they call hundreds and the divisions into tenths called tithings, so that every law-abiding Englishman had his century and his tenth [. . .]. By this new system (*Hoc commento*) Alfred spread peace throughout the province so that on public highways he ordered gold bracelets to be hung up at crossroads, to mock the greed of passers-by, for no one dared steal them'.[44] There is an obvious parallel with Bede's picture of Edwin's rule. But whereas

40 *Annals of Winchester* in *Annales Monastici*, ii, ed. H.R. Luard (Rolls Series, 1865), p. 3. But on this entry and on the pre-519 annals, still unprinted, see John Gillingham, 'Richard of Devizes and a "rising tide of nonsense": How Cerdic met King Arthur,' in *The long twelfth-century view of the Anglo-Saxon past*, ed. M. Brett and D.A. Woodman (forthcoming).   **41** Ibid., pp 8, 10, 15. His comments on Cnut's policy are clearly based on William of Malmesbury, *Gesta regum*, chs 181 and 183.   **42** Geoffrey of Monmouth, *The history of the kings of Britain*, ed. Michael D. Reeve, trans. Neil Wright (Woodbridge, 2007), ch. 47.   **43** 'Iste instituit hundredos et tethingas ad latrinos investigandos', *Annals of Winchester*, p. 10.   **44** 'Centurias quas dicunt hundrez et decimas quas tithingas vocant instituit, ut omnis Anglus legaliter dumtaxat vivens haberet et

Bede had simply ascribed Edwin's peace to the king's power, William of Malmesbury has made it the consequence of administrative innovation enabling law to be implemented. There has been some difference in opinion as to whether the attribution of hundreds and tithings to Alfred was William's anachronistic invention (the view taken by Stubbs and Whitelock) or whether there is some truth in it, a 'remarkable example of William's historical insight' (Wormald).[45] What no one, so far as I know, has hitherto remarked, is that here William of Malmesbury was writing a new kind of history, the history of institutions. Later in the century there emerged a new kind of literature, the administrative manual, *The dialogue of the exchequer*, composed by an author, Richard FitzNigel, who was interested in the history of the institution.[46] In this new environment, William of Malmesbury's innovative approach caught on. It seemed, as we have seen, plausible to Richard of Devizes; and it was followed by the London Collector. Indeed the latter once again supplied the 'missing' documents, in this case the Alfredian laws establishing tithings and peace gilds.[47]

Some administrative arrangements were in the collector's view even older. His British empire had been established by King Arthur.[48] Nothing new in that, but in choosing to give an administrative slant to Arthur's achievement, he took a path foreign to Geoffrey of Monmouth. He credited Arthur with the creation of folk-moots and annual meetings on May Day at which all the king's subjects had to join together as sworn brothers and take an oath of allegiance.[49] According to the collector, this practice later fell into disuse until revived by Edgar, together with the order that all subjects were to possess appropriate weapons, and bring them to an annual weapon show, on the morrow of Purification (3 February), on the same day throughout the whole kingdom.[50] Indeed it was these institutions, established in the name of peace-keeping and the defence of the realm, that the collector believed enabled Æthelred to organize and command the St Brice's Day massacre on one and the same day.[51] Is this new history of administrative institutions a

centuriam et decimam.' Malmesbury, *Gesta regum*, ch. 122. **45** Wormald, *Making of English law*, pp 5, 14, 137. See also William of Malmesbury, *Gesta regum Anglorum*, ii, introduction and commentary by R.M. Thomson (Oxford, 1999), p. 98. **46** Hudson, 'Administration, family', pp 77–8. **47** Liebermann, *Über die Leges*, pp 16–20. 'Alfred's' law on tithings was intended to create a band of sworn brothers (*coniurati fratres*), bound together to keep the peace *pro regni communi utilitate*. His concept of citizens as sworn brothers also figured in his account of King Arthur's achievement. See below n. 49. **48** Ibid., pp 22–3, 25–6. The empire, according to the collector, remained largely intact until Cnut gave much away. **49** 'insimul confederare et consolidare sicut coniurati fratres ad defendendum regnum. Hanc legem invenit Arturus [...] et ita consolidavit et confederavit regnum Britannie universum in unum', Liebermann, *Gesetze*, p. 655; *Über die Leges*, pp 57, 59. **50** Liebermann, *Gesetze*, p. 655; *Über die Leges*, pp 59–60. **51** 'Huius legis auctoritate Aldredus rex subito uno eodem die per universum regnum Danos occidit', Liebermann, *Gesetze*, p. 656

reflection of a changing society – the authors' recognition of the rise of what has been called 'administrative kingship', and hence of a genuine widening in the scope of royal government? It was this development, this 'intensification of lordship' which, as Rees Davies observed, helps to explain the contrast between, on the one hand, there having been in 'a pre-bureaucratic age' little or no attempt to introduce English administrative machinery into Wales and, on the other, royal policy towards Ireland, when 'for the first time the institutions of English governance had been transported en bloc to a conquered country'.[52]

Another sphere in which past kings were thought to have had a role was that of education. According to Richard of Devizes, King Egbert of Wessex became a teacher. 'Having been driven into exile in Gaul, rather than waste time there, he instead he chose to be taught and exercised every day in the school of military science'. On his return as king in 800, 'he made soldiers out of all the strong and active young men of his kingdom [...] the former pupil now became the teacher'.[53] King Alfred's concern for book-learning was well-known, but not well-evidenced in the surviving record, so once again the London Collector supplied what was needed – an Alfredian law requiring all freemen with two hides or more of land to put their children to school until they were fifteen years old: *Verum liberum hominem illiteratum pro bruto et cephalo et stulto reputamus.*[54] Richard of Devizes noted that Alfred translated 'many books' as well as the British laws. For him, Alfred's reign marked the pivotal point in the civilizing of the English. 'This kingdom which before his time was uncultured and underdeveloped, he taught and entirely refashioned, bringing it up to a proper standard'.[55] The civilizing Alfred of Richard's Winchester Annals is recognizably similar to Aelred's King David of Scotland: a gentle (*mansuetus*) king who knew how to entice a whole people, once rough and rustic (*rudem et agrestem*), to adopt manners which were civilized and domesticated (*ad mores compositos et edomitos*).[56]

---

52 Davies, *Domination and conquest*, pp 121–2. In Ireland, with the long term consequences summed up in Seán Duffy, *Ireland in the Middle Ages* (Dublin, 1997), pp 96–8.   53 *Annals of Winchester*, pp 6–7.   54 Liebermann, *Über die Leges*, pp 16, 19.   55 'Iste regnum Anglorum ante dies suos rude et incompositum, totum erudivit et informavit ad regulam', *Annals of Winchester*, p. 10. On this whole theme see John Gillingham, 'Civilizing the English? The English histories of William of Malmesbury and David Hume', *Historical Research*, 74 (2001), 17–43. 56 'Unde non immerito velut mansuetus hereditabat terram [...] quam inter barbaras gentes, et diversitate linguarum et morum sibi contrarias, et propter mutuas mortes et vulnera sibi inimicissimas, tanta cautione composuit [...] Ita enim populum illum, rudem et agrestem, ad mores compositos et edomitos illicere satagebat [...] Ipse barbaros mores tuos Christiana religione composuit. Unde tota illa gentis illius barbaries mansuefacta, tanta se mox regi benevolentia et humilitate substravit, ut naturalis oblita saevitiae, legibus quas regia mansuetudo dictabat, colla submitteret'. *Eulogium Davidis* by Aelred of Rievaulx in *Pinkerton's Lives of Scottish saints*, ed. W.M. Metcalfe (Paisley, 1889), pp 271, 279; translated in Aelred, *Historical works*, pp 47–8, 52.

According to William of Malmesbury, David used fiscal policy to that end, offering tax exemptions to all those Scots who were prepared to 'live in a more cultivated fashion, dress more elegantly and eat with more refinement'.[57]

Historically minded twelfth- and early thirteenth-century English authors evidently believed that there were a number of ways in which royal policy and leadership had had a marked impact upon the past of their own country – and in Aelred's case, of Scotland – not just in war and conquest, but also in education, economic life and in the maintenance of peace by encouraging intermarriage as well as by means of legislation and administrative innovation. For all manner of well-rehearsed reasons, the kings of England for a very long time failed to bring peace to Wales, and failed for an even longer time in Ireland.[58] But if their conquering kings were thought to have successfully shaped British society in the past, then the confidence, however misguided, with which the English expected to be able to re-shape neighbouring countries is more readily comprehensible.

---

57 'David iuvenis ceteris curialior et qui, nostrorum convictu et familiaritate limatus a puero, omnem rubiginem Scotticae barbariei deterserat. Denique regno potitus mox omnes compatriotas triennalium tributorum pensione levavit qui vellent habitare cultius, amiciri elegantius, pasci accuratius', William of Malmesbury, *Gesta regum*, ch. 400.   58 See, for example, R.R. Davies, 'The English state and the "Celtic" peoples 1100–1400', *Journal of Historical Sociology*, 6 (1993), reprinted in *Twenty years of the Journal of Historical Sociology*, i: *essays on the British state*, ed. Y-S. Wong and D. Sayer (Oxford, 2008), pp 157–71.

Domination and conquest?: the Scottish experience in the twelfth and thirteenth centuries

MATTHEW HAMMOND

If the kingdom of the Scots was never invaded outright[1] between William the Conqueror's sojourn to Abernethy in 1072 and Edward I's more definitive romp in 1296, from our third-millennium vantage point, the scholar can hardly escape the conclusion that the *study* of this definitive period in Scottish medieval history, in contrast, has succumbed no fewer than fours times to successive waves of what may be dryly termed 'process-driven models', or, perhaps more satisfactorily, the '-zations'.[2]

According to the *Oxford English dictionary*, the term 'Normanization' has been in use at least since 1901, when it was employed in a Welsh context, but it seems to have made its Scottish début in 1954 with R.L. Graeme Ritchie's volume, *The Normans in Scotland*, which began with the memorable line, 'there was a Norman conquest of Scotland'.[3] Ritchie's book garnered generally positive reviews in its day, although one reviewer commented (perhaps unfairly) that 'the story of Normanization is an unexciting account of a slow, peaceful introduction of more efficient methods of administration, and of French *elegantia* among a new feudal aristocracy'.[4] The reviewer's attempt to relay the book's central thesis to an American audience reveals unwittingly the inherent flaws in applying any process-driven model to the Scottish situa-

1 A paper with this title was given at the First English Empire Conference at Trinity College Dublin on 14 November 2007; however, the substance of this published version owes more to a second outing in the form of a Denys Hay seminar paper at the University of Edinburgh, delivered on 25 November 2008, which was entitled 'Scotland in the twelfth and thirteenth centuries: anglicization or Scotticization; or, a whirlwind tour of the four "zations"'. I would like to thank my hosts, Dr Seán Duffy and Dr Tom Brown, for their gracious invitations on both of these occasions. I would also like to offer my gratitude to Professors David Carpenter, Archie Duncan and John Gillingham for useful discussions on topics relating to this paper, and especially to Professor Dauvit Broun for reading and commenting on drafts of this chapter. As far as invasions go, I am of course omitting to mention King John's harrying of Lothian, which occurred early in 1216, but was a short-lived punitive expedition rather than an outright invasion, with all of the implied political ramifications. 2 Of course, technically, the relevant suffix is '-ization', but I must confess to being unable to resist the punnical attraction of the 'four zations'. 3 "Normanization, n." *OED Online*. Dec. 2003. Oxford University Press. *http://dictionary.oed. com/cgi/entry/00327063*, 9 Jan. 2009. The first example quoted therein is John E. Morris' *The Welsh wars of Edward I* (Oxford, 1901), i. 4; R.L. Graeme Ritchie, *The Normans in Scotland* (Edinburgh, 1954). 4 Richard A. Newhall, *American Historical Review*, 60 (1955), 876.

tion: 'The basic assumptions upon which his interpretation of the scanty record rests are that the process of Normanization in Scotland was very similar to the process in England, that the England of Henry I served as a model for the Scottish kings, and that native Scottish conditions, can, if necessary, be surmised from probably similar conditions in Wales and Ireland'.[5] In the same pithy sentence, the reviewer notes the obvious similarity between the processes driving change in Scotland and in England, as well as the frequently-held presumption that Scotland was nevertheless so similar to Ireland and Wales that evidence for one could be substituted for the other. It was this complicated if not paradoxical scenario, that Scotland could find analogues in both the English experience on the one hand, and the Irish and Welsh experiences on the other, that has prevented any model (or at least any model very firmly tied to the British political dimension) from adequately reflecting the nature of changes and continuities in the Scottish kingdom.

If 'Normanization' seems hopelessly outdated today, it is probably due to its easy association of ethnic identity with various characteristics of civilization, from writing and centralized royal administration to more effective military practices and increased trade, affiliations still redolent of nineteenth-century assumptions.[6] For the following generation of scholars, Ritchie's unleashing of Normanization on Scotland may have seemed uncomfortably close at times to the progressivist history of an earlier era.[7] Thus we can guess that Professor Duncan had a sarcastic tongue in cheek when he titled his extremely thorough review of Ritchie's book '*Gesta Dei per Francos*'! Duncan thus dismissed Ritchie's effort as somewhat overenthusiastic, staking his claim that the introduction of burghs, castles, coins and sheriffs were 'not from a deliberate policy of Normanizing'.[8] Similarly, in light of Professor Barrow's fondness for all things feudal and his

5 Ibid.   6 It should be noted that 'Normanization' has enjoyed a somewhat more fruitful life in Ireland than elsewhere in the four nations, a life that has been abruptly ended by Professor John Gillingham. In 'The English invasion of Ireland', ch. 9 in *The English in the twelfth century: imperialism, national identity and political values* (Woodbridge, 2000) [initially published in B. Bradshaw, A. Hadfield and W. Maley (eds), *Representing Ireland: literature and the origins of conflict, 1534–1660* (Cambridge, 1993), pp 24–42], Gillingham makes clear that the view of the Irish invasion as a 'Norman' one is a modern invention, and argues that 'the best reason for saying that the invaders were English is that this is what contemporary narrative sources say they were'. Gillingham, *English in the twelfth century*, p. 151. In 'Normanizing the English Invaders of Ireland', he has traced the use of the term 'Norman' in reference to Ireland back as far as the 1780s. Huw Pryce and John Watts (eds), *Power and identity in the Middle Ages: essays in memory of Rees Davies* (Oxford, 2007), pp 85–97.   7 For an exploration of the effects of nineteenth-century attitudes on Scottish history, see Matthew H. Hammond, 'Ethnicity and the writing of Scottish medieval history', *Scottish Historical Review*, 85 (2006), 1–27.   8 Archibald Duncan, *Scottish Historical Review*, 34 (1955), 150–3.

publication of works with titles like *The Anglo-Norman era in Scottish history* and 'Scotland's "Norman" families', scholars may be surprised to note that upon close examination, his *oeuvre* contains little if any mention of the process-driven Normanization. Many of Barrow's most important articles are aimed at pointing out the broad and diverse points of origin – from Brittany to Burgundy – of many of the families too often lumped together as 'Normans'.[9]

With Normanization thus tending to be superseded by a much more nuanced approach, albeit one that tended to favour the Anglo-French dimension of the era, scholars may have been tempted by the 1980s to declare the ascendency of process-driven models as over and done with. They, of course, would have been mistaken, as two new '-zations' with implications for the world far beyond Scotland emerged by the century's final decade. Professor Rees Davies' volume *Domination and conquest: the experience of Ireland, Scotland and Wales, 1100–1300* appeared in print in 1990, and consisted of his 1988 Wiles Lectures from Queen's University, Belfast. As Davies explicitly stated, no attempt was made in this concise work to construct a narrative of 'the story of Anglo-Norman and English penetration and domination of Ireland, Scotland and Wales'. Rather, he would focus on the 'strategies of domination which underpin the narrative accounts'.[10] Moreover, this book marked a clear departure from the Norman-dominated analyses of the past; part of Davies' enduring, daring, departure, was his insistence on transcending national boundaries and nationalist narratives. When one does this, he claimed, the scholar would be left with an impression less of Norman conquests of these three countries than 'a second tidal wave of Anglo-Saxon or English colonization'.[11]

In 1993, Robert Bartlett's book, *The making of Europe: conquest, colonization and cultural change, 950–1350*, was published, containing a chapter with the striking title 'The Europeanization of Europe', which highlighted the spread of universal European saints and personal names, underpinned by the adoption of coins and charters in peripheral parts of Europe.[12] If Normanization placed emphasis on the spread of French culture, and angli-

---

9 G.W.S. Barrow, *The Anglo-Norman era in Scottish history* (Oxford, 1980); G.W.S. Barrow, 'Scotland's "Norman" families', appears as ch. 13 in *The kingdom of the Scots: government, church and society from the eleventh to the fourteenth century* (2nd ed., Edinburgh, 2003) and first appeared as 'Les familles normandes d'Ecosse' in *Annales de Normandie* 15e année (1965). See also 'The beginnings of military feudalism', ch. 12 in *Kingdom of the Scots* (originally published as 'The beginnings of feudalism in Scotland', *Bulletin of the Institute of Historical Research*, 29 (1956)), wherein Barrow makes reference to Ritchie's work. 10 R.R. Davies, *Domination and conquest: the experience of Ireland, Scotland and Wales, 1100–1300* (Cambridge, 1990), pp ix–x. 11 Ibid., p. 12. 12 Robert Bartlett, *The making of Europe: conquest, colonization and cultural change, 950–1350* (London, 1993).

cization, the uneven nature of power relations in the British Isles, Europeanization had the advantage of combining these two elements. The genius of Bartlett's book is that it is played out on such a large stage that its broader points are less subject to the whims and vicissitudes of the relations between any two kingdoms. It was not until his 1999 offering, *The first English empire* (which, like Barrow's *Anglo-Norman era*, was the printed manifestation of a series of Ford Lectures at Oxford) that Davies first seems to have employed the term 'anglicization', with a chapter entitled 'The anglicization of the British Isles'.[13] Moreover, it was apparently in reaction to Bartlett that Davies decided to apply the anglicization label to his *Domination and conquest* paradigm. With characteristic openness, Davies reveals in *The first English empire* (2000):

Just as Robert Bartlett can talk about the Europeanization of Europe as the distinctive feature of the centuries 950–1350, so likewise it may not be improper to refer to the anglicization of the British Isles during the period covered by this book. Indeed anglicization may be interpreted as the distinctively insular version of this process of Europeanization.[14]

If Davies coined 'anglicization' in response to Bartlett, it nevertheless seems evident that the structure and organization of *Domination and conquest* are suggestive of a process–driven model. Moving through the chapters, aristocratic domination is followed by native submission, the kings of England and the domination of the British Isles, the intensification of lordship and, finally and irrevocably, conquest. This process seems to fit neatly with the steps leading from the establishment of the Welsh March to the capitulation of the independent Welsh principality, and to a lesser extent with Ireland, where the process of conquest eventually ran out of steam. For all the sweeping grandeur and brilliance of Davies' model, and for all the inherent advantage in taking a cross-border approach to this period, there remains a nagging feeling that the fledgling ship of anglicization was in danger of running adrift on the reef of nationalist narrative. This anxiety clearly drove a certain hesitancy on the part of Davies, particularly when it came to Scotland. In the preface to *Domination and conquest*, Davies voiced his worries: 'I have been aware [. . .],' he wrote, 'that it may be misleading to juxtapose Scotland on the one hand with Wales and Ireland on the other in an analysis of these two centuries'. He was careful to note that 'Scotland was a separate, unitary

13 R.R. Davies, *The first English empire: power and identities in the British Isles, 1093–1343* (Oxford, 2000). 14 Davies, *First English Empire*, p. 170. See also Huw Pryce, 'Welsh rulers and European change, c.1100–1282' in Huw Pryce and John Watts (eds), *Power and identity in the Middle Ages: essays in memory of Rees Davies* (Oxford, 2007), pp 37–51. Pryce makes a similar claim for the principality of Wales on p. 37, where he states that the 'transformation of Welsh society' highlighted by Rees Davies can 'be seen as exemplifying what Robert Bartlett has called Europeanization'.

kingdom whose status was recognized by the kings of England and the rulers of the Continent; its institutional and political development in the twelfth and thirteenth centuries placed it in a league altogether different from that of the native polities of Wales and Ireland'. Thus, Davies was at pains to show that he understood Scotland's unique position, somewhere between the 'full domination and conquest paradigm' of Wales and Ireland, and the role of dominator filled by England. Nevertheless, he concluded that 'the Scottish experience [...] does illuminate the story of Anglo–Norman expansion in, and English domination of, the British Isles in a significant fashion'.[15]

Despite Davies' understanding of Scotland's unique place, and his concern to fence it round with caveats, I must express doubts as to the extent to which the role of the Scottish kingdom in Davies' paradigm is sustainable. One suspects that Scotland would have needed its own separate and distinct section in the two books, but under constant and unremitting comparison to Ireland and Wales, with the contrasts not receiving a full-throated airing, the structure begins to fall apart. If we look at the twin themes of domination and conquest that underpin the anglicization model, one first notes the extent to which the 'conquest' experience in Scotland fails to fit the model. Certainly, all three countries were conquered to great extent by the kings of England. There are two problems with comparing the Edwardian conquest of Scotland with the English invasions of Ireland and Wales, however. First, the Scottish conquest was extremely short-lived; even during the wars of independence period, there were only two relatively short phases when a reasonably effective English administration was operating in large parts of the kingdom.[16] Second, the Edwardian takeover of Scotland stands outside the processes that Davies seeks to tie to English conquests in Ireland and Wales. In other words, Davies suggests that the processes of aristocratic domination, native submission and the overlordship of the English kings were precursors to the eventual conquest of Ireland and especially Wales. In Scotland, this was not the case. The processes of anglicization were firmly marshalled to increase the power of the kings of Scots, and the influx of colonial aristocracy did nothing to further the cause of the English king. Indeed, Edward's foes – first Balliol, with his supporters the Comyns, then Bruce – were all members of longstanding Anglo–French families with lands in England. The takeover of Scotland was avowedly not the culmination of a process of domination, but rather ruthless opportunism on the part of Edward after the precipitous collapse of what had been a remarkably successful 'native' dynasty.

---

15 Davies, *Domination and conquest*, p. x.   16 Fiona Watson, *Under the hammer: Edward I and Scotland, 1286–1306* (East Linton, 1998), esp. chs 2 and 7.

The theme of domination is more nuanced and deserves greater attention. Simply put, the relationship between dominator and dominated in, for example, Wales, is relatively straightforward. The main difference between Scotland and Ireland or Wales is that Scotland, like England, had a centralizing and modernizing monarchy, which means that effective comparisons can be drawn between Scotland and England in ways that are not true for their neighbours. Indeed, the kings of Scots, in addition to inviting and controlling the forces of Europeanization and using them to augment their own power, were also capable of using the same techniques as the kings of England and acting as the dominator, for example, in their dealings with Galloway, Orkney or the kingdom of Man and the Isles.

The bedrock principle of Davies' argument is that the kings of England used the same techniques, albeit as often typified by flattery and subtlety as by brute force, when dealing with their client rulers in Scotland, Ireland and Wales. This is undoubtedly true at times in the twelfth century, although the comparisons wear thin in the reigns of Alexander II and III.[17] Nevertheless, the English kings were capable of sometimes subtly undercutting the Scottish kings, as with Henry II and Mael Coluim IV at Chester, sometimes publicly humiliating them, as with Henry II and William I after his capture at Alnwick, and tested the limits of their power in various ways while at the same time making sure that the pope did not allow the Scots to acquire episcopal anointment for their royal inaugurations.[18] At the same time, Davies acknowledges that 'Scotland, of course, was in a different league altogether from Wales and Ireland. Whereas the latter two were part of the king of England's dominions, Scotland was, and was recognized to be, a separate kingdom with its own independent monarchy'.[19]

Despite the similarities in the dynamics of power between the kings of England and the rulers of their neighbouring polities, there are two factors relevant to the Scottish situation that not only muddy the waters of the anglicization paradigm, but also explain why the course of Scotland's history diverged so much from that of Ireland and Wales. First, there was a single king of Alba by the early twelfth century who was able to dominate most of Northern Britain, as compared to the myriad of Irish and Welsh rulers. Perhaps more crucial to their success than has been acknowledged was that the marriage of Mael Coluim III to Margaret of England conferred a new importance to the kingdom in the broader European political scene, as well as a certain legitimacy from an ethno-nationalist standpoint. The naming of their sons was not so much evidence of the kind of Europeanizing

17 *The kingship of the Scots, 842–1292: succession and independence* (Edinburgh, 2002), ch. 8; Dauvit Broun, *Scottish independence and the idea of Britain: from the Picts to Alexander III* (Edinburgh, 2007), ch. 7. 18 Davies, *Domination and conquest*, pp 75–87. 19 Ibid., p. 81.

tendencies in royal names that Bartlett has written about (in fact none of them had conventional French or Norman names) than an attempt to replicate the prestige of the late Anglo–Saxon dynasty.[20] They were named after Margaret's father (Edward), her grandfather (King Edmund), her great-grandfather (Ethelred) and her great-great-grandfather (King Edgar), in that order; only then did they resort to two grandiose royal – yet still not French – names: Alexander and David. Ultimately, it can be argued, the marriage of Mael Coluim and Margaret had the effect of raising the kingdom of the Scots above the level of, for example, the king of Man and the Isles, or even that of the king of Connacht, with his pan-Irish aspirations.

The second factor complicating any comparison of Scotland with Ireland and Wales is that the Scots kings used the powers of Europeanization – from charters and coins to knights and Cistercian monasteries – to their own advantage. Consequently, the kings of Scots had their own retainers of knights to draw upon. Davies uses the example of hostage-taking from 'Celtic' rulers as evidence of native submission.[21] He is surely right to suggest that there are similar forces at work in terms of the personal relations between the rulers. For example, Davies compares the hostages given over by King William at the Treaty of Falaise in 1174 to Henry II's taking of hostages from the Welsh princes following his military campaigns of 1157 to 1165.[22] The difference is revealed in who the hostages were and how the English treated them. There are no known instances regarding Scottish hostages to compare with Henry's mutilation of the sons and daughters of the Welsh princes in 1165 or John's hanging of Welsh hostages in 1212.[23] The reason for this should not be a mystery. When an English king took hostages from a 'native' Welsh or Irish ruler, he was taking 'native' Welsh and Irish aristocrats and their sons, and presumably he took the opportunity to expose them to the benefits of chivalric culture, as well as to prevent the marriage and procreation of 'native' aristocrats. When William handed over twenty-one men to Henry II in 1174, only four were 'native earls', who, like William's brother David, had grown up with exposure to various Europeanizing or anglicizing trends.[24] The remaining sixteen hostages were immigrant Anglo-French knights or the sons of immigrants, people like Richard de Morville, Richard Comyn, Hugh Giffard and William de la Haye.[25] The symbolism of handing

20 Bartlett, *Making of Europe*, pp 274–7.   21 Davies, *Domination and conquest*, p. 57.
22 Ibid., p. 76.   23 Davies, 'Keeping the natives in order', 216; John Gillingham, 'Killing and mutilating political enemies in the British Isles from the late twelfth century to the early fourteenth century: a comparative study' in Brendan Smith (ed.), *Britain and Ireland, 900–1300: insular responses to medieval European change* (Cambridge, 1999), p. 132.   24 Dauvit Broun, 'Anglo-French acculturation and the Irish element in Scottish identity' in Smith (ed.), *Britain and Ireland, 900–1300*, pp 135–53, esp. pp 137–8, 153.   25 *Anglo-Scottish Relations, 1174–1328: some selected documents*, ed. and trans. E.L.G. Stones (Oxford, 1965), pp 2–11, no. 1.

over Anglo–French knights and 'acculturated' Scottish earls who probably spoke French and partook of chivalric culture[26] must have spoken volumes, and the message would have been: treat these men as you would the sons of your own Anglo–French barons, not as 'uncivilized' Gaels from the ends of the earth.

The case of the Treaty of Norham, 1209, is a good illustration. The Close Rolls for 13 June 1213 (in John's fifteenth regnal year) reveal the names of fourteen hostages taken at Norham. The nature of Anglo–Scottish baronial families allowed for markedly different arrangements than with Irish and Welsh hostages. Saher de Quincy, earl of Winchester, but also a major landholder in Scotland, was actually holding his own son, Reginald, who was a hostage for the king of Scots, as well as the son of William de Vieuxpont. King William's brother, Earl David of Huntingdon, who himself had been a hostage after Falaise, was now in custody of a hostage, the son of David of Lindsey, on behalf of the English king. Moreover, there were several cross-border baronial families the English representatives of which were allowed to look after their Scottish relatives. This was true of the de Vaux, de Moubray and de Brus sons held hostage. Of the 'native' hostages taken in 1209, the son of Earl Gillebrigte of Strathearn was in the custody of his mother's family, the d'Aubignys, while the son of Laurence of Abernethy was held by the Prior of Durham (the family's names are in the *Liber Vitae* there), the son of Thomas of Galloway by the bishop of Winchester, and the son of the earl of Dunbar, for no apparent reason, by Robert de Vieuxpont.[27] As John Gillingham has pointed out, 'when men of high status were defeated in the conflicts within the English and French parts of the Angevin Empire, they were in little danger of suffering bodily harm – not even when they were dealt with as traitors'.[28] *Magna Carta* offers a clue to our understanding of these events: Alexander II was promised the return of his sisters and hostages 'in the same manner in which we will act towards our other barons of England'.[29] We thus have an alternative analogue for the kings of Scots; if

---

26 There is a good deal of evidence to suggest that chivalric French literature was well known in the Scottish east midlands. One example among many is individuals named Tristram and Ysenda (a form of Iseult) in Strathearn. Mark A. Hall and D.D.R. Owen, 'A Tristram and Iseult mirror-case from Perth: reflections on the production and consumption of romance culture', *Tayside and Fife Archaeological Journal*, 4 (1998), 150–65; R.L. Graeme Ritchie, *Chrétien de Troyes and Scotland* (Oxford, 1952), p. 16.   27 *Rotuli Litterarum Clausarum in Turri Londinensi asservati*, ed. Thomas D. Hardy, i (London, Record Commission, 1833), p. 137; Archibald C. Lawrie, *Annals of the reigns of Malcolm and William kings of Scotland* (Glasgow, 1910), p. 392. Partially printed in Thomas Rymer (ed.), *Foedera, conventiones, litterae et cuiuscunque generis acta publica* (London, Record Commission, 1816–69), i, 1, p. 113. See also Joseph Bain (ed.), *Calendar of documents relating to Scotland*, i (Edinburgh, 1881), no. 574; A.A.M. Duncan, *Scotland: the making of the kingdom* (Edinburgh, 1975), p. 246.   28 Gillingham, 'Killing and mutilating political enemies', p. 119.   29 J.C. Holt, *Magna Carta* (Cambridge, 1965), p. 333 (Clause 59).

they were sometimes treated as 'Celtic rulers',[30] they were also owed certain dignities as English barons.

Another important plank of Davies' argument regarding the domination of 'Celtic' rulers is based on the obligation of military service and the tendency to look to the king of England as the prestigious bestower of knighthood, posing the question, 'what better way was there in a military society for a dependent ally to demonstrate his loyalty and to do so in the most public and useful manner?'.[31] Davies reasonably compares the service of Scottish kings like Alexander I and Mael Coluim IV to that of the Irish and Welsh rulers, but these Scottish examples are somewhat exceptional. Two incidents from the mid-twelfth century reveal the nature of the Scottish situation. The events of Stephen's reign and the need to secure an Angevin succession showed that in a time of crisis the English were capable of looking to a king of Scots as a force with sufficient prestige and dignity to confer upon the heir the belt of knighthood. For Aelred of Rievaulx, the symbolism went well beyond Henry's knighting at Carlisle in 1149; he appended a lauda-tory eulogy of King David as a prologue to the *Genealogy of the kings of English*, which he composed for the soon-to-be king Henry. 'Since I have written a little concerning the outstanding habits of the holy King David', he wrote, 'I think it worthwhile briefly and truthfully to add his genealogy, which is also yours, most illustrious Duke Henry'.[32] Maybe David I was an exception; still, it seems unthinkable that a Welsh or Irish ruler would ever be asked to knight the future ruler of the Angevin realms. All the same, there is no point ignoring the 'almost indecent anxiety to be girded with the belt of knighthood' by young Mael Coluim, only a decade later.[33] That Mael Coluim's actions, in following Henry II to Toulouse after being snubbed by the king at Carlisle, provoked such a firestorm domestically as to cause his own earls to hold him in the castle at Perth surely signals that there were limits in the extent to which the king of Scots could be seen as the Angevin ruler's lapdog.

Another crucial distinction between the kings of Scots and other rulers was that the king of Scots could call up his own knights to perform military service for him, often against the king of England. The Scottish monarchs routinely knighted men of both 'Anglo-Norman' or 'native' background within their own kingdom, although at times sons could be knighted *en masse*

30 Rees Davies, '"Keeping the natives in order": the English king and the "Celtic" rulers 1066–1216', *Peritia*, 10 (1996), 212–24.   31 Davies, *Domination and conquest*, p. 57.   32 D.E.R. Watt (gen. ed.), *Scotichronicon by Walter Bower in Latin and English*, vol. iii, ed. and trans. John and Winifred MacQueen, and D.E.R. Watt (Edinburgh, 1995), pp 172–3; Marsha L. Dutton (ed.) and Jane Patricia Freeland (trans.), *Aelred of Rievaulx: The historical works*, Cistercian Fathers Series 56 (Kalamazoo, 2005), p. 71.   33 Davies, *Domination and conquest*, 51.

by the English king, as when twenty new knights were made alongside the young Alexander III at his marriage in York on Christmas, 1251.[34] These differences illustrate the notion of the paradox of medieval Scotland. Davies lays out this concept in the *First English empire*: while Scotland was the most heavily anglicized part of the British Isles outwith England, it was also the one country that was able to maintain its political independence. As with the Anglo–French hostages for the Scots king after Falaise or Norham, or the knights of Anglo–French and other backgrounds in their armies, what we seem to have here is anglicization turned on its head. The notion of a king of Scots offering up a panoply of Anglo–Norman knights as hostages on the one hand highlights the extent to which that kingdom had become anglicized; at the same time, it was the sons of immigrant knights who were acting as the guarantors of an independent kingdom. Of course, it was largely the descendants of these Anglo–French knights[35] who ensured the survival of that kingdom after the attempted takeover of Edward I.

The effect of the arrival of Anglo–French aristocrats in Ireland and Wales, of course, was notably different. Davies included chapters in *Domination and conquest* on 'aristocratic domination' and 'the intensification of lordship', but he makes very little mention of Scotland within this context. In the collected volume *Medieval frontier societies* (1989), Bartlett draws a line between countries where a 'colonial aristocracy [...] intruded into and was imposed upon the indigenous society' and those where 'foreign aristocrats came to settle [...] at the invitation of native ruling dynasties'.[36] Thus, Bartlett finds more that is comparable to Scotland in Pomerania or Silesia than in Ireland or Wales. Presumably, the French-speaking colonial aristocracies who took over large parts of Ireland and Wales can be considered 'anglicizing' chiefly because they were ultimately (in some cases, eventually) under the control of the English king. If the French-speaking colonial aristocracies invited into Scotland were ultimately under the control of the Scottish king, should they not be considered 'Scotticizing'? Still, this realization should not lead us to deny the underlying truism that these men and women were often members of the same families that were intruding themselves into Ireland and Wales, and that Davies could have undoubtedly found more examples in the Scottish kingdom of some of the tactics used by these families, such as marriage to local heiresses, a topic which clearly deserves more study.

The importance of the crucial role of Queen Margaret in providing the

34 Matthew Paris, *Chronica majora*, ed. H.R. Luard (London, 1882), v, pp 266–70; *Scottish annals from English chroniclers*, ed. A.O. Anderson (London, 1908), pp 364–5. 35 Andrew of Moray and William Wallace, however, were descended from Flemings and Welsh speakers, respectively. 36 Robert Bartlett, 'Colonial aristocracies of the high Middle Ages' in Robert Bartlett and Angus MacKay (eds), *Medieval frontier societies* (Oxford, 1989), pp 23–4.

dynasty with their European bona fides should always be kept in mind. It was her blood, after all, which allowed David I to have a sister married to an English king and a niece married to a German emperor. This allowed the Scots to present a strong argument for 'full kingship' in a broader European sense by implying that they were the more genuine heirs to the house of Wessex. Due to their inability to acquire papal sanction for royal anointment, however, the kings of Scots had to resort to alternative means of highlighting the status of their kingship and kingdom. Henry II ascribed the capture of William at Alnwick to the martyred Thomas Becket, as the king had recently done public penance to the newly canonized Thomas.[37] William's response was to establish a richly endowed monastery – indeed his only foundation – at Arbroath in 1178, at the same time seeking to placate the powerful new saint who had allowed him to fall into calamity as well as to outdo the English king in terms of public piety and devotion. Even more significantly, William endowed the *Brecbennach* – the reliquary of St Columba that went before the Scots army into battle – on the house of St Thomas the Martyr of Arbroath.[38] The granting of the custody of the reliquary of a major – indeed a 'national' – saintly patron of Gaelic pedigree on a house staffed by Tironensian monks devoted to a brand-new English saint is a quintessential case in Europeanization, but in this case the motives behind it were clearly to bolster the preservation of an independent kingdom of Scotland. After William's death, his widow Ermengarde and his son King Alexander II endowed a Cistercian abbey at Balmerino in Fife. In similar fashion, this house was dedicated to St Edward the Confessor.[39] We again see the motive of shoring up the top-tier monarchical bona fides by expressing devotion to an English saint whose cult was becoming increasingly important: in this case, it drew attention to the Scottish royal house's right to be 'real kings', based on their descent through Margaret. Furthermore, it showed them beating the English to the punch, as the foundation prefigured Henry III's own devotion by a few years.[40] In this context it is also worth noting that the canonization of Margaret in 1249 was in one way a political act: if the kings of England would block the kings of Scots from obtaining papal sanction for anointment, they could at least get papal recognition of the saintly status of the woman who was very much their ticket into the élite club of European monarchy.

37 Frank Barlow, *Thomas Becket* (London, 1986), pp 269–70; Richard Barber, *Henry Plantagenet* (Ipswich, 1964), p. 179.   38 *Regesta regum Scottorum, ii: The acts of William I King of Scots 1165–1214*, ed. Geoffrey W.S. Barrow with the collaboration of William W. Scott (Edinburgh, 1971), no. 499.   39 Matthew Hammond, 'Queen Ermengarde and the Abbey of St Edward, Balmerino', *Citeaux –Commentarii Cistercienses*, 59 (2008).   40 David Carpenter, 'King Henry III and Saint Edward the Confessor: the origins of the cult', *English Historical Review*, 122 (2007), 865–91.

While it may be appropriate to talk of Scotland being anglicized in certain well-defined contexts – linguistically, for example, or in terms of the legacy of Queen Margaret – it seems wise at this point to suggest that anglicization should not be interpreted as the process of Europeanization operating in the northern part of the British Isles.[41] Indeed, a strong case can be made that these processes can be better summed up as 'Scotticization'. The remainder of this chapter will deal with an exploration of this fourth 'zation'.

The effects of Scotticization on various constituencies and geographical regions must be considered. How does the invited 'colonial aristocracy' fit into the model? It is remarkable that this group began self-identifying as 'Scottish' by the thirteenth century. An early example is Thomas de Coleville, described as *cognomento Scoto* in one charter, who died in 1219.[42] The legend of his seal reads 'Sigill Thome de Collevilla Scotti'.[43] We also have the mid-century seal of one Alan the Scot, who on closer inspection turns out to be Alan de Candela (of Caundle, Dorset), a member of the Malherbe family.[44] Similarly, Guy de Balliol, a knight on Simon de Montfort's side at the Battle of Evesham, is described in the Chronicle of Melrose as 'by race, a Scot'.[45] This transformation in national identity is all the more remarkable when one considers the strong negative associations with barbarism the word held for English people, at least in the twelfth century, according to John Gillingham.[46] Other scholars, such as David Carpenter, however, doubt the extent to which these stereotypes survived into the thirteenth century.[47] Therefore, it is clear that the immigrant aristocracy were becoming Scotticized, at least in terms of loyalty to the Scottish king and a realignment in national identity. But what about culturally? One remarkable difference between Scotland and Ireland was the tendency for immigrant knights who married daughters of the native élite to adopt local personal names, either through imitation of the royal family or local magnates. This led to de-Gaelicized forms of names which nonetheless

41 This is not to suggest that the anglicization model is not useful for other parts of Britain and Ireland, as continuing research makes clear. See, for example, Max Lieberman, 'Anglicization in high medieval Wales: the case of Glamorgan', *Welsh History Review*, 23 (2006), 1–26; Freya Verstraten, 'The anglicization of the Gaelic Irish nobility *c.*1169–*c.*1366' (PhD, University of Dublin, 2008). 42 *Liber Sancte Marie de Melros* (Bannatyne Club, 1837), no. 192. 43 Edinburgh, National Archives of Scotland, GD 55/192. 44 J. Raine, *The history and antiquities of North Durham* (London, 1852), App., no. 379. Durham, seal HB 2773. For more on de Coleville and de Candela, see Matthew Hammond, 'The use of the name Scot in the central Middle Ages, Part One. Scot as a by-name', *Journal of Scottish Name Studies*, 1 (2007), 52–5. 45 Dauvit Broun and Julian Harrison, *The chronicle of Melrose Abbey: a stratigraphic edition*, vol. i, *Introduction and facsimile edition* (Woodbridge 2007), DVD, Faustina B IX, fo. 67r; A.O. Anderson, M.O. Anderson and W.C. Dickinson (eds), *The chronicle of Melrose* (Facsimile Edition) (London, 1936), p. 131. 46 Gillingham, *The English in the twelfth century* (Woodbridge, 2000), esp. chs 1 and 3. 47 David Carpenter, *The struggle for mastery. The Penguin history of Britain, 1066–1284* (London, 2003), pp 16–17, pp 22–4.

remained firmly Scottish, like Duncan and Malcolm.[48] Beyond just onomas-
tics, however, it should be noted that the most successful families of the
thirteenth and fourteenth centuries were those that were able to bridge the
gap between the Gaelic and Anglo–French cultural orbits. Some of these, like
the Galloway brothers, Alan and Thomas, or the powerful Alan Durward,
came from Scottish or Galwegian backgrounds, but others, namely the
Comyns, the Stewarts and the Murrays, were successful in places like
Sutherland, Badenoch and Bute because they were able to 'go native' to a
certain extent. This tendency can also be considered an aspect of
Scotticization.

It is equally necessary, of course, to consider the effects of Scotticization
on the 'native' (perhaps 'domestic' would be a less loaded term) aristocracy.
As Dauvit Broun has pointed out, one distinguishing element of the Scottish
situation was the ability of *mormaír* or earls to adopt the French chivalric
culture and, presumably, language, without giving up their Scottish
identity.[49] These acculturated Scots inhabited a transitional zone stretching
from the Forth to the Highlands, and were able to straddle the cultural
divide. Here, Scottish earls tended to keep their distinctive Gaelic names, like
Donnchad, Mael Coluim, Mael Ísu and Gillebrigte, and European names
tended to be adopted through marriage, based on custom. Earl Gillebrigte of
Strathearn, who married Matilda d'Aubigny, was followed in the earldom by
Robert, named for Matilda's father, but there had been an older son, named
for his father, Ferteth. Families of both Scottish and immigrant origin were
able to give some children Scottish names, others English or French names,
and it was typical to copy the names used by the royal family, including
Henry, William and Alexander.[50]

Crucially, the opportunities that were open to younger sons of Anglo–
French aristocracy in the kingdom of the Scots were equally available to the
younger sons of acculturated Scottish nobles. For example, Earl Gillebrigte
of Strathearn's younger brother, Mael Ísu, married Ada, an illegitimate
daughter of Earl David of Huntingdon.[51] Younger sons of the earls of Fife
and Strathearn obtained charters for large lordships in the north of the
country, and the earldoms of Atholl and Carrick were for a time held by cadet
branches of 'native' families from elsewhere in the kingdom.[52]

Alan Durward, despite his French-sounding name, was an acculturated

48 Freya Verstraten, 'Naming practices among the Irish secular nobility in the high Middle
Ages', *Journal of Medieval History*, 32 (2006), 45.   49 Broun, 'Anglo–French acculturation', p.
153.   50 Matthew Hammond, 'Ethnicity, personal names and the nature of Scottish
Europeanization', *Thirteenth Century England*, 11 (2007), 90–1.   51 Keith Stringer, *Earl David
of Huntingdon, 1152–1219: a study in Anglo-Scottish history* (Edinburgh, 1985), p. 41, pp 81–2.
52 Duncan, *Making of the kingdom*, p. 585; Barrow (ed.), *Regesta regum Scottorum*, ii, no. 474;
Registrum episcopatus Moraviensis (Bannatyne Club, 1837), nos. 16, 47, 50, 62, 63.

Scot who made the best of the opportunities available to him. Alan's great-grandfather was Earl Gillecrist of Mar; his grandfather Mael Coluim was lord of Lundie in Angus. He had an uncle with the Gaelic name Eógan (Scots Ewen) and a brother with the name Colin. His mother was probably a daughter of Earl Mael Coluim of Atholl. His father, who either inherited or was invested with the office of royal usher or doorward, was probably named after St Thomas Becket around the time of King William's veneration of the saint, and Alan was perhaps named after Alan son of Walter, the royal steward. Alan laid unsuccessful claim to the earldoms of Mar and Atholl, but succeeded in carving out a substantial lordship for himself and his family, marrying a bastard daughter of Alexander II and running a rival government to Walter Comyn's in the minority of Alexander III. Alan typifies the cultural mix of Gaelic and French on display in the thirteenth century, and it was probably his ability to span both worlds that largely enabled his success.[53]

If Scotticization could seem at times like a win-win scenario for the kingdom's eastern core, those living in the kingdom's more peripheral regions were as likely to see its hard edge. In particular, the regions inhabited at the beginning of the twelfth century by the *Gall-Goídil* – not only Galloway but also much of Ayrshire, Renfrewshire and the Hebrides – were likely to see a side of Scotticization that looked much more like Ireland's and Wales' experience of Davies' anglicization.[54] Certainly, David I's grants of huge lordships to the Steward, de Morville and de Brus look much like the speculative grants made by Henry II in Ireland, especially that of Meath to Hugh de Lacy.[55] Contemporary accounts make abundantly clear that the *Gall-Goídil* were considered to be at the bottom of the pile of the peoples of Britain, and it is possible that the kings of Scots may have looked on the region with the same kind of condescension that some in England held for the neighbours they saw as less civilized.[56] In any event, the combination of planting Anglo-French knights, occasional subdual by military force, and

---

53 Matthew Hammond, '*Hostiarii Regis Scotie*: the Durward family in the thirteenth century' in Steve Boardman and Alasdair Ross (eds), *The exercise of power in medieval Scotland* (Dublin, 2003), pp 118–38. 54 On the evolving meaning of the term *Gall-Goídil*, see Thomas Owen Clancy, 'The Gall-Ghàidheil and Galloway', *Journal of Scottish Name Studies*, 2 (2008), 19–50. 55 Seán Duffy, *Ireland in the Middle Ages* (Basingstoke and London, 1997), p. 82. 56 See for example John Gillingham's statement that Roger of Howden 'showed himself to be acutely aware of the differences between Scotland and Galloway, of the high level of killing and mutilating that characterized Galwegian politics, and of the tensions that existed between Scots and Galwegians'. Gillingham, *English in the twelfth century*, p. 82. This chapter (5) was first published as 'The travels of Roger of Howden and his views of the Irish, Scots and Welsh', *Anglo-Norman Studies*, 20 (1998), pp 151–69. See also William M. Aird, '"Sweet civility and barbarous rudeness": a view from the frontier. Abbot Ailred of Rievaulx and the Scots', *Imagining frontiers contesting identities* (CLIOHRes Net e-book, 2007), pp 59–75.

intermittant meddling in internal affairs that the kings of Scots used in Galloway look remarkably like the *Domination and conquest* techniques employed by the English kings in Ireland and Wales. Even there, in time, loyalty and acculturation had their rewards: Lachlan of Galloway changed his name to Roland and inherited the de Morville estates and the office of the Scottish king's constable.[57] One of his sons was given a Scottish earldom; the other became a major Anglo–Scottish magnate whose name appears in *Magna Carta*.[58]

One aspect of Scotticization is that, as with anglicization, the kings were able to use a combination of flattery and violence to achieve their goal of extending their power over the most intractable part of their lands. The MacWilliam threat to Scottish kingship drew its chief support from the province of Ross.[59] In the attempt of Domnall Bán MacWilliam after the death of King William in 1214, a local strongman from a clerical dynasty, Fearchar Maccintsacairt, 'cut off the heads of the king's enemies' and 'presented them as new gifts to the new king', Alexander II. It is telling that the response of the teenage king (no doubt advised by his household officers) was to immediately confer the order of knighthood on Fearchar.[60] Within a few years, Alexander II had revived the defunct earldom of Ross and Fearchar became the progenitor of a long line of earls of Ross.[61] Significantly, in 1235, when Thomas, the illegitimate son of Alan son of Roland of Galloway, led an armed revolt against the splitting up of the lordship between three heiresses, it was Fearchar who led the attack for King Alexander.[62] Fearchar serves as an example of how quickly this process of

57 Richard D. Oram, 'Roland, lord of Galloway (*d.* 1200)', *Oxford dictionary of national biography*, Oxford University Press, 2004 [http://www.oxforddnb.com/view/article/49361, accessed 2 Feb. 2009]. 58 Holt, *Magna Carta*, p. 317. Keith Stringer sums up the multifaceted milieu that Alan of Galloway inhabited in 'Scottish foundations: thirteenth-century perspectives' in Alexander Grant and Keith Stringer (eds), *Uniting the kingdom? The making of British history* (London, 1995), p. 88. Thomas of Galloway, who was earl of Atholl from *circa* 1210 to 1231, was also a major player in Irish Sea zone politics. See Keith Stringer, 'Periphery and core in thirteenth-century Scotland: Alan son of Roland, lord of Galloway and constable of Scotland' in Alexander Grant and Keith Stringer (eds), *Medieval Scotland: crown, lordship and community* (Edinburgh, 1993), pp 82–113, esp. pp 83–9. 59 For a new interpretation of the evidence on the MacWilliams, see Alasdair Ross, 'Moray, Ulster, and the MacWilliams' in Séan Duffy (ed.), *The world of the galloglass: kings, warlords and warriors in Ireland and Scotland, 1200–1600* (Dublin, 2007), pp 24–44. 60 Broun and Harrison, *Chronicle of Melrose Abbey*, vol. i, DVD, Faustina B IX, fo. 31r-v; Anderson et al., *Chronicle of Melrose*, pp 59–60. 61 George Broderick (ed.), *Chronicles of the kings of Man and the Isles* (3rd ed., Douglas, 2004), fo. 42v; *Registrum episcopatus Moraviensis*, no. 258; Alexander Grant, 'The province of Ross and the kingdom of Alba' in E.J. Cowan and R. Andrew McDonald (eds), *Alba: Celtic Scotland in the medieval era* (East Linton, 2000), pp 122–3; R. Andrew McDonald, 'Old and new in the far North: Ferchar Maccintsacairt and the early earls of Ross, *c.*1200–74' in Boardman and Ross (eds), *Exercise of power*, pp 23–45. 62 D.E.R. Watt (gen. ed.), *Scotichronicon by Walter Bower in Latin and English*, vol. v, ed. and trans. Simon Taylor and D.E.R. Watt with Brian Scott (Aberdeen, 1990), pp 148–51.

acculturation could occur, as well as the extent to which Alexander could rely on his own (in this case 'native') knights for military support. For those who did not – or could not – play along, however, like the infant MacWilliam heiress executed in Forfar's marketplace in 1230, acculturation and acceptance were not an option.

Summing up the elements of Scotticization, then, we can describe the process as a local form of Europeanization linked closely to a Scottish identity based on the figure of the king. The effects of this process were the following: 1) the maintenance of the Scottish identity of the acculturated native élites, despite the spread of French and English languages; 2) the redefinition of English-speaking parts of the kingdom as Scottish; and 3) the adoption of Scottish identity among Anglo–French immigrant knights, merchants and clergy. Scotticization can be described as an expansionist force, using the same techniques as anglicization to spread Scottish power, authority and identity into regions which could be seen as more barbarous, especially the lands of the *Gall-Goídil*. As with Davies' model, this process could lead to conquest, and the Scottish takeover of the old kingdom of Man and the Isles in the 1260s can be seen as a culminating event.

Whereas Scotticization seems to best characterize the nexus of political and cultural change in north Britain in the twelfth and thirteenth centuries, it would perhaps be salutary to finish on a note of caution. In an academic milieu inhabited by four 'zations', surely we should consider the limits of process-driven models – indeed any paradigm at all – to adequately do justice to the complex social, political and cultural arrangements in central medieval Britain and Ireland. Indeed, one could probably argue fairly convincingly that all four 'zations' were at work in the kingdom of the Scots: administrative Europeanization, linguistic anglicization, cultural Francization and political Scotticization. Such a multi-layered approach, however, would surely obscure the point of constructing models in the first place: to elucidate and clarify. Scotland's elusiveness at categorization is surely something to be admired and explored. Its kings were at once dominated and dominator, anglicized and Scotticizer. It was this paradox of medieval Scotland that Professor Davies bequeathed on the discipline, long may it endure.

A second England? Scotland and the monarchy of Britain in *The first English empire**

DAUVIT BROUN

The first English empire is chiefly an exploration of the growth of England's political power and her cultural and social influence in Britain and Ireland in the twelfth and thirteenth centuries. As such it represents a deeper and broader investigation of a theme Rees Davies tackled a decade earlier in *Domination and conquest: the experience of Ireland, Scotland and Wales, 1100–1300*. As well as dealing with all aspects of English expansion, *The first English empire* is also a cogent attempt to explain why this trajectory of ever greater peaks of achievement was not sustained after the last hope of Welsh independence had been mercilessly extinguished in 1282–3, and the kingdom of Scotland had been abolished by Edward I in 1296. According to Rees Davies, the precocious development of kingship and society in southern England and the early self-assurance of an exclusively English identity – already apparent in the tenth century – was at once the secret of England's success and the cause of its inability to create what he called a 'meaningful monarchy of the British Isles'.[1] Instead of an all-embracing British kingdom in which lesser rulers retained their local power under English overlordship and cultural differences were tolerated, the political dominance of England was asserted on English terms and became increasingly associated with English social and cultural norms. Leaders of localities across the islands of Britain and Ireland, instead of enjoying the opportunity to participate in political and social networks close to the king of England – limited only by fortune and ambition – either had to conform to a sense of Englishness that became 'raucously strident during the thirteenth century' or suffer exclusion.

The alternative vision of what might have been – a 'meaningful unity, of a single British Isles at a measure of ease with itself' – is a particularly striking feature of the book. It throws the growth of English power into relief, and gives purpose to the argument that England's chief strengths made it incapable of achieving the ultimate goal of a monarchy of Britain. This is not just a rhetorical device. Rees Davies occasionally went further and

* I would like to thank Professor Keith Stringer for his comments, and Dr Nerys Ann Jones for her constant support and encouragement. I am, of course, solely responsible for any flaws.
1 R.R. Davies, *The first English empire* (Oxford, 2000): see, for example, p. 112.

referred to an inclusive English–dominated kingdom of Britain as a possible development. At one point he stated that 'the prospect of a single, albeit loose–limbed, unit of power [. . .] seemed to be very much on the cards from the 1090s onwards, and particularly so during Henry I's reign';[2] on another occasion he suggested that 'it looked periodically in the late twelfth and early thirteenth centuries as if the high kingship of the British Isles might evolve into a federative, loose–limbed, composite monarchy'.[3] But in his view the possibility of this alternative trajectory was finally snuffed out in the thirteenth century. As he himself put it: 'as the Angevin power contracted mainly into the confines of an English state and its annexes, and as the ideology and institutions of that state became more stridently and defiantly English, so the prospect of the kingship of the English converting itself into the monarchy of the British Isles other than on its own terms largely disappeared'.[4]

Because this putative 'loose–limbed' monarchy of the British Isles never materialized it is, of course, difficult to envisage what it might have looked liked. Rees Davies invited readers to think of 'composite assemblies of peoples and territories under the presidency of a single multi–titled ruler' comparable to the 'so–called Norman and Angevin empires'.[5] Presumably for Rees Davies this would have become a more 'meaningful' unity as the momentum of business, literacy and charter–defined power took hold in the thirteenth century.[6] The inevitable uncertainty of trying to envisage something that did not happen raises the question of why Rees Davies decided to make this such a key element in the argument of his book. Is it possible that his vision of a kingdom of Britain that would not have belonged exclusively to the English owes more to the Welsh imagination than anything else – particularly when this is tinged with a sense of unfulfilled promise?

In fact, there is no need to speculate that Rees Davies was passionately committed to the ideal of a 'loose–limbed' Britain. In the same year as he gave the Ford lectures, which were published as *The first English empire*, he gave the annual Syr Thomas Parry–Williams lecture in Aberystwyth, delivered and published in Welsh. He argued there that the words 'Britain' and 'England' had become synonymous because 'Britain' had been usurped by medieval kings of England who had claimed, on account of their power and authority, that it was one–and–the–same to be the king of England and king of Britain. He described this as a 'kind of ideological hijack'[7] – a point that

2 Ibid., pp 145, 142, 201 and 10. 3 Ibid., p. 140: see also pp 78–9. 4 Ibid., p. 141. The only point of comparison he offered was the Angevin Empire, but that was neither a monarchy nor an overkingship. 5 Ibid., p. 141. 6 Note, however, that he saw charter-defined power becoming part of the problem, because 'the written formulae of the law and governance restricted the sphere of freedom of action to allow for local circumstances' (ibid., p. 195). 7 R.R. Davies, *Beth*

can also be found in *The first English empire*.[8] On this occasion, however, he
developed it with a Welsh public very much in mind. He proposed that this
'ideological hijack' should be reversed in order to stop the crumbling
timeworn edifice of the Anglocentric British state from collapsing altogether.
Here, he suggested, historians have a crucial role to play. By showing that
'Britain' could be something else apart from England writ large, they can
help to build a vision of a 'new Britain' that, as a state, is held together not
by English power and authority, but by embracing the distinctiveness of
Britain's historic nations – Wales and Scotland as well as England. 'What do
I care for Britain?' he asked at the end of his lecture. 'I care a great deal', he
said to his Welsh-speaking audience, 'especially for our children's generation,
and the children of their children, and indeed their children.'[9]

Here, it seems, is a direct link between Davies' historical imagination and
his aspirations for Wales in the future. The inclusive and diverse kingdom of
Britain he saw as an achievable goal today is strikingly similar to the culturally diverse and politically variegated kingdom of Britain he argued was on
the cards in the twelfth century. But the modern Welsh cultural context is not
as straightforward as it may seem. The title of Rees Davies' lecture, *Beth yw'r
ots gennyf fi am—Brydain?*, 'What do I care for—Britain?', is a calculated
echo of the first line of the famous poem, *Hon*, 'Her', by Syr Thomas Parry-
Williams, in whose memory the lecture was given. Instead of Britain,
Parry-Williams asked the question of Wales: 'What do I care for Wales?' His
answer at the end of the poem also reveals what he meant by 'her' in the
poem's title: 'And I feel the claws of Wales torturing my breast. May God
deliver me, I cannot escape from her.'[10] It is clear, when you read his lecture,
that Rees Davies expected his cry for redefining Britain to be challenging for
his Welsh audience, too. The claws of Britain that tortured Rees Davies'
breast were what he saw as the inescapable lessons of history. It was this that
informed his vision of the future, not the other way round.

In this chapter, Rees Davies' idea of a potential loose-limbed kingdom of
Britain will be examined from the perspective of Scotland's experience of
anglicization. This was fundamentally different from anglicization in Ireland
and Wales in ways that Keith Stringer, in particular, has drawn attention to
in his contribution to the collection of essays, *Uniting the kingdom? The*

yw'r ots gennyf fi am—Brydain?, Darlith Goffa Syr Thomas Parry-Williams 1998 (Aberystwyth,
1999), p. 11.   8 Davies, *The first English empire*, p. 202.   9 Davies, *Beth yw'r ots gennyf fi
am—Brydain?*, p. 13. Compare the final sentences of Davies, *The first English empire*, p. 203: 'the
English empire of the British Isles was not a united kingdom, either in pretension or in reality.
That was the legacy that the advance of English power in the British Isles in the twelfth and
thirteenth centuries had left as a bequest for future generations.'   10 T.H. Parry-Williams,
'*Hon*', from Thomas Parry, *Blodeugerdd Rhydychen o Farddoniaeth Gymraeg* (Oxford, 1962), no.
282.

making of British history.[11] There he emphasized how key aspects of anglicization – be it the immigration of knights and leading churchmen, the
adoption of English offices and legal practices, or the establishing of burghs
which were the engine driving the spread of the English language – took
place under the direction of the king of Scots and increased his power. As a
result, Britain developed not one 'core', but two: the anglicized inner core of
the Scottish kingdom as well as the larger and more wealthy heartlands of
England. It has to be said that little attention is given in *The first English
empire* to this striking element in Stringer's argument.[12] If British history in
this period is to be seen in terms of the emergence of 'not one, but *two*
dominant states or "superpowers"',[13] as Keith Stringer has argued cogently,
then that would surely be inherently inimical to any notion that a united
kingdom of Britain was, in any meaningful sense, on the cards. But Keith
Stringer also explained how a loose-limbed polity like the Scottish kingdom
was much more effective as a force for unity than the awesome might of a
centralized power like England. He pointed out that the intrusive nature of
government in England made it incapable of incorporating its 'peripheral'
zones effectively, and contrasted this with the less bureaucratic and more
decentralized style of government in Scotland where the king depended on
established local and regional powers.[14] This, Stringer argued, meant that the
spreading of royal control into the north and west of Scotland involved
cooperation with some, at least, of the most prominent rulers of local society
who 'themselves became leading actors in the process of expansion'.[15] As a
result, 'the two Alexanders presided over one of the most successful
programmes of territorial consolidation and expansion to be seen in the
British Isles since the Norman Conquest itself'.[16]

It is not difficult to see how the emergence of Scotland as a sovereign
kingdom can of itself be seen as a key cause for the failure of a monarchy of
Britain in this period. The main significance of Scotland in relation to *The
first English empire*, however, is that it provides a model for what an inclusive
kingdom of Britain might have looked like. In this chapter, this question will
be addressed not only with Keith Stringer's discussion in mind, but also with

11 Keith J. Stringer, 'Thirteenth-century perspectives' in Alexander Grant and Keith J. Stringer
(eds), *Uniting the kingdom? The making of British history* (London, 1995), pp 85–96. 12 Note
also Robin Frame, *The political development of the British Isles, 1100–1400* (Oxford, 1990), p. 72,
where he observes that, despite the differences between Scotland and England, 'nevertheless
there is much to be said for viewing the development of administration in the interwoven realms
as a single story'. 13 Stringer, 'Thirteenth-century perspectives', p. 96 (his emphasis). 14
The contrast between English and Scottish royal government within a British context has also
been discussed by Robin Frame (*The political development of the British Isles*, pp 89–97), although
he associated territorial expansion not so much with this as with the emergence of a royal dynasty
(ibid., pp 103–7). 15 Stringer, 'Thirteenth-century perspectives', p. 95. 16 Ibid., p. 93.

particular emphasis on what can be discerned about the identity of the kingdom's inhabitants. To what extent did anglicization mean self-identification as English? How, and when, did those who were ethnically English become Scottish? Although the information for answering these questions is severely limited – the best source is the Chronicle of Melrose which, at most, only offers good access to changing perceptions among leading members of society in the south-east – this can, at least, throw into sharper relief the Scottish dimension of the British question posed by Rees Davies' image of a meaningful monarchy of Britain. Is it conceivable, for example, that those who were ethnically Scottish could have become English within an inclusive British kingdom? In what follows I should confess that, unlike Rees Davies, I have no vision to offer of what Britain as a country might need to become today in order to thrive (or simply survive) in the future, and I certainly lack any trace of his literary sophistication. This is not a case of 'a drunk man looking at a – rose'.

Rees Davies regarded Scotland as something of a puzzle. He evidently expected to find a clear border between anglicized and not-so-anglicized areas that would be comparable to the division he described in Wales and Ireland, but the examples he cited are unconvincing. Scotland was different: instead of a fault-line, there was what Kenneth Nicholls has memorably described as a 'transitional zone'.[17] Rees Davies was, however, perfectly aware that anglicization in Scotland lacked some of the key ingredients of the Welsh or Irish experience. He observed that 'It is not the least of the paradoxes in the history of the British Isles that it was in the kingdom of the Scots – the very area in which the English kingship did not directly impose its military and political power and in which English settlers and institutions were absorbed comfortably into the existing society and polity – that the English language and with it English culture arguably made its greatest and most enduring advances in the twelfth and thirteenth centuries'.[18] He made a similar observation about the 'triumph' of English law in Scotland, and quoted F.W. Maitland's famous observation: 'We may doubt whether a man who crossed the river [Tweed] felt that he had passed from the land of one law to the land of another.'[19] Rees Davies also drew attention to the fact that Scotland at the end of this period stood in a radically different relationship with England compared to Ireland and Wales. He noted that, 'paradoxically, the most extensively English-settled and anglicized part of the British Isles was the country which retained its political independence'.[20]

17 Kenneth Nicholls, 'Celtic contrasts: Ireland and Scotland', *History Ireland*, 7:3 (Autumn 1999), 22–6, at 24.   18 Davies, *The first English empire*, p. 157.   19 Ibid., p. 160 n. 70; F. Pollock and F.W. Maitland, *The history of English law before the time of Edward I* (Cambridge, 1968 ed.), vol. i, pp 222–3.   20 Davies, *The first English empire*, p. 170.

Rees Davies did not go on to try and explain these paradoxes. His chief concern was to show how the power of the king of England in the British Isles became exclusively English; how, in his own words, 'the fault-line of cultures, economies, and societies [...] become the frontier line of political and legal exclusion'.[21] It was enough to point out that Scotland was, in some key respects, different. Scotland, indeed, must seem rather puzzling for anyone who, of necessity, depends chiefly on secondary works as a guide. To the discerning reader it must seem as if each historian of Scotland in the twelfth and thirteenth centuries navigates their own particular path through what has been described rather bluntly as 'the whole continuity-versus-change debate'.[22] Matthew Hammond has pointed out that the many and profound ways in which Scottish society changed has tended to be seen through the prism of an ethnic dualism, which relegates the Celtic or Gaelic to the 'old' world that had largely passed away by the thirteenth century and survived merely as 'fossils'.[23] This has been heightened by Ted Cowan's characterization of the resistance to the king of Scots in Moray, Argyll and the Isles, and Galloway as evidence for an 'anti-feudal faction' – an idea that has been discussed (but not wholly endorsed) by Andrew McDonald.[24] McDonald's work has focused on the north, west and south–west of what is now Scotland, rather than on areas where royal authority had been established for centuries. In the regions he examined in detail, he continues to see native resistance to Anglo–Norman penetration and influence, albeit as only one factor in explaining the risings against kings of Scots.[25] Cynthia Neville has taken this further by presenting Strathearn in the kingdom's historic heartlands as a 'Celtic enclave' whose earl in the early thirteenth century

---

21 Ibid., 141. 22 Richard Oram, *David I. The king who made Scotland* (Stroud, 2004), p. 9, where he explains that his book (despite its sub-title) does not engage with this central issue. 23 Matthew H. Hammond, 'Ethnicity and the writing of medieval Scottish history', *SHR*, 85 (2006), 1–27. 24 E.J. Cowan, 'The historical MacBeth' in W.D.H. Sellar (ed.), *Moray: province and people* (Edinburgh, 1993), at p. 131, discussed in R.A. McDonald and S.A. McLean, 'Somerled of Argyll: a new look at old problems', *SHR*, 71 (1992), 3–22, at 21: 'it is possible to discern what Professor E.J. Cowan has termed an "anti-feudal faction" determined to resist Anglo–French culture at any cost'. For fuller discussions by McDonald, see next note. 25 R. Andrew McDonald, *Outlaws of medieval Scotland: challenges to the Canmore kings, 1058–1266* (East Linton, 2003), pp 82–4, 106 and 119–21. McDonald warns (at p. 106) that 'there is also the very real danger of polarizing these insurrections into a sort of "Celt versus Norman" rugby match played on a grand scale, which would surely be too fatuous an explanation'. Putting this together with his comments about natives 'resisting the Anglo–Norman penetration of Scotland' (at p. 84), I understand him to mean that he sees 'Celt versus Norman' as a factor, but not the only (or necessarily chief) factor in these risings. He also points out that Fergus of Galloway was open to European influence. For a more condensed discussion, see R. Andrew McDonald, '"Soldiers most unfortunate": Gaelic and Scoto-Norse opponents of the Canmore dynasty, *c*.1100–*c*.1230' in R. Andrew McDonald (ed.), *History, literature and music in Scotland, 700–1560* (Toronto, 2002), pp 93–119, esp. pp 105–7.

preferred to withdraw from the Anglo–Norman circles of the royal court.[26] Archie Duncan at one stage went so far as to sum up this period by saying that 'Scotland in 1286 was an independent kingdom with a western monarchy [. . . but] its unity was nonetheless flawed by a marked geographical division as its Celtic character had retreated before modernizing and anglicizing influences [. . . .] Scotland, which had been created as a Celtic kingdom, had become an English kingdom'.[27] At the same time, there is widespread recognition that there were important strains of continuity; that changes were gradual and geographically varied, and that imitation of English practices and institutions was discerning rather than slavish – no-one, for example, would disagree with Keith Stringer's observation that 'it is increasingly clear that there was considerable interaction between Gaelic tradition and "modernization",'[28] or with Hector MacQueen when he says, 'The evidence does not suggest that the old native system was being destroyed or displaced as a matter of deliberate policy; rather, it was being assimilated, so that [. . .] old functions were made to serve in new surroundings'.[29] Some, like me, might go further and query whether it is necessary, in order to explain the motives of those who fought against royal authority in the north and west, to look beyond their immediate political objectives in the highly competitive world of west-coast and North Channel politics that has been illuminated so effectively by Seán Duffy.[30] As for the earl of Strathearn's absence from the charters of William I after 1200, this coincides with the end of his time as justiciar of Scotia. It is possible that this marked a return to managing the affairs of Strathearn, which may have been necessary following the death of his son and heir at whose grave he and his wife founded Inchaffray Priory.[31] In making these points I am, of course, charting my own path through this difficult terrain, and thereby, no doubt, potentially adding to the confusion of the general reader confronted by so many criss-crossing tracks in the secondary literature. Those of us who are intimately acquainted with Scotland in this period may feel we can get ourselves through the challenges posed by this formative period in Scotland's past to

26 Cynthia J. Neville, 'A Celtic enclave in Norman Scotland: Earl Gilbert and the earldom of Strathearn, 1171–1223' in Terry Brotherstone and David Ditchburn (eds), *Freedom and authority: Scotland c.1050–c.1650. Historical and historiographical essays presented to Grant G. Simpson* (East Linton, 2000), pp 75–92. 27 A.A.M. Duncan, *The nation of Scots and the Declaration of Arbroath*, Historical Association Pamphlet (1970), p. 9. 28 Keith J. Stringer, 'Thirteenth-century perspectives', p. 91. 29 Hector MacQueen, 'Scots law under Alexander III' in Norman H. Reid (ed.), *Scotland in the reign of Alexander III, 1249–1286* (Edinburgh, 1990), pp 74–102, at p. 82. 30 The most complete treatment remains his unpublished PhD thesis: Seán Duffy, 'Ireland and the Irish Sea region, 1014–1318' (PhD, Trinity College Dublin, 1993). 31 William Alexander Lindsay, John Dowden and John Maitland Thomson (eds), *Charters, bulls and other documents relating to the Abbey of Inchaffray*, Scottish History Society (Edinburgh, 1908), no. 9.

our own satisfaction, but it cannot be said that we have sign-posted our basic assumptions and disagreements with sufficient clarity for any visitor to the subject to find their way at all easily. Instead of condemning Rees Davies' treatment of Scotland, therefore, it might be more profitable for Scottish historians like myself to view his discomfort as a barometer for the state of our subject, and take heed.

It will need more than a single chapter to pursue these thoughts to much purpose. Fortunately the mass of available charter material is being made more manageable for research in a three-year project, 'The paradox of medieval Scotland: social relationships and identities before the wars of independence'. The 'paradox' in the title is, of course, taken from Rees Davies' *First English empire*. A prosopographical database for Scotland 1093–1286 (www.poms.ac.uk) should make it possible to begin to tackle the transformation of Scottish society from the sources up (as it were). The database was published in 2010, it has since been extended to 1314. As a result, it may not be necessary to depend so heavily on pre-existing concepts like anglicization or Europeanization, feudalism or kin-based society, or ethnic labels like Gaelic/Celtic or Norman/English/French, as a way of navigating a way through this period. Huw Pryce, in a magnificently lucid and perceptive essay in the memorial volume to Rees Davies, has commented on the complex interplay in this period between innovation and continuity, and between external influences and internal pressures, as those who ruled in *pura Wallia* sought to sustain and extend their power.[32] The same could be said of Scotland, where not only the king of Scots, but also the *mormaír* or earls in the kingdom's heartlands managed to consolidate and extend their authority. The evidence of thousands of charters should make it possible to gain a focus on key aspects of this process in some of its variety. Other sources are needed, of course, for those parts of Scotland where charters are few and far between. It is striking, though, that in these areas the basic conti-nuity of a family retaining power over generations was broken with the creation of new lordships by Somhairle (Somerled) and his descendants in Argyll and the Isles; by the progenitors of the MacSweens, Lamonts and MacLachlans in Cowal and Knapdale;[33] and arguably also by the descen-dants of the shadowy Cairbre mac Airbheartaigh further north in and around the Isle of Mull.[34] In a number of cases these new arrivals are specifically

---

32 Huw Pryce, 'Welsh rulers and European change, *c.*1100–1282' in Huw Pryce and John Watts (eds), *Power and identity in the Middle Ages: essays in memory of Rees Davies* (Oxford, 2007), pp 37–51. 33 W.D.H. Sellar, 'Family origins in Cowal and Knapdale', *Scottish Studies*, 15 (1971), 21–37. 34 John Bannerman, commentary on sculptured stone no. 12 in K.A. Steer and J.W.M. Bannerman, *Late medieval monumental sculpture in the west highlands*, Royal Commission on the Ancient and Historical Monuments of Scotland (Edinburgh, 1977), pp 103–5.

associated with the erection of early stone castles, which suggests that their power may have depended on the appearance or reality of a new form of military might.[35] A case could be made that the tendency of historians to depend on ethnic labels has obscured a contrast between what may, crudely, be described as radical political change in the west and basic political continuity in the east.

This is not to deny, of course, that anglicization could mean radical change in other ways. This is particularly apparent if we take contemporary perceptions as our guide. John Gillingham, in his seminal essay on the beginnings of English imperialism, drew attention to a passage in *Gesta Stephani*, written in the 1140s, in which England's special qualities were poignantly described. England, we are told, was 'the seat of justice, the abode of peace, the apex of piety, [and] the mirror of religion'. As far as this anonymous author was concerned, Wales was rather different; but according to him, by 1135 the efforts of Richard fitz Gilbert 'had made the country so abound in peace and varied productivity that it might easily have been thought a second England'.[36] Turning to Scotland, it is striking that Aelred of Rievaulx, in his account of David I's achievements, also talked of justice, peace, religion and productivity.[37] In one place he praised David for taming the 'total barbarity of that people' so that, 'forgetting its natural fierceness, it submitted its neck to the laws which the king's meekness dictated, and gratefully accepted peace, of which it knew nothing up to that point'.[38] In another extended

---

35 G.W.S. Barrow, *The Anglo-Norman era in Scottish history* (Oxford, 1980), p 137. Note the comment, apropos the castles of the thirteenth and early fourteenth centuries – Castle Sween and Skipness, Dunchonnell and Inchconnell, Dunstaffnage and Castle Tioram, Kisimul and Mingarry – that 'even in ruin they are eloquent witnesses to a thoroughgoing, one might indeed say harsh, form of lordship', and the observation that place-names such as Ardlamont (residence of the chief of the Lamonts), Castle Lachlan in Strathlachan, home of the chief of the MacLachlans, and the MacSween fortress of Castle Sween on the shore of Loch Sween, 'suggest that proprietary feelings were, if anything, more developed in the west highlands than in other parts of the kingdom'.   36 K.R. Potter (ed. and trans.), *Gesta Stephani*, with introduction and notes by R.H.C. Davies (Oxford, 1976), pp 14–17, cited in John Gillingham, *The English in the twelfth century* (Woodbridge, 2000), p. 7.   37 For an excellent discussion of Aelred's ideals and his attitude to (Gaelic) Scots and Galwegians, see Keith J. Stringer, 'Reform monasticism and Celtic Scotland: Galloway, *c.*1140–*c.*1240' in Edward J. Cowan and R. Andrew McDonald (eds), *Alba: Celtic Scotland in the Middle Ages* (East Linton, 2000), pp 127–65, at pp 134–6.   38 D.E.R. Watt (gen. ed.), *Scotichronicon by Walter Bower in Latin and English*, vol. iii, ed. and trans. John and Winifred MacQueen, and D.E.R. Watt (Edinburgh, 1995), pp 144–5; Marsha L. Dutton (ed.) and Jane Patricia Freeland (trans.), *Aelred of Rievaulx: The historical works*, Cistercian Fathers Series no. 56 (Kalamazoo, 2005), pp 47–8. For a brief explanation of *Scotichronicon* as a witness to part of the unpublished full version of Aelred's *Genealogia regum Anglorum* (including the eulogy of David I), see Dauvit Broun, 'Attitudes of *Gall* to *Gaedhel* in Scotland before John of Fordun' in Dauvit Broun and Martin MacGregor (eds), *Mìorun Mòr nan Gall, 'The great ill-will of the lowlander'? Lowland perceptions of the highlands, medieval and modern* (http://www.arts.gla.ac.uk/scottishstudies/ebooks/miorunmor.htm), at 69 n. 60. These problems are briefly outlined by Marsha Dutton in Dutton (ed.) and Freeland (trans.), *Aelred of Rievaulx: The*

passage he described how David had transformed Scotland from a harsh land of famine into a fertile country with trading ports, castles and cities. The people, he said, were no longer naked or clothed with rough cloaks, but wore fine linen and purple cloth. Their savage behaviour had been calmed by the Christian religion. Chastity in marriage and clerical celibacy, which were largely unknown beforehand, had been imposed by King David, and church-attendance and payment of offerings and teinds to the church had been made regular.[39] Aelred did not go on to call Scotland a 'second England', but there is no doubt that he would have seen the radical changes he ascribed to David I in terms of bringing Scottish society into line with what in his time were regarded as normal aspects of English society.

There is room for debate about how Aelred's account of David I might best be read. All that needs to be stressed on this occasion is that he betrays much the same view of Scottish barbarity as John Gillingham has identified as a particular feature of English attitudes to their Celtic neighbours from the second quarter of the twelfth century.[40] This English perception of themselves as 'civilized' and of their Celtic neighbours as 'barbarians' is, of course, a powerful manifestation of the sense of exclusive Englishness that Rees Davies regarded as ultimately responsible for the failure of the English kingdom to develop into a more culturally inclusive and politically variegated monarchy of Britain. Aelred was not like most English writers in one crucial respect: he had long-lasting ties with the Scottish kingdom.[41] It is well known that, early in his career, he held a position in the household of David I, and that he maintained close links with David and his son, Earl Henry.[42] His views are likely to have been influential, not only in royal circles, but especially among the new Cistercian monasteries in Scotland founded as daughter or granddaughter houses of Rievaulx while he was abbot there. Perhaps it is possible to go further and consider the occasion when his lengthy account of David I is likely to have first taken shape. It survives only as part of a text consisting also of an account of generations of kings of England, and was addressed to Henry fitzEmpress as the future king. It must have been packaged this way sometime after the Treaty of Winchester, 6 November 1153, and before Henry's accession the following year. Could the material on David be slightly earlier? When reading the lamentation for

historical works, pp 35–6. 39 Watt (gen. ed.), *Scotichronicon*, iii, 158–9; Dutton (ed.) and Freeland (trans.), *Aelred of Rievaulx: The historical works*, pp 59–60. This section is repeated from Broun, 'Attitudes of *Gall* to *Gaedhel*', 70. 40 The theme is explored in a series of papers republished in John Gillingham, *The English in the twelfth century* (Woodbridge, 2000). 41 This might also explain why he emphasized that Scottish barbarity could be softened: see Broun, 'Attitudes of *Gall* to *Gaedhel*', 70; see also 73. 42 David N. Bell, 'Ailred of Rievaulx (1110–1167)', *Oxford dictionary of national biography*, ed. H.C.G. Matthew and Brian Harrison, vol. i (Oxford 2004), pp 491–3, at p. 493.

David I, one of the most striking features is the astonishingly vivid and detailed account of David's last days, which was surely set into writing not long after David's death on 24 May 1153. Presumably it is so vivid because Aelred was himself present; and if he was at David's deathbed in Carlisle, then it would have been natural for him to have taken a prominent part in the funeral at Dunfermline shortly afterwards. Was this, then, the occasion when Aelred first wrote his eulogy of David? Should we imagine that, when he warmed to the subject of David's introduction of 'civilized' ways to his 'barbarous' realm, his attentive audience included the great and the good of the kingdom at large?

Be this as it may, there is no doubt that ideas of Scottish barbarity were shared by important elements within the kingdom, not least the new monasteries that owed their existence to David I himself.[43] It is apparent, for example, that the monks of Melrose who drafted material for inclusion in their chronicle in 1259 (or soon thereafter) regarded 'Scots' not only as Gaelic-speaking people from north of the Forth, but as savages who despoiled Melrose's neighbourhood and ate meat on Good Friday. Melrose Abbey did not, however, identify itself with the cause of kings of England. English overlordship, either in Scotland or Wales, was regarded as servitude and oppression.[44] Presumably, however, even as late as *c.*1260, monks of Melrose would still normally have seen themselves as English, in the same way as when they referred to Bede as 'the honour and glory of our people'

43 For what follows in this paragraph, see Dauvit Broun and Julian Harrison, *The Chronicle of Melrose Abbey: a stratigraphic edition*, vol. i, *Introduction and facsimile edition* (Woodbridge, 2007), pp 10–11. The next four paragraphs summarize or repeat more detailed discussion of the themes of antipathy to Gaels, the spread of 'Scottish identity', and the extension of royal authority in relation to property and possessions, in (respectively) Broun, 'Attitudes of *Gall* to *Gaedhel*', 73–9; 'Becoming Scottish in the thirteenth century: the evidence of the Chronicle of Melrose' in *West over sea. Studies in Scandinavian sea-borne expansion and settlement before 1300. A festschrift in honour of Dr Barbara E. Crawford*, ed. Beverley Ballin Smith, Simon Taylor and Gareth Williams (Leiden, 2007), pp 19–32, at pp 25–7; and Broun, 'Becoming a nation: Scotland in the twelfth and thirteenth centuries' in Hirokazu Tsurushima (ed.), *Nations in medieval Britain* (Donington, 2010).   44 Under the year 1190, the Quitclaim of Canterbury is described as lifting 'the heavy yoke of domination and servitude' from the kingdom of the Scots: BL Cotton Faustina B.IX fo.25r; Stratum 5, probably entered into the chronicle-manuscript sometime in the first decade of the thirteenth century (certainly after 17 March 1199): Broun and Harrison, *The Chronicle of Melrose Abbey*, vol. i, pp 129–30. Under the year 1241 (BL Cotton Faustina B.IX fo.46r; Stratum 22, probably entered into the chronicle-manuscript sometime in the 1250s: Broun and Harrison, *The Chronicle of Melrose Abbey*, vol. i, pp 153–5), there is a comment that the Welsh, whose cases had since the days of Brutus been determined by their own rulers, are now required to have their cases decided in London by the English. This is described as an oppression. Presumably this is a reference to the submission of Dafydd ap Iorwerth to Henry III at Gwerneigron in August 1241 (repeated in London in a document dated 24 October), whereby Dafydd (among other grave concessions) recognized that the case of his half-brother, Grufudd (who Dafydd had imprisoned) should be determined in the king's court, where the question of Gruffudd's inheritance would be decided. See J. Beverley Smith, *Llywelyn ap Gruffudd, prince of Wales* (Cardiff, 1998), pp 32–5.

when their chronicle was created in 1173 and/or 1174. This, obviously, did not prevent them from being loyal subjects of the king of Scots, whose own descent from English kings was celebrated in dynastic histories and the cult of St Margaret.

The existence within the Scottish realm of an English self-identification with civilization and a corresponding view of Scots as barbarians may seem surprising – especially if it was shared by members of the royal household, or those who otherwise had close ties with the king. It did not, however, develop in the legal sphere into what Hector MacQueen has described as an 'institutional form of apartheid similar to the exceptions of Irishry and Welshry'.[45] Gaels and non-Gaels acted together in regulating society through royal authority. This can be seen at a local level (in rare detail for its date, around 1200) when at the king's command the Cistercian abbey of Coupar Angus was put in possession of some moorland in Blairgowrie by Earl Donnchadh of Fife (presumably in his capacity as justiciar), Hugh of Calder and Roger de Mortemer (local landholders, the last only recently given his estate in the area for knight service by the king),[46] Mac Beathadh who held the long-established position of judge of the region, a certain Donnchadh son of Domhnall, and other men of standing (*probi homines*).[47] It is striking that Gaels across the spectrum of free society are so prominent in performing this act of royal authority in a 'lowland' location not more than 20 kilometres from Perth, one of the main centres of trade and royal government. This can also be seen at the highest level when assizes were promulgated by the king in assemblies which expressly included *judices* – members of a long-established caste of judge-arbitrators who sported predominantly Gaelic names until well into the thirteenth century.[48]

The law may have been, in key respects, barely distinguishable from English law; it could even be referred to as *lex Anglicana* in 1285 when monks of Melrose claimed that it gave then exemption from the time-honoured arrangements for law enforcement in Carrick: but it was not limited to the king's English (or anglicized) subjects.[49] The king and those closest to him

---

45 MacQueen, 'Scots law under Alexander III', 95.   **46** G.W.S. Barrow with the collaboration of W.W. Scott (eds), *Regesta regum Scottorum*, vol. ii, *The acts of William I, King of Scots, 1165–1214* (Edinburgh, 1971), pp 341–2, pp 370–1 (nos. 338, 375).   **47** Ibid., p. 399 (no. 420): charter of William I to Coupar Angus Abbey recording the grant of a marsh (including what is now Muirton of Ardblair), 15 February 1198–7 July 1202 (from the abridgement (in Latin) of Coupar Angus Abbey's cartulary by Sir James Balfour of Denmilne (d.1657)).   **48** See Alice Taylor, '*Leges Scocie* and the lawcodes of David I, William the Lion and Alexander II', *SHR*, 88 (2009) on examples from the reign of William I. Barrow includes a list of known *judices* in his *The kingdom of the Scots. Government, church and society from the eleventh to the fourteenth century* (2nd ed., Edinburgh, 2003), pp 61–5.   **49** Cosmo Innes (ed.), *Liber Sancte Marie de Melros. Munimenta Vetustiora Monasterii Cisterciensis de Melros*, Bannatyne Club, 2 vols (Edinburgh 1837), no. 316 (cited in Barrow, *The Anglo-Norman era*, p. 119).

imagined that it applied to everyone. When Magnús VI king of Norway resigned the Western Isles and Mann to Alexander III in the Treaty of Perth in 1266, it was explained that 'all the men of the said islands [...] as well lesser as greater, shall be subject to the laws and customs of the kingdom of Scotland and be judged and dealt with according to them from now on'.[50] Scottish society was far from uniform, of course, and kin-based custom remained an important aspect of social regulation outside the royal courts for centuries to come not just in the west but also in the kingdom's heartlands.[51] It was inconceivable, however, that the *Gàidhealtachd* should become a separate entity with its own laws. When the western highlands and islands were shired in 1293, for example, the head of the MacDubhghaill branch of Clann Shomhairle was assigned the sheriffdom of Argyll. Politically, too, the most powerful men in the West, the heads of the three kindreds descended from Somhairle (Somerled), were now counted among the 'barons of Scotland'– although they are conspicuously the last to be named in the long list of those who, in 1284, issued a document recognizing Alexander III's granddaughter, Margaret, as heir to the throne.[52]

The idea that all the king's subjects were under one law – the law of the kingdom of Scotland[53] – may have contributed to an important change that is visible in the Chronicle of Melrose in annals for the 1260s. This material was added to the chronicle-manuscript probably before May 1291, and no earlier than Easter 1286.[54] On a couple of occasions people who belonged to Melrose's home county of Roxburghshire are identified as Scots. Does this mean that the old distinction between civilized English or anglicized Scots and barbaric Scots had disappeared by the late 1280s? For an answer we might turn to the mortal remains of a major history of the Scots completed in 1285.[55] Here we find the earliest traceable reference to 'highland Scots'.[56] In one place *Scotus montanus* denotes a Gaelic-speaker; in another it refers to pillagers who, we are told, are otherwise called 'brutes'. It is tempting, there-fore, to put this together with the adoption of Scottish identity by monks of

---

50 Thomas Thomson and Cosmo Innes (eds), *The acts of the parliament of Scotland*, vol. i, *1124–1423* (London, 1844) [hereafter *APS*, i] 420 col.b; Gordon Donaldson, *Scottish historical documents* (Edinburgh, 1974), p. 35.   51 W.D.H. Sellar, 'Celtic law and Scots law: survival and integration', *Scottish Studies*, 29 (1989), 1–27.   52 *APS*, i, 424; Donaldson, *Scottish historical documents*, pp 37–8.   53 Hector L. MacQueen, '*Regiam Majestatem*, Scots law and national identity', *SHR*, 74 (1995), 1–25, at 10.   54 Broun and Harrison, *The chronicle of Melrose Abbey*, vol. i, pp 168–9.   55 This is *Gesta Annalia* I. For a full discussion of its date and place within the textual tradition culminating in John of Fordun's chronicle, see Dauvit Broun, *Scottish independence and the idea of Britain from the Picts to Alexander III* (Edinburgh, 2007), pp 216–68. For a brief summary, see Broun, 'Attitudes of *Gall* to *Gaedhel*', 50–3.   56 I am grateful to Matthew Hammond for pointing out to me that *gens montana* appear on Matthew Paris' map of Britain (Cotton MS Claudius D. vi., fo.12v), *c.*1250. This appears in what may be intended to be Argyll.

Melrose and suggest that what had been a dichotomy between 'barbaric' Scots and 'civilized' English or anglicized Scots was now expressed in terms of 'highland' Scots as opposed to other Scots like the monks of Melrose (who were presumably already identified as 'lowlanders').

The process of adopting a Scottish identity by monks of Melrose can be traced back to around 1220. In material entered into the chronicle-manuscript around that time the south-east and south-west of the kingdom were referred to as parts of 'Scotland'. In other contexts the south-east had earlier been referred to as part of England, and Glasgow as in the northern part of Wales.[57] If we wish to explain how Scottish identity spread in the thirteenth century the most likely place to start is the legal, political and economic mechanisms that meant that royal authority became increasingly meaningful for a significant section of society under Alexander II (1214–49) and Alexander III (1249–86). A modern scholar of legal history may in his mind's eye have crossed the Tweed and wondered whether he had passed from the land of one law to the land of another; but anyone living in the mid-thirteenth century would have spotted an important and obvious change if they experienced the law in action. North of the Tweed the law embodied the authority of the king of Scots, not the king of England. In the mid-thirteenth century new species of written instructions to royal courts were introduced (modelled on English exemplars), which were designed to provide a definitive way of establishing the enjoyment of property by an individual and his successors. As a result, royal authority became routinely accessible as a potential safeguard of wealth and position.[58] At the same time, the opportunity to improve one's lot by exchanging surplus produce for cash became increasingly available through the establishing of burghs – chiefly royal burghs – in all areas except the Hebrides, west highlands and the extreme north. As a result, the livelihoods not only of merchants, but also of peasants and craftsmen with produce to sell would have become increasingly dependent on trade. This in turn would have depended on the relatively secure conditions that prevailed with the effective administration of the king's peace. The dramatic growth in money supply – from about £50,000 to £60,000 at the beginning of Alexander III's reign to something in the region of £130,000 to £180,000 (or more) by the early 1280s[59] – gives an indication

---

57 Broun, *Scottish independence*, pp 126, 165. 58 The classic study is Hector L. MacQueen, *Common law and feudal society in medieval Scotland* (Edinburgh, 1993). MacQueen focuses particularly (but by no means exclusively) on pleadable brieves. For a perceptive summary of the development of royal justice before 1300, see ibid., pp 34–50, 247–53. For a summary, including early evidence of brieves of inquest as well as pleadable brieves, see Ian Douglas Willock, *The origins and development of the jury in Scotland*, Stair Society (Edinburgh, 1966), pp 31–6. 59 N. Mayhew, 'Alexander III—a silver age?: an essay in Scottish medieval economic history' in N.H. Reid (ed.), *Scotland in the reign of Alexander III, 1249–1286* (Edinburgh, 1990), pp 53–73.

of how widespread the cash economy must have become at much the same time as people (in the south-east, at least) began to identify themselves as Scots for the first time. Being within the trading liberty of a burgh – usually a royal burgh – must now have become vital for the wellbeing of many more people. By the time the royal line became extinct in 1290, the enhanced experience of royal protection and increasingly widespread economic dependence on royal authority could well have played an important part in the realignment of Scottish identity so that (potentially) all the kingdom's inhabitants regarded themselves as Scots.

According to this scenario, it could be said that one of the most important consequences of anglicization was the 'Scoticization' of Scotland, when our modern sense of Scotland as a country and the Scots as its people was first established in the minds of those who lived in the kingdom. A key dimension of this – as many, including Keith Stringer, have explained – is that anglicization did not mean that English institutions, practice and culture were replicated slavishly. In particular, Scottish royal government in this period did not become a replica of English government. It remained a small-scale affair which (it will be recalled) depended on the cooperation of regional powers and local communities. For example, the justiciar was typically a magnate, and cases were heard and determined by major landowners in the region. An equivalent dependence on men of standing in local communities is also a feature of sheriff courts. As Hector MacQueen has pointed out, 'where the English royal justices came into the local community and imposed their own view of the law and of the correct way to settle disputes, so to speak from above, in Scotland decision-making in court combined views from above with those from below who would be affected by it'.[60] 'Scoticization' seems to have been a result of this balance between royal and local power, so that local interests may have been more inclined to see themselves as protected rather than threatened by their experience of royal authority. As such, this may be viewed as more of a spontaneous process rather than something that was promoted centrally.

It could be argued, then, that Scotland offers an example of what anglicization could mean in the context of a loose-limbed polity. Here, it seems, is the culturally inclusive and politically variegated outcome that Rees Davies proposed as a lost trajectory of English – and British – history. It is particularly striking that, at much the same time when (to use Rees Davies' words) 'the ethnic lines *vis-à-vis* the Welsh and especially the Irish [were] drawn more clearly and intolerantly than before',[61] Scottish identity was embraced even by those who had once regarded Scots as savages. This was not the same

60 MacQueen, *Common law and feudal society*, p. 253.   61 Davies, *The first English empire*, p. 141.

as newcomers adopting the identity of their hosts. The idea of 'Scotland' that emerged in the early thirteenth century – and the corresponding redefinition of 'Scots' two or three generations later – was something new that related to the society that had been transformed through anglicization. There is nothing to suggest that the 'English' in the south-east of the Scottish realm thereby lost their English identity, or that Gaels lost theirs. The new identity embraced older ethnic identities: it did not replace them. Could something equally dramatic, if not necessarily exactly the same, have happened in Britain as a whole if circumstances had been different? Could the English have become 'British' pure-and-simple, or might Scots and Welsh have even become 'English' – without any suggestion that ethnic identities were compromised in the process?

Rees Davies was not inclined to engage in such counter-factual speculations. Indeed, when it came to the final summing up of *The first English empire*, the idea of a 'multiple kingdom' or 'broader-based polity' was only touched on.[62] Instead, what was emphasized was 'the paradox [...] at the heart of the book', which was how the precocious power, cohesion and 'self-definition of the English state' which made England so dominant in this period also 'disabled [it] from reaching out effectively and constructively to the other peoples and power centres of the British Isles'.[63] If this line of argument is followed, then it might be said that the Scottish kingdom succeeded in becoming a 'meaningful monarchy' embracing a range of regional powers and ethnicities chiefly because it was *not* English. England may have been the source and inspiration for what Aelred of Rievaulx regarded as 'civilized' ways, but Scotland did not, in the end, become a 'second England'. An association with England may have been routinely acknowledged in the contemporary designation as *Inglis* of what modern linguists call Older Scots – the language akin to English which by the thirteenth century had taken root in burghs and surrounding countryside; the reigning dynasty may have boasted of its ancestry from pre-Conquest English kings;[64] and the law, in certain contexts, might still be referred to as 'English': none of this, however, was linked to the 'self-definition of the English state' described by Rees Davies. Instead a new self-definition of 'Scotland' had emerged which was quite self-consciously separate from England.[65] By the time of the inauguration of the boy Alexander III in 1249,

62 Ibid., pp 196, 199.   63 Ibid., p 201.   64 Alice Taylor, 'Historical writing in twelfth- and thirteenth-century Scotland: the Dunfermline compilation', *Historical Research*, 83:220 (May 2010), 228–52.   65 For the twelfth century, see John Reuben Davies' perceptive summary of recent work (by himself and David Howlett) in John Reuben Davies, 'Bishop Kentigern among the Britons' in Steve Boardman, John Reuben Davies and Eila Williamson (eds), *Saints' cults in the Celtic world* (Woodbridge, 2009), pp 66–90, at p. 89, where he observes that (mainly) English writers, as subjects of the Scottish king, 'were deliberately supplying the new kingdom of the

there was a clear sense, among those who identified most closely with the kingship, that Scotland was a sovereign kingdom.[66] The legal, social, economic and cultural changes in Scotland that Rees Davies saw as part of his bigger picture of anglicization belonged – as Keith Stringer has made clear – to a different nexus of power and authority focused from the outset on the king of Scots. It is striking that the 'three crucial factors' named by Davies in the 'social and economic matrix', which played an integral part in making and determining the 'identity of the English state' had also become key elements of 'anglicized' Scotland by the mid-thirteenth century:[67] a 'well-entrenched gentry class' is visible, for example, in the small landholders who adopted the place-name of their estate as their surname; 'the rapid circulation of money and goods' is witnessed by the rapid growth in money supply during Alexander III's reign;[68] and the 'close liaison between kingship and the locality' is readily represented in the relationship between the king and the sheriff courts.[69] These were arguably all essential elements in the making and determining of the new sense of 'Scotland' and 'Scots' that had emerged by the end of Alexander III's reign in 1286: crucial factors, that is, in the 'Scotification of Scotland'. It was because the king of Scots, and not the king of England, stood at the apex of 'anglicized' Scotland that even those in the south-east or in the burghs who regarded themselves as ethnically English eventually became 'Scots'. They might still have maintained their claim to be 'civilized' in opposition to other Scots, but the 'English' themselves were now seen as foreigners. For example, those who originally coined 'Ingliston' (i.e., 'English settlement/estate') as the name of numerous places in Scotland must have spoken English; but they plainly did not regard themselves as 'English', for otherwise the designation of a particular site as inhabited by English would have been meaningless.[70]

The paradox of the anglicization of Scotland identified by Rees Davies, if it is confronted, has the potential, therefore, to raise questions about key aspects of his *First English empire*. The Scottish experience shows that, for contemporaries, there was nothing inherently English about anglicization

---

Scots with a defined range of literary compositions [...]' which he saw as '[...] a response by Englishmen to the Norman Conquest of England. Englishmen successfully defined Scotland as a place in which to preserve their Englishness [...]' (i.e., in opposition to what had become the kingdom of England). **66** Broun, *Scottish independence*, pp 179–82, 189. **67** The three factors are summarized in Davies, *The first English empire*, p. 199. **68** Ibid., p. 61. **69** See above, p. 92. **70** G.W.S. Barrow, 'The Anglo-Scottish border: growth and structure in the Middle Ages' in Wolfgang Haubrichs and Reinhard Schneider (eds), *Grenzen und Grenzregionen/Frontières et régions frontalières/Borders and border regions* (Saarbrücken, 1993), pp 197–212, at pp 210–12 (reprinted in his *The kingdom of the Scots*, 2nd ed., pp 296–311, at pp 310–11); Alexander Grant, 'Aspects of national consciousness in medieval Scotland' in C. Bjørn, A. Grant and K.J. Stringer (eds), *Nations, nationalism and patriotism in the European past* (Copenhagen, 1994), pp 68–95, at p. 78. I follow Alexander Grant's interpretation, rather than Professor Barrow's.

once it was divorced from the power of the king of England. It could become something quite different, such as the loose-limbed kingdom that became 'Scotland' in the thirteenth century. It was possible – as Keith Stringer saw – for a kingdom and identity to embrace not only the social and economic matrix of anglicization, but also the society that was increasingly less anglicized the further west or north you travelled. This suggests that the root cause of England's failure to achieve a monarchy of Britain was not so much because there was something inherently exclusive about English identity or English society. The main factor that remains is the increasingly invasive practices of royal government in England. As Rees Davies himself observed, the exclusivity of the English was essentially 'a state of mind that was bolstered by reference, conscious or unconscious, to the norms of Englishness in England itself, be it by collective memory or by the language and assumptions of English government'.[71] Perhaps the root of the contrast between Scotland and England, therefore, lies in the fundamentally different expectations of royal government, leading to increasing bureaucratization and centralization in England, as opposed to Scotland, where the greater use of documents and royal courts led to a more even balance between kingship and locality. In this respect Scotland in its modern sense could not become a second England, for all that it was itself a product of anglicization.

A meaningful monarchy of Britain may have ceased to be possible in the thirteenth century, but what of a 'high kingship'? Perhaps a case could be made that Henry III in his last two decades began to establish a pattern of relationships with Scotland and Wales that might have evolved into an over-kingship of Britain along the lines suggested by Rees Davies. According to the Scottish history datable to 1285 (which we have met earlier), Henry kept his agreements with the Scots more faithfully than had any previous king of the English or even king of the Britons, and was regarded by Alexander II and Alexander III as a 'most trusty advisor and neighbour [. . .] which had previously happened but rarely'. In the same text we are also told that in 1265, Alexander III 'from motives of sheer goodwill' (*ex sua mera voluntate*) levied three men per hide for an expedition to assist Henry III against Simon de Montfort, but this force was not required due to Simon's defeat and death.[72] But there was at least one core issue that could bring such spontaneous goodwill to an end. The homage owed by the king of Scots could no longer remain ill-defined and had become contentious. At York on Christmas Day 1251, the day before his daughter's marriage to the 10-year-old Alexander III, Henry raised the issue of Alexander's homage for Scotland, but a definite

71 Davies, *The first English empire*, p. 194.   72 W.F. Skene, *Johannis de Fordun Chronica gentis Scotorum*, 2 vols (Edinburgh, 1871–2), i, p. 302

response was politely but firmly declined, and Henry never raised the subject again. But could the issue be postponed indefinitely? The arrangement for the festivities at York betrayed an awareness of potential friction. Matthew Paris tells us that precautions were taken to minimize conflict by lodging the followers of the king of Scots in one street, keeping them apart, presumably, from the English.[73] This attempt to segregate the visiting supporters was perhaps deemed to be advisable because of incidents like the ill-tempered stand-off in 1245 between Scottish and English jurors when they failed to agree on the border between the kingdoms where it heads south from the Tweed across the bog at Carham.[74] Be this as it may, there are indications that leaders of Scottish society had begun to think of their king as a sovereign ruler who was, in law if not in political reality, the equal of the king of England.[75] In such circumstances the continuation of a high kingship of Britain would depend on the willingness of kings of England and kings of Scots to avoid engaging with a legal conceptualization of their relationship, something which Edward I found impossible to resist.

In the end, then, we return to Keith Stringer's penetrating analysis of Scotland's place in Britain's political development in this period. He pointed out that Scotland's social, legal and cultural convergence with England was not the same as unity. The result was the emergence of two core areas; despite England's far greater resources, this meant that a permanent conquest of Scotland was ultimately impossible. In this essay Stringer's analysis has been amplified by examining what 'Scotland' and 'Scots' meant to the kingdom's inhabitants, insofar as this can be discerned. What this suggests is that anglicization in this period is not simply about the 'first English empire'; it is also about the 'Scoticization' of Scotland.

---

73 H.R. Luard (ed.), *Matthæi Parisiensis Monachi Sancti Albani Chronica majora*, vol. v, *A.D. 1248 to A.D. 1259*, Rolls Series (London, 1880), 267. Unfortunately there seems to have been insufficient space and violence broke out. 74 E.L.G. Stones (ed.), *Anglo-Scottish relations, 1174–1328: some selected documents* (Oxford, 1970), no. 8 (pp 54–7). 75 Broun, *Scottish independence*, pp 170–212.

The emergence of national identity among the religious of Britain in the thirteenth and fourteenth centuries

NIAV GALLAGHER

In his introduction to *The first English empire*, R.R. Davies stated that the histories of England, Ireland, Scotland and Wales had 'largely gone their separate ways, and plotted their development along their own individual trajectories'.[1] His research sought to re-integrate them, and his example has been followed by historians such as Robin Frame, Seán Duffy and Brendan Smith.[2] Their research has begun carefully reconstructing links that were apparent in the medieval world, but which have slipped from common consciousness in the intervening years. In a similar fashion, many histories of the religious orders of the British Isles have been written, but again these generally fall into two categories: either they concentrate mostly on the activities of a single order in a single country, or they examine an order from a purely theological perspective.

The intention of this chapter is to follow the example set by Davies, using the religious orders to explore the links that existed between the four countries during the medieval period. Although my primary intention is to look at the emergence of national identity among the religious of these islands, the logical starting point for this chapter is with the secular church. Rees Davies states that 'it was among churchmen [. . .] that the ideas of an all-Britain – indeed an all-British Isles – unit of authority were most fondly cherished in the early twelfth century'.[3] This theme is taken up in his *Age of conquest*, when he claims that 'control of the church was the natural corollary of political conquest'.[4] Certainly Archbishop Lanfranc and his successor

---

1 R.R. Davies, *The first English empire: power and identities in the British Isles, 1093–1343* (Oxford, 2000), p. 3. 2 See, for example, R.R. Davies, *Domination and conquest: the experience of Ireland, Scotland and Wales, 1100–1300* (Cambridge, 1990); idem, *The British Isles, 1100–1500: comparisons, contrasts and connections* (Edinburgh, 1988); idem, 'Frontier arrangements in fragmented societies: Ireland and Wales' in Robert Bartlett and Angus MacKay (eds), *Medieval frontier societies* (Oxford, 1989), pp 77–81; S. Duffy, 'Ireland and the Irish Sea region, 1014–1318' (PhD thesis, Trinity College Dublin, 1993); idem, 'The Bruce brothers and the Irish Sea world', *Cambridge Medieval Celtic Studies*, 21 (Cambridge, 1991), 55–86; R. Frame, *Ireland and Britain, 1170–1450* (London, 1998); B. Smith (ed.), *Britain and Ireland, 900–1300: insular responses to medieval European change* (Cambridge, 1999); idem, *Colonization and conquest: the English in Louth, 1170–1330* (Cambridge, 1999). 3 Davies, *The first English empire*, pp 11–12. 4 Davies,

Anselm had aspirations towards becoming *totius Britanniae primas*,[5] and in this the church can be seen as the forerunner of what became English political aspirations.

One of Lanfranc's first acts upon becoming archbishop in 1070 was to investigate his rights and metropolitical powers.[6] This included a reading of Bede's *Ecclesiastical history* which, he claimed in a letter to the pope in 1072, stated that '[...] until the last years of Bede himself, which is a period of almost 140 years, my predecessors exercised primacy over the church of York and the whole island which men call Britain and over Ireland as well; they extended pastoral care to all: they ordained bishops and held councils where they thought fit [...]'.[7] Whether this desire to extend his jurisdiction arose out of concern for the spiritual welfare of these countries, or from the desire to extend his personal metropolitical power can only be guessed at. Regardless, Canterbury's hopes for primacy over the British Isles were in vain. Although it had successfully extended its jurisdiction over Wales by 1143, in 1152 Ireland received four pallia and was placed beyond Canterbury's metropolitical control. Later in the century it seemed inevitable that the Scottish church would go the way of Wales. As part of the Treaty of Falaise of 1174, William the Lion was forced to accept that the Church of Scotland should henceforth owe subjugation to the Church of England.[8] Two years later, William and his bishops were summoned to Northampton where Henry III claimed that, as they had bound themselves to him by an oath of fealty, the bishops must also be subject to the Church of England. This was something the Scottish bishops vehemently denied, and they appealed to the pope. In a bull dated 1176, Alexander III called Henry's actions 'an attack upon ecclesiastical liberty' and he freed Scotland from York's metropolitical claims. This independence was cemented in 1192, when Celestine III proclaimed the Scottish church *filia specialis*, subject directly to the papal see and free from the claims of York and Canterbury. Thus the expansionist aspirations of the English secular church were ended, with only Wales fully incorporated into Canterbury's metropolitical jurisdiction.

The religious orders fared differently. In the late eleventh and early twelfth centuries, new monastic orders such as the Cistercians, Augustinians and Premonstratensians spread from the Continent and established foundations throughout the British Isles. The Cistercians in particular held

Age of conquest, p. 179.   5 *Calendar of entries in the papal registers relating to Great Britain and Ireland: papal letters*, ed. W.H. Bliss (London, 1893), pp 302–3.   6 M.T. Flanagan, *Irish society, Anglo-Norman settlers, Angevin kingship* (Oxford, 1998), p. 13.   7 H. Clover and M. Gibson (eds), *The letters of Lanfranc, archbishop of Canterbury* (Oxford, 1979), pp 48–57.   8 B. Webster, *Medieval Scotland: the making of an identity* (London, 1997), p. 68.

enormous appeal and quickly gained support within the native populations. Towards the end of the twelfth century, however, the reforming zeal of these monastic orders had faded and men such as Dominic Guzman and Francis Bernadone sought to introduce a new wave of reform. Throughout the thirteenth century, Franciscan, Dominican, Carmelite and Augustinian friars came into England, Ireland, Scotland and Wales and, with their arrival, changed the ecclesiastical landscape of these countries. Hitherto, those taking holy orders had been confined to a monastery or lived the solitary life of a hermit. By contrast, the individual friar was attached to the organization as a whole, rather than to one monastic settlement. His poverty was not merely personal but was also institutional and, because the order was subject directly to the pope, individual friars were in theory free of diocesan authority.[9] Yet because they were also religious, they were granted preaching, burial and confessional rights.[10]

Possibly because of their location within the urban centres of the British Isles, the new mendicant orders came to identify closely with the towns-people upon whom they depended for alms and gifts of property. A possible side-effect of this was a sense of, if not national identity, then native exclusivity creeping into the mendicant orders towards the end of the thirteenth century. This 'racialism' was not new in the wider church, however. In Ireland, several attempts were made by the English government to impose bans on Irishmen taking benefices, while religious orders were accused of barring entry to holy orders on the grounds of ethnicity. The most dramatic illustration of this is the so called 'Mellifont Conspiracy' that arose in Ireland during the early thirteenth century. Mellifont was the oldest Cistercian house in Ireland: it had been established in 1142, and its foundation was at the invitation and encouragement of one of Ireland's leading churchmen, St Malachy. The order proved popular with both native Irish and Anglo-Irish founders, and by the end of the century there were at least thirty-two houses established.[11] This racial harmony proved short-lived however. Starting in 1216 and lasting into the 1230s and beyond, Cistercian visitors to Irish

---

9 J.H. Moorman, *A history of the Franciscan order from its origins to the year 1516* (Oxford, 1968); R. Brooke, *Early Franciscan government: Elias to Bonaventure* (Cambridge, 1959); E.B. Fitzmaurice and A.G. Little (eds), *Materials for the history of the Franciscan province in Ireland, 1230–1450* (Manchester, 1920); F.J. Cotter: *The Friars Minor in Ireland from their arrival to 1400*, ed. R.A. McKelvie (New York, 1994); R.W. Emery, *The friars in medieval France: a catalogue of French mendicant convents, 1200–1550* (London, 1962); R.C. Easterling, 'The friars in Wales', *Archaeologia Cambrensis*, 6th series, 14 (1914), 323–57.   10 For examples of contemporary complaints regarding these rights see M. Paris, *Chronica majora*, ed. H.R. Luard (London, 1872–83); B. Cotton, *Historia Anglicana, AD 449–1298*, ed. H.R. Luard (London, 1859); 'Annales Prioratus de Wygornia' in H.R. Luard (ed.), *Annales monastici* (London, 1869), iv; *Memorials of St. Edmund's Abbey*, ed. T. Arnold (London, 1892).   11 A. Gwynn and R.N. Hadcock (eds), *Medieval religious houses: Ireland* (Dublin, 1988), pp 121–44.

monasteries faced rebellious Irish monks barring their way.[12] J.A. Watt, when examining the issue, notes that the order informed Pope Gregory IX that such visitors were chosen from a variety of nationalities – "'Irish, Welsh, English, Flemish, French, Lombard, and many from Clairvaux itself" – in order to avoid suggestion that disciplinary action was being influenced by any national bias'.[13] The visitation by Stephen of Lexington in 1228 attempted to address the issue of rebellion and, in tandem with this, the issue of race. Stephen exiled those monks guilty of rebellion and, among other things, insisted that the monks of the order have a good knowledge of both Latin and French. It was, as Watt says, 'a combination of administrative, coercive, pastoral, and educational devices'.[14] It is especially interesting that Stephen focused on language – Latin was the universal language of the church while French was the language of communication within the order. By clinging to their native language, Irish Cistercians were defining themselves by nationality first and order second. Stephen's remedy was to insist that all learn those languages that would internationalize them.

There is evidence also that exclusions based on race were becoming manifest in the Irish church as a whole during the thirteenth century. In 1217, the minority government of Henry III, acting no doubt on the direction of William Marshall, lord of Leinster, decreed that 'no cleric from Ireland, no matter how educated or good-living' should be elected to any ecclesiastical office.[15] Three years later Pope Honorius III condemned this mandate and ordered that Irish clergy should be freely admitted to ecclesiastical offices, provided that their learning and conduct were fitting and their election was canonical.[16] In 1250, papal intervention was required once again. This time Innocent IV was forced to rebuke the archbishops and bishops of Ireland for issuing a statute excluding Englishmen from their benefices. Again, in 1258, a royal mandate recommended that native Irishmen should be excluded from bishoprics and archbishoprics. The stated reason here was that they had a predilection for choosing from among their own so as 'to maintain their language'.[17] This equation of language to race mirrors closely Stephen of Lexington's assessment of the Irish Cistercians earlier in the century, when he cited language, among other things, as both cause and solution to the 'Mellifont Conspiracy'.

---

12 See B. Smith, 'The Armagh-Clogher dispute and the "Mellifont Conspiracy": diocesan politics and monastic reform in early thirteenth-century Ireland', *Seanchas Ardmhacha* (1991), 26–38; J.A. Watt, *Church and the two nations in medieval Ireland* (Cambridge, 1970), pp 87–8; B.W. O'Dwyer, *The conspiracy of Mellifont, 1216–1231* (Dublin, 1970). 13 Watt, *Church and the two nations*, pp 88–9. 14 Ibid., p. 97. 15 *Calendar of documents relating to Ireland*, ed. H.S. Sweetman (London, 1875), vol. i, p. 112. 16 M.P. Sheehy, *Pontificia Hibernica: medieval chancery documents concerning Ireland, 620–1261* (Dublin, 1965), vol. i, p. 226. 17 *Materials*, p. xxii; Sheehy, *Pontificia Hibernica*, i, pp 159–60.

It is clear, therefore, that by the middle of the thirteenth century, language and nation were becoming interchangeable, and as the century wore on such racial delineations became more frequent. In 1284 or 1285, in the period after Edward I had conducted his war against the Welsh prince, Llywelyn ap Gruffudd, Irish mendicant friars were singled out as promoters of the Irish language. No doubt racial tensions were running high across the British Isles as a result of the conflict, but it is interesting that religious would be thus singled out. An English official, conducting an investigation into the affairs of Nicholas Mac Mael Iosa,[18] archbishop of Armagh, recommended to the king that no Irishman should ever be an archbishop or bishop because they always preached against the king, and they always provided their churches with Irishmen so as to 'maintain their language'. He named the Dominican and the Franciscan friars as the worst offenders. In Scotland, racial tensions were clearly emerging also. On 1 April 1289, Pope Nicholas IV wrote complaining about the 'detestable' custom whereby Scottish religious houses were only admitting native Scots to holy orders.[19] In Ireland, further to the complaints made in the 1280s, was a letter from the Franciscan bishop of Kildare, Nicholas Cusack. Dated probably to the 1290s, the bishop warned Edward I that 'certain [...] Irish-speaking religious' were holding 'secret counsels [...] with the Irish'.[20] He claimed that rebellion was being encouraged at these secret meetings, advised that religious of Irish sympathies should be replaced with 'good and select Englishmen'.[21] In his work on Gerald of Wales, Robert Bartlett defines nationality not as 'a matter of objective classification' but rather 'a matter of identification', that is, 'a social process in which self-identification exists in a close relationship with identification by others and identification of others'.[22] James Kellas concurs,

---

18 The allegations came after an investigation into the archbishop of Armagh, Nicholas Mac Maol Íosa. On 9 September 1284, he was ordered to present himself for examination at Drogheda regarding charges that he had committed misdemeanours, appropriated temporalities of vacant sees, had consecrated the Anglo-Irish Walter de Fulburn as bishop of Meath without the king's licence and that he had held pleas which belonged to the crown. 'Fratres predictores et minores de lingua illa faciunt (multum?) [...]', *Cal. documents Ireland*, iii, p. 10.   19 T. Rymer, *Foedera, conventiones, litterae, et cujuscunque generis acta publica inter reges Angliae*, ed. A. Clarke and F. Holbrooke (London, 1816), i, part ii, p. 707; R. Nicholson, *Scotland: the later Middle Ages* (Edinburgh, 1974), p. 32.   20 *Materials*, pp 52–3.   21 'Suggerunt enim iidem religiosi lingue hibernice et precipue magis famo [...] et in officiis constituti eisdem regulis hibernice lingue et eorum subditis et asserunt quod secura [...] licite secundum jus humanum et divinum possunt iidem reguli et eorum subditi lingue hibernice [...pro patria?] nativa pungnare et anglicos hibernie conquis[itores...] pro viribus (?) impugnnare eorumque mobilia invadere et sibi penitus applicare canonice [...] boni et electi anglici [...cu*] sociis anglicis [...]'. Ibid. See also C. Mooney, 'Racialism in the Franciscan order in Ireland, 1224–1700' (PhD thesis, University of Louvain, 1951), pp 4–5; Watt, *Church and two nations in Ireland*, pp 181–2.   22 R. Bartlett, *Gerald of Wales* (Oxford, 1982), p. 10; J. Gillingham, 'Henry of Huntingdon and the English nation' in *Concepts of national identity in the Middle Ages*, ed. S. Forde, L. Johnson, A.V. Murray

stating that 'A nation is a group of people who feel themselves to be a community bound by ties of history, culture and common ancestry'.[23] Clearly the Irish Cistercian monks in the 1220s, and later in the century the mendicant friars of Ireland were engaging in a process of self-identification as defined by Bartlett and language – that is, the Irish language – marked them as a danger to the hegemony of English governance.

In an article published in 1986, Robert Colls states that 'the first stirrings of a popular national consciousness [in England] occurred in the fourteenth century in the writings and fightings of the Hundred Years War'.[24] In other words, fighting against 'the other' forged a sense of identity and common purpose that became 'Englishness'. This experience of war came earlier to Wales, Scotland and Ireland. From the 1280s onwards, Edward I waged war throughout the British Isles almost continuously, leading to a gradual politicization of not just the general populace but also the religious of these countries. There is little extant evidence for a rising sense national identity among the religious of Wales at this time, although there are tantalizing glimpses. In 1274, a dispute arose between Llywelyn ap Gruffudd and Anian, bishop of St Asaph, regarding the matter of secular versus ecclesiastical liberties, mainly relating to the 'bishop's men'. It was the Cistercian abbots of Whitland, Strata Florida, Cwm Hir, Ystrad Marchell, Aberconwy, Cymer and Valle Crucis who strongly defended the prince against Anian's charges. They proclaimed him a vigorous champion of the Cistercian order and declared him a special protector of them and of all ecclesiastical persons and orders in Wales. They humbly begged the pope not to believe such allegations as were made by the bishop of St Asaph concerning the prince.[25] Davies says that this, 'the most international of monastic orders, had become fiercely patriotic in its outlook'.[26] Similarly, at least one Franciscan friar appears to have acted on behalf of Llywelyn in the build up to war with Edward I, although it is hard to say if he was motivated by patriotism or by a desire for peace. About July 1282, William de Merton, warden of the Franciscan friary at Llanfaes, came before the king to negotiate on behalf of the prince. Subsequently he wrote to Edward stating that although 'it might seem presumptuous for him, a poor mendicant, to address the king's majesty'; he was motivated by zeal for the continuance of the peace between Edward and the prince.[27] Declaring Llywelyn to be the king's 'faithful and

(Leeds, 1995), pp 75–6. **23** J.K. Kellas, *The politics of nationalism and ethnicity* (Cambridge, 1992), pp 2–3. **24** R. Colls, 'Englishness and political culture' in *Englishness: politics and culture, 1880–1920*, ed. R. Colls and P. Dodd (Oxford, 1986), p. 29. **25** *Councils and ecclesiastical documents relating to Great Britain and Ireland*, ed. A.W. Haddan and W. Stubbs (Oxford, 1869), i, p. 499. **26** Davies, *Age of conquest*, p. 201. **27** *Calendar of ancient correspondence concerning Wales*, ed. J. Goronwy Edwards (Cardiff, 1935), pp 99–100.

devoted vassal', he stated that the prince nonetheless had very great occasion of complaint and he urged the English king to deal swiftly with his grievances.[28]

In the context of Scotland, Robin Frame phrases the emerging sense of Scottishness most eloquently. According to him in *The political development of the British Isles*, 'the Scottish sense of national identity was sharpened, not so much through interaction between a demanding government and those it taxed and drilled, as by the response of a small, conservative society to the sustained threat presented by an external enemy'.[29] And, harking back to my earlier assertion, he states that it was the Scottish church that had been the leading proponent of independence which was 'vital to its own freedom from control by York and Canterbury'.[30] Geoffrey Barrow, too, sees the Scottish church as the bulwark behind the cause of Scottish independence. 'Their nationalism', he says, 'was both informed and self-interested; it stemmed from two centuries and more of intermittent claims of various parts of the English church to jurisdiction over them'.[31] In far more colourful language, the nineteenth-century author, Andrew Lang wrote: 'The clergy saved Scotland's freedom. They later preached for it, spent for it, died for it on the gibbet and imperilled for it their immortal souls by frequent and desperate perjuries'.[32] While Lang may be overstating the case somewhat, there is evidence that the secular clergy – most especially the bishops of St Andrew's and Glasgow[33] – were very active in propping up the cause of an independent Scotland. But what of the religious? Again, the sources are scarce but provide glimpses of individuals acting in a partisan fashion. There is mention of Patrick of Selkirk, the abbot of Melrose, and John Morel, abbot of Jedburgh, travelling as envoys to the French court in 1299,[34] while in August of the same year Richard, abbot of Kelso, was said to have been absent from his monastery for a long time and was now 'an aider, abettor and counsellor of King Edward's enemies'.[35]

In the early years of the fourteenth century, evidence of religious support for the Scottish cause – increasingly Robert Bruce's cause – is more tenuous. On 10 February 1306, Robert Bruce murdered John Comyn in the Franciscan church at Dumfries.[36] The fact that there was no sentence of

28 Ibid., pp 99–100.   29 R. Frame, *The political development of the British Isles, 1100–1400* (Oxford, 2003), p. 193.   30 Ibid., p. 1193.   31 G. Barrow, *The kingdom of the Scots* (Edinburgh, 2003), pp 233–54.   32 A. Lang, *History of Scotland* (Edinburgh, 1900), i, p. 165. Barrow, *Kingdom of the Scots*, p. 214.   33 William Lamberton of St Andrew's and Robert Wishart of Glasgow.   34 *Documents illustrative of the history of Scotland*, ed. J. Stevenson (Edinburgh, 1870), ii, no. 1071.   35 Ibid., pp 392–3.   36 See the Chronicle of Walter of Guisborough previously edited as the *Chronicle of Walter of Hemingford*, ed. H. Rothwell (London, 1957), pp 366–7; N. Trivet, *Annales sex regum Angliae*, ed. A. Hall (Oxford, 1719), p. 342; W. Rishanger, *Chronica et annales*, ed. H.T. Riley (London, 1865), p. 229; T. Gray, *Scalachronica, the reigns of*

excommunication passed against Bruce, or condemnation of his actions published, indicates that while the Scottish church as a whole might not have approved of the murder, it was unwilling to denounce him.[37] By 1309, however, this ambiguity was gone. On 16 and 17 March 1309, Bruce held his first parliament at St Andrews.[38] At the same time a declaration was issued from the 'the bishops, abbots, priors and others of the clergy duly consti-tuted in the realm of Scotland', and it declared that Bruce was the legitimate king and that Balliol had been imposed on the people.[39] The following year there was allegedly a general Scottish council held in the Church of the Friars Minor of Dundee.[40] D.W. Hunter Marshall, in his paper for the *Scottish Historical Review* in 1926, provided a detailed and thoroughly researched argument as to why this meeting could never have taken place,[41] but Geoffrey Barrow does not believe the tradition can be easily dismissed, stating that it possibly took place during the Anglo-Scottish truce in early 1310.[42] A final piece of possible evidence for religious support is a reference dated to 1307. In May of that year, an eyewitness[43] to the battle between Bruce and Aymer de Valence sent a letter in which a reference is made to 'les faus prechours'. Seán Duffy has argued that these 'false preachers' were, in fact, Friars Preachers or Dominicans, who were stirring up the people with tales of Merlin's prophecy.[44] Alexander Grant, on the other hand, believes the translation is 'false prophets',[45] and thus bypasses the religious connec-tion. It is possible that Duffy is correct and that these men were Dominicans, but the use of the lower case letter 'p' for *prechours* seems to indicate other-wise. In most instances, where Dominicans are referred to as preachers it is usually in the form 'Friars Preachers' or 'fratres Praedicatorum'; only very occasionally do the words appear in the lower case, and then 'preachers' is usually preceded by the defining word 'friar'. Of course, it is possible that capital letters are sometimes the product of editorial intervention and that

Edward I, Edward II and Edward III, trans. H. Maxwell (Ceredigion, 2000), pp 28–30; 'Annales prioratus de Wygornia', p. 557; 'Annales Londonienses' in W. Stubbs (ed.), *Chronicles of the reigns of Edward I and Edward II* (London, 1882), i, p. 147; 'Annales de Osney', pp 341–2.   37 A. Grant, *Independence and nationhood: Scotland, 1306–1469* (London, 1984), pp 7–8.   38 G. Barrow, *Robert Bruce and the community of the realm of Scotland* (Edinburgh, 1988), p. 183.   39 Barrow, *Robert Bruce*, p. 184; Grant, *Independence and nationhood*, pp 8–9.   40 Barrow, *Robert Bruce*, pp 268–9, gives the source as the Scottish Record Office, HM General Register House, Edinburgh: State Papers, no. 4 (written in a chancery hand of the earlier fourteenth century) but I have been unable to view it in person. There is also another version provided in *Acts of the parliament of Scotland*, i, p. 460 but this is reportedly flawed in its dating: see H. Marshall, below. 41 D.W. Hunter Marshall, 'A supposed provincial council of the Scottish church at Dundee in February 1310', *Scottish Historical Review*, 23 (1926), pp 280–94.   42 Barrow, *Robert Bruce*, pp 268–9.   43 Alexander Abernethy has been proposed by Geoffrey Barrow. See Barrow, *Robert Bruce*, pp 172–3.   44 Duffy, *Ireland and the Irish Sea region*, p. 178.   45 Grant, *Independence and nationhood*, pp 7–8.

the original manuscript, on which the printed source is based, may have used the lower case.

In 1315, the Anglo–Scottish war crossed the Irish Sea with Edward Bruce. In September of that year, Edward II ordered the justiciar, Edmund le Botiller, to take information concerning the residence of Irish friars and clerks among the English in Ireland, whereby danger might arise to the cities, boroughs and towns of the country.[46] There is ample evidence to show that his concerns were well founded. In 1315, for example, Brother Robert, prior of the Augustinian abbey of St Mary's in Louth, was accused of entertaining Edward Bruce and other Scottish enemies of the king, as well as warning them that the justiciar was gathering an army to destroy them. He was fined £40.[47] In August 1316, Edward II wrote the minister general of the Franciscan order, Michael of Cesena. In a letter entitled 'Correcting the friars of the order of Minors in Ireland', Edward complained that friars of the Irish province were in confederation with the Scots, instigating rebellion and exhorting the people to support Bruce.[48] He informed the minister general that he was sending Friars Geoffrey of Aylsham, whom he proposed for the archbishopric of Cashel, and Thomas Godman, the provincial minister, to provide the minister general with full information regarding the activities of these rebellious friars.[49] There is further evidence that Edward II was correct in his concerns for the activities of Irish friars. In 1316, a messenger from the bishop of 'Enadens' was caught with 'litteris suspectis' at Caernarvon. This 'suspect letter' was most probably the letter written by Edward Bruce and addressed to the Welsh magnates and to all of that country who desired to be 'freed from servitude'.[50] Seán Duffy has argued that this bishop of 'Enadens' was most probably the bishop of Annaghdown, the Franciscan Gilbertus Ó Tigernaig,[51] something that would lend credence to Edward II's complaints that friars were promoting the Scottish cause in Ireland.

On 10 April 1317, John XXII wrote to the newly appointed archbishops

---

46 *Materials*, pp 94–5.   **47** *Medieval religious houses: Ireland*, p. 186; Smith, *Colonization and conquest*, p. 110; J.F. Lydon, 'The Bruce invasion of Ireland', *Historical Studies*, 4 (1963), 115. **48** 'Quia, ex frequentibus relatibus diversorum fidelum nostrorum, didicissem quod quidam Fratres Hibernici de vestro Ordinis, suae professionis immemores, et rejecta propriae honestate, quosdam, de ligeantia nostra, in Terra nostra Hiberniae, ad Confoederationes cum Scotis, inimicis nostris, faciendas, fuis persuasionibus instigarunt (ex quibus jam in eadem Terra, tam nobis, quam fidelibus nostris, diversa dampna et dispendia contigerunt) et adhuc, de die in diem, Hibernicos laicos ad rebellandum nobis et ad adhaerendum dictis Scotis, jam dictam Terram hostiliter ingressus, modis, quibus poterunt, non definint incitare ...', Rymer, *Foedera*, ii, part i, p. 294.   **49** Ibid.   **50** J. Beverly Smith, 'Edward II and the allegiance of Wales', *Welsh History Review*, 8 (1976), 139–71; idem, 'Gruffydd Llywd and the Celtic alliance, 1315–18', *Bulletin of the Board of Celtic Studies*, 26 (1976), 477–8.   **51** Duffy, *Ireland and the Irish Sea region*, p. 218.

of Cashel and Dublin, William FitzJohn and Alexander Bicknor, about certain friars of the mendicant orders, as well as rectors, vicars and chaplains who stirred up the Irish people against the king. Their 'secret persuasion and base counsel' through preaching and public advice, had promoted rebellion and provided absolution for those guilty of homicides, burnings, sacrileges and rapine'.[52] The pope decreed that all such offenders were to be publicly excommunicated if these activities did not cease within eight days of issuing his mandate.[53] There is also an obscure reference in the Annals of Inisfallen to an incident at Cork: 'The Friars Minors at Corcach are cited as defendants; they are summoned to appear in the king's court contrary to the common and ecclesiastical law.'[54] This is an entry that has puzzled two of the foremost contemporary historians of the order. A.G. Little, in *Materials*, notes merely that 'the events referred to in the last sentence remain obscure'[55] but Canice Mooney believes that they must have been indicted for encouraging the king's enemies.[56] In the 1933 facsimile version, Eóin Mac Neill and R.I. Best provided an analysis of the script in their introduction.[57] According to their interpretation, the scribe responsible for this entry, 'hand 35', was a copyist. The editors believe that because this scribe made so many errors, he was obviously working from a defective source. By contrast the editor of the 1953 edition, Seán Mac Airt, believes that a different scribe was responsible for this entry and that the entry came about for a completely different reason. He believes 'hand 30' was an orthodox Franciscan friar who added entries to the annals under several years as well as dealing with his own period. In other words, this was a rogue entry included by a copyist with an interest in recording such an event involving Franciscan friars.[58] It is interesting to note that it is the friars in the house at Cork who were named as coming before the king's court, since it was at their friary that the alleged incident in 1291 took place. Indeed Munster as a whole must have been causing grave concern to the Dublin administration since it was in reference to the postulation of Geoffrey of Aylsham to the archbishopric of Cashel that Edward II had written to the cardinals and new pope the previous year.

The death of Bruce in 1318 did not, it appears, end the political activities and national sympathies that had come to the fore during his three-year war

---

52 'nedum persuasiones occultas, et prava consilia, quinetiam per praedicationes et monita publica, temerariis ocusibus retrahunt, et ad impugnandum jura Regalia, et Rebellionis calcaneum, guerram turbinibus concitatis, erigendum in Regem eundem, potenter inducunt [...] ac etiam perpetrandis in hujusmodi prosecutione guerrum homicidiis, incendiis, sacrilegiis, et rapinis, absolvere rebrobra temeritate praesumunt [...].' 53 Rymer, *Foedera*, ii, part i, p. 325. 54 *Annals of Inisfallen*, ed. S. Mac Airt (1951), p. 429. 55 *Materials*, p. 102. 56 Mooney, *Racialism in the Franciscan order*, pp 22–3. 57 The Annals of Inisfallen, reproduced in facsimile from the original manuscript (Rawlinson B 503) in the Bodleian Library, with a descriptive introduction by R.I. Best and E. Mac Neill (1933). 58 See *Annals of Inisfallen*, pp xxxvi–vii.

in Ireland. In 1322, the Cistercian order in Ireland was cited for admitting no one to the order unless they had taken an oath swearing that they were not of the English nation nor related to the English. Edward II complained to their general chapter that the house at Mellifont and others were acting 'in contempt of the king, in opprobrium of all his nation and in subversion of his lordship.'[59] In response the abbot of Cîteaux sent the abbots of Dore and Margam to Ireland 'to dispose and ordain concerning houses of the order, and to compel the abbots of these houses to receive without distinction any who wish[ed] to enter the religious life, so long as they are able and suitable.'[60] An investigation into the Franciscan order two years later found that certain native Irish friars continued to constitute a serious danger to the king's peace and recommended that such friars living in these places were to be scattered about the country, ensuring that no more than three or four of the least suspect remained behind in these rebellious houses.[61] In the following year, Friar John Clyn complained that there was 'discord, as it were universally, amongst almost all the poor religious of Ireland, some of them upholding, promoting and taking the part of their own nation, and blood and tongue'.[62] It appears that racial tensions were still present at the end of the decade when John XXII felt obliged to address the matter. In a letter dated July 1330, he wrote that 'some impartial person(s) should be sent [to Ireland], as there are in that country two sorts of people, pure Irish and those of mixed race' and that care should be taken to have governors and officers of the same respectively.[63]

In Scotland, also, the issue of troublesome clergy continued to dog English aspirations in that country. In 1333, the Treaty of Edinburgh–Northampton was finally abandoned when Edward III came out from behind Balliol's cause to make his war with Scotland official.[64] In July, a Scottish army, attempting to relieve the English siege of Berwick, did battle with the

59 *Calendar of close rolls, 1318–23*, p. 404. In 1274, Irish Cistercian houses had been restored to the control of Mellifont, following the petitions of the archbishop of Cashel, David Mac Carwell, to the chapter-general of the order in that year. See J.R.S. Phillips, 'David Mac Carwell and the proposal to purchase English law, *c*.1273–*c*.1280', *Peritia*, 10 (1996), 258. 60 *Close rolls, 1318–23*, p. 404. 61 See Watt, *Church and two nations*, pp 190–2. 62 'Fuit discordia ut communiter inter religiosis pauperes Hybernie quasi omnes, quidam eorum nacionus sue et sanguinis et lingue partem tenentes et foventes ac promoventes [. . .] 1325 in Pentecoste capitulum generale celebratum Lugduni: ubi loca de Cork, Boton (Buttevant), Lymyric et Tartdart (Ardfert) auferentur ab Hybernicis fratribus et Anglicis et Quinta custodia assignatur, cum ante tantum fuissent quatour custodie [. . .]'. *The annals of Ireland by Friar John Clyn*, ed. B. Williams (Dublin, 2007), p. 183; *Materials*, p. 120; Watt, *Church and two nations*, p. 192; K. Walsh, 'Franciscan friaries in pre-Reformation Kerry', *Journal of the Kerry Archaeological and Historical Society*, 9 (1976), 24–5. 63 *Calendar of papal letters, 1305–42*, p. 500. 64 W.M.Ormrod, *The reign of Edward III: crown and political society in England, 1327–1377* (New Haven and London, 1990), p. 8; R. Nicholson, *Edward III and the Scots: the formative years of a military career, 1327–1335* (Oxford, 1965), p. 177.

English army at Halidon Hill, two miles to the north-west of the town, and were soundly defeated.[65] Berwick fell to the English,[66] and King David fled first to Dumbarton Castle and then to France.[67] The Lanercost chronicler reports that following the surrender of Berwick it was found that the clergy of the town had 'given great offence to the king during the siege'.[68] To certain religious houses clemency was granted but the mendicant orders were singled out for their strong Scottish sympathies and expelled from border houses. In a letter addressed to the provincial minister of the order in England, the king blamed the 'preaching of certain religious mendicants of the Scottish nation who, under a fictitious cloak of sanctity, encouraged the Scots in their tyranny'. Having inquired 'into the means by which the source of this malice and disorder [might] be removed', Edward felt that all Scottish Franciscans dwelling in the town and county of Berwick should be sent to the houses of the order in England and that 'there be put in their place wise and capable English friars who, by their salutary ministrations, may instruct the people, win them to our allegiance and affection and, under the guidance of God, implant a true friendship between the nations'.[69] The house at Berwick, founded by English friars in 1231, reverted to being an English house and remained so for the rest of its history. According to the Lanercost chronicler, however, the Scottish friars did not go meekly into England. He claims that when two English friars arrived at the Berwick friary 'the Scottish friars prepared for them a good breakfast [and] during the meal some entertained the English friars in comfort and familiar talk whilst others broke into the storehouse, gathered together all the books, chalices and vestments, and bound them up in silken and other cloths, alleging that all those things were the deposits of the lord, earl Patrick.'[70]

The Hundred Years War brought conflict closer to home for the religious

---

65 Nicholson, *Edward III and the Scots*, p. 177; Prestwick, *The three Edwards*, p. 59.   66 *Chron. de Lanercost*, pp 274–5; Nicholson, *Edward III and the Scots*, ch. 9; idem, *Scotland: the later Middle Ages*, pp 128–9; Grant, *Independence and nationhood*, p. 19; John Edwards, 'The Grey Friars and their first houses in Scotland', *Transactions of the Scottish Ecclesiological Society*, 1906–7 (Aberdeen, 1907), 10.   67 M. Prestwich, *The three Edwards: war and state in England, 1272–1377* (London, 1980), p. 60; Ormrod, *The reign of Edward III*, pp 8–9; W.C. Dickinson, *Scotland from the earliest times to 1603* (London, 1965), p. 179.   68 '[. . .] sed quia viri religiosi de villa tempore obsidionis ejusdem animum regis multum offenderant [. . .]'. *Chronicon de Lanercost*, ed. J. Stephenson (Edinburgh, 1839), p. 275.   69 *Rotuli Scotiae in Turri Londinensi et in domo capitulari Westmonasteriensi asservati* (London, 1814, 1819), i, p. 258; *Chron. de Lanercost*, p. 275; W. Moir Bryce, *The Scottish Grey Friars* (Edinburgh, 1909), i, pp 33–4; J. Edwards, 'The Grey Friars and their first houses in Scotland' in *Transactions of the Scottish Ecclesiological Society*, 1–26, 10.   70 Ninth earl of Dunbar. '[. . .]quod fratres Scotti, quum tunc oppotiut eos exire conventum Berwici et duo fratres Anglici essent introducti, fecerunt eis Scotti bonum festum, et tempore prandii aliqui tenuerunt in solatio et garulatione donec alii, fracto armario, librorum et calicum et vestimentorum omnia congregabant, et in pannis sericis et aliis colligabant et asportabant, dicentes quod omnia illa erant deposita domini comitis Patricii.' *Chron. de*

of England. In 1369, Edward III ordered the Dominican priory at Oxford to expel those friars who came from 'enemy' countries. The charge was that they were there on pretence of engaging in study, but actually came to spy out the king's plans, discover the state of the realm and pass on such information to the king's enemies.[71] In a similar fashion, and taking advantage of the schism throughout Christendom, in July 1378 Robert II of Scotland seized the chance to expel English monks from the Benedictine priory at Coldingham and replace them with monks from Dunfermline abbey. In the following year a consistory court was held at St Andrews and the charges made against the expelled monks sound remarkably similar to those made against French and Irish Dominican friars at Oxford. The English monks were accused of spying, of smuggling bullion and relics and of terrorizing the border area with a hired retinue.[72] In 1382, a second writ from Edward III stated that French and Irish friars were spying on behalf of their respective countries and that they were to be expelled without delay. This second writ was reissued in 1401. In it the guardian and convent of the Friars Minors of London were ordered not to permit alien friars of the order, whether sent at the mandate of superiors or others, to remain at the house for more than two days and they were to remove all such friars there at present, with the exception of those who were necessary and 'for whom they are willing to answer at their peril.'[73] Presumably this time the writ was aimed at Welsh friars acting on behalf of Owain Glyn Dŵr, rather than French or Irish friars spying for their countries.

Where religious support for Llywelyn ap Gruffudd had been muted in the 1280s, it appears that the religious were among Glyn Dŵr's staunchest supporters when he led Wales in a revolt against English governance at the end of the fourteenth century. The Franciscan house at Llanfaes, for example, was destroyed by the English army, its goods seized and the friars 'separated and dispersed as rebels'.[74] There is also a record of one John ap Hywel, prior of the Cistercian house at Llantarnam, who fell in battle in 1405.[75] Courtesy of Walter Bower we have a description of this prior

---

Lanercost, p. 275.   **71** *Calendar of close rolls, 1369–74*, p. 517; Rymer, *Foedera*, iii, part ii, p. 991; Hinnebusch, 'Foreign Dominican students and professors at the Oxford Blackfriars' in *Oxford studies presented to Daniel Callus* (Oxford, 1964), pp 101–34, 123.   **72** W. Bower: *Scotichronicon*, ed. D.E.R. Watt (Aberdeen, 1990–8), ii, pp 161–3; *Papal letters*, iv, p. 236; A. Goodman, 'Religion and warfare in the Anglo-Scottish marches' in R. Bartlett and A. MacKay (eds), *Medieval frontier societies* (Oxford, 1989), p. 256; R.B. Dobson, 'The last English monks on Scottish soil', *Scottish Historical Review*, 46 (1967), p. 3.   **73** *Patent rolls, 1399–1401*, p. 482.   **74** Ibid., p. 418.   **75** On 11 March 1405, the Welsh were defeated in the valley of Monnow and in May of the same year Glyn Dŵr's eldest son Gruffudd was defeated and captured at Pwell Melyn in Usk. *Annales Ricardi Secundi et Henrici Quarti*, ed. H.T. Riley (London, 1866), p. 399; J.E. Lloyd, *Owen Glendower* (Oxford, 1966), p. 96.

preaching to the Welsh troops, praying and speaking until 'his throat was sore and his sight failed.' According to Bower's account, he urged them to 'fight for their fatherland, and to defend their lands and possessions, to save their children and wives, and to suffer even death for their ancestral freedom.' Finally, not content with mere words, he joined in the battle where he 'met his temporal end along with seven hundred Britons.'[76] In 1952, Glyn Roberts published two documents,[77] the first of which named large numbers of the inhabitants of Anglesey who had adhered to Glyn Dŵr, but who now submitted to the special commissioners appointed. The second document was a list of those 'indicted [...] for being in arms and rebellion'.[78] Among the names in the former document are thirty-three clergy, while the latter contains five more.[79] There are six friars in all named as supporters of Glyn Dŵr and these are the brethren that had been removed from the friary at Llanfaes in 1400.[80] Among the other clergymen named in the documents were the bishop of Bangor,[81] the archdeacon of St Asaph,[82] the abbot of Conway[83] and the dean of Bangor.[84] By 1414, Glyn Dŵr was no longer a threat to the English presence in Wales, and friars were permitted to return to the deserted house at Llanfaes. However, in a manner reminiscent of the treatment received by rebellious friars in Ireland almost a century before, Henry V stipulated in his charter of restoration that only two of the eight friars housed there were to be of native Welsh origin.[85]

This chapter began with Canterbury's attempts to claim all the British Isles as its primatial right. The secular church had sought to extend England's spiritual rule into Wales, Scotland and Ireland and in doing so foreshadowed England's political aspirations. It is only fitting therefore, to conclude with another churchman attempting to claim the British Isles for England. Thomas Polton, future bishop of Hereford, spoke at the Council of

---

76 Bower: *Scotichronicon*, viii, pp 106–8.   77 G. Roberts, 'The Anglesey submission of 1406', *Bulletin of the Board of Celtic Studies*, 15 (1954), 39–61.   78 Ibid., 40; T. Roberts, '"An ancient record?" Anglesey adherents of Owain Glyndŵr', *Bulletin of the Board of Celtic Studies*, 38 (1991), 129.   79 Roberts, 'The Anglesey submission of 1406', 41.   80 Tudur Cayn; Tegw ap Blethy; Madog Dewi; Gruffith Nannay; William Conway and Gron ap dd Jthel . They are clearly native Welsh names. R.R. Davies, *The revolt of Owain Glyn Dŵr* (Oxford, 1995), pp 60, 212, 279. 81 Lewys Byford.   82 Gruffydd Young.   83 Hywel ap Gwilym.   84 David Daron. Roberts, '"An ancient record?" Anglesey adherents of Owain Glyndŵr', p. 130.   85 'Concessimus pro nobis et haeredibus nostris quantum in nobis est, quod in eadem domo sint imperpetuum octo fratres ibidem divina sevitia celebraturi, et Deum, pro salubri statu nostro, ac carissimorum fratrum nostrorum, et aliorum de sanguine et progenie nostris, et pro anumabus patris et matris nostrotum et progenitorum nostrorum et eorum qui in domo praedicta, it praedictum est, sunt sepulti, et omnium fidelium defunctorum, exorature imperpetuum. Quorum quidem octo fratrum volumus quo duo sint de natione Wallensi, ratione victus sui et aliorum, ad sustentationem sui necessariorum adquirendorum.' M. Holbeche Bloxam, 'Some account of the friary of Llanvaes', *Archaeologia Cambrensis*, 4th series, 11 (1875), pp 138–9; *Patent rolls, 1413–16*, p. 234.

Constance convened in 1414. Polton, responding to French claims that the English had no right to nationhood, replied lengthily and eloquently and, in doing so, has left us with a medieval English definition of a nation:

These people [that is, the French] claim that Wales and the prelates and clergy of those parts do not pay any attention to the king of England, nor do they want to be part of the English nation [...]. The answer is that they can blush for putting out such a flagrant untruth. For the whole of Wales is obedient to the archbishop of Canterbury (as its primate) in spiritual matters, and to the most serene king of England in temporal matters, peacefully and as a matter of routine [...]

Similarly, they are just as mistaken about Ireland, which embraces four provinces and sixty spacious dioceses. It is well known and undoubted that these provinces are recognized parts of the English nation [...]

When they go on to propose that the suffragan bishops of Scotland are not and have no wish to be in the English nation [...] the answer is that they undoubtedly are and ought to be, part of the English nation, since they have no way of denying that Scotland is part of Britain – though it is not so large a part.[86]

---

86 Text of English protest, 31 March 1417 (31st session of Council of Constance). See C.M D. Crowder (ed.), *Unity, heresy and reform, 1378–1460: the conciliar response to the Great Schism* (London, 1977), pp 110–26.

Anglicization in medieval Ireland: was there a Gaelic Irish 'middle nation'?*

FREYA VERSTRATEN VEACH

Domhnall Ó Néill's vociferous remonstrance to Pope John XXII, written in the early fourteenth century, is remembered mostly for its spirited plea for the termination of Ireland's dependence on the king of England and his non-Gaelic subjects. In his letter, Domhnall enumerated crimes committed against the Gaelic Irish and the appalling influence of a, as he called them, perfidious group of people. This group, distinct from others not, surely, by their supposed perfidy, but by their unique culture, were the Anglo-Irish.[1] They were of English descent, but born in Ireland, and over time heavily influenced by the Gaelic Irish language and customs. They were consequently viewed as a group separate from the English born in England, and, of course, from the Gaelic Irish. Falling between these two nations, they were collectively termed 'the middle nation'.[2]

The transformation of this group's culture from 'English' to 'Anglo-Irish' as a core subject of studies has attracted the attention of several eminent scholars of late, who have discussed the phenomenon under such terms as hibernicization, gaelicization and degeneracy.[3] Their works have shed

---

* This paper was written while I was a scholar at the Dublin Institute for Advanced Studies, and I would like to thank those at the School of Celtic Studies for their support. I would also like to thank Dr Colin Veach and Dr Peter Crooks for their comments on drafts of this article and apologize for not implementing *all* of their expert advice. All remaining errors are, of course, my own.
1 In this article, I use 'English' for the colonists of Ireland born in England (in spite of their varied backgrounds), 'Anglo-Irish' for colonists born in Ireland, and 'Gaelic' or 'Irish' for the Irish born in Ireland. 'Anglo-Norman' is used below when referring to surnames, as this concerns language, not origin.   2 James Lydon, 'The middle nation' in idem (ed.), *The English in medieval Ireland* (Dublin, 1982), pp 1–26, at pp 1–2, discusses why, even though the term 'middle nation' is only found in the Remonstrance, it should nevertheless be taken as a reflection of contemporary attitudes. For the Remonstrance itself (and a copy of Laudabiliter, attached), see Walter Bower: *Scotichronicon*, ed. D.E.R. Watt, 9 vols (Aberdeen, 1987–98), vi, pp 384–405, plus notes on pp 465–83.   3 See, for instance, Art Cosgrove, 'Hiberniores ipsis Hibernis' in idem and Donal MacCartney (eds), *Studies in Irish history* (Dublin, 1979), pp 1–14; Lydon, 'The middle nation', pp 1–26; idem, 'Nation and race in medieval Ireland' in Simon Forde, Lesley Johnson and Alan V. Murray (eds), *Concepts of national identity in the Middle Ages* (Leeds, 1995), pp 103–24; Robin Frame, '"Les Engleys nées en Irlande": the English political identity in medieval Ireland', *Transactions of the Royal Historical Society*, 3 (6th ser.) (1993), 83–103; idem, 'Exporting state and nation: being English in medieval Ireland' in Len Scales and Oliver Zimmer (eds), *Power and the nation in European history* (Cambridge, 2005), pp 143–65; and Seán Duffy, 'The problem of degeneracy' in James Lydon (ed.), *Law and disorder in thirteenth-century Ireland: the Dublin*

important light on acculturation in medieval Ireland. It is therefore unfortunate that very little research has been done on the much neglected – indeed, often ignored – corresponding Gaelic trend, anglicization, in the medieval period.[4] The neglect is all the more lamentable, because this phenomenon was present even in the early stages of the English invasion and was a major influence on many throughout the medieval period. Investigation into this topic is admittedly hampered by the fragmentary nature of the evidence, but piecing together the various nuggets of information can be a very illuminating exercise. It shows, among many other things, that acculturation in one geographical region or within a particular family can, on occasion, be linked with similar findings in another region or family. Such discoveries tempt us to question whether there was a Gaelic counterpart to the Anglo-Irish middle nation. It is hoped that the following very tentative findings will draw some much-deserved attention to the subject of anglicization and perhaps provoke a discussion about its spread, its development, and its place in medieval Ireland.

FINDING ACCULTURATION IN MEDIEVAL IRELAND

Most Anglo-Irish noblemen, although born and bred in Ireland, related as a matter of principle mainly to English culture and identified themselves as the 'English born in Ireland'.[5] Many of them were not keen to intermarry with their Irish neighbours, actively learn the Irish language, or adapt to anything Gaelic. This reluctance to acclimatize was not exclusively directed towards Gaelic culture, but was part of a more general colonial approach.[6] In

parliament of 1297 (Dublin, 1997), pp 87–106. For their culture see, amongst others, Kenneth Nicholls, *Gaelic and gaelicized Ireland in the Middle Ages* (Dublin, 1972) and Katharine Simms, 'Bards and barons: the Anglo-Irish aristocracy and the native culture' in Robert Bartlett and Angus MacKay (eds), *Medieval frontier societies* (Oxford, 1989), pp 177–97.   **4** An exception is Freya Verstraten [Veach], 'The anglicization of the Gaelic Irish nobility, *c*.1169–*c*.1366' (PhD thesis, Trinity College Dublin, 2008). For anglicization in the early modern period, see, for instance, David Edwards, 'Collaboration without anglicization: the MacGiollapadraig and Tudor reform' in Patrick J. Duffy, David Edwards and Elizabeth FitzPatrick (eds), *Gaelic Ireland* c.*1250*–c.*1650: Land, lordship and settlement* (Dublin, 2001), pp 77–97.   **5** A phrase found in, amongst others, three mid-fourteenth-century statutes (*Statutes and ordinances, and acts of the parliament of Ireland. John–Henry V*, ed. Henry F. Berry (Dublin, 1907), pp 417 and pp 436–7, and *Foedera, conventiones, litterae, et cujuscunque generis acta publica*, ed. Thomas Rymer, 4 vols (London, 1816–25), iii, part ii, p. 738), quoted in Lydon, 'The middle nation', pp 10–11.   **6** See, for example, the comments made at the time of the First Crusade by an Arabic observer by the name of Usama ibn Munqid. Clearly frustrated by the apparent stubbornness of western colonists, he remarked that: 'The Franks are an accursed race, who do not assimilate with any but their own kin.' Joshua Prawer, 'The roots of medieval colonialism' in Vladimir P. Goss and Chistine Verzár Bornstein (eds), *The meeting of two worlds: cultural exchange between east and west during the period of the crusades*. Studies in Medieval Culture XXI (Kalamazoo, 1986), pp 23–38, at p. 34.

spite of this stance, and as happened elsewhere, the settlers in Ireland nevertheless found that local customs and language gradually, but irreversibly,
impacted on their own ring-fenced culture. Many colonists lived side by side
and were in daily contact with the Irish through, for instance, trade, lordship
or diplomacy, and this meant that they could hardly avoid a degree of acculturation.[7] Like it or not, the Gaelic culture that surrounded the Anglo-Irish
and that they in many cases had so heavily defended themselves against, was
rubbing off on theirs. Over time, the colonists' adaptation became more and
more of a concern to the Dublin administration. So much so, that by the end
of the thirteenth century, legislation was put in place to halt the spreading
acculturation among the Anglo-Irish. The parliament of 1297 used the term
degeneres for the Anglo-Irish, 'meaning that they had departed from their
race'.[8] They came to be regarded as a group quite distinct from both the
English of England and the Gaelic Irish,[9] and thus a 'middle nation'.[10]

A 'nation' in this context indicates a number of people connected by
significant similarities in culture and language, and cemented by a feeling (on
part of both the people within the group as well as outsiders) that its
members form an identifiable group.[11] The 'middle nation', then, was
characterized by the identification with English culture, the adoption of Irish
customs and an origin in conquest and settlement.

What took place, however, was not merely the adaptation of Irish customs
by the colonists: many of the Irish inhabitants acculturated to some degree
to their new neighbours as well. One can therefore expect not only a degree
of gaelicization in and outside of the frontier or marcher regions, but also a
degree of anglicization. As was stated above, the latter of the two is the more
difficult to uncover, as contemporary sources typically did not concern
themselves with Gaelic acculturation. While gaelicization was clearly a
problem that had to be legislated against and is hence mentioned in official
documents, anglicization was, conversely, something to be applauded and
presumably stimulated where possible. However, records of the English
administration of Ireland, including those concerning the dispensing of
justice but also the patent and close rolls, do in fact display significant
examples of anglicization. For instance, many anglicized Irishmen mentioned
in court cases are hidden behind adopted Anglo-Norman (sur-)names, and

7 Professor Lydon remarked on this in his 'The middle nation', pp 2–3 and pp 13–18.
8 Lydon, 'The middle nation', p. 18 and idem, 'Nation and race', p. 104: 'meaning that they had
lost their racial identity.'   9 For the use of the Gaelic language among the Anglo-Irish see
Lydon, 'The middle nation', pp 13–14; for their interest in Gaelic literature, see ibid., pp 16–17.
10 For the text of the 1297 parliament see *Statutes and ordinances*, pp 194–213. For a discussion
of its contents, context and its importance, as well as a newer edition, see James Lydon (ed.), *Law
and disorder in thirteenth-century Ireland: the Dublin parliament of 1297* (Dublin, 1997).   11 See
discussion of medieval concept of *natio* in Lydon, 'The middle nation', pp 3–4.

these can be very difficult or impossible to identify. Whenever they are identified, however, they often are wonderful examples of acculturated men. First, of course, by virtue of their anglicized names, but also because they often feature in legal sources as having received a grant of English law. For example, the patent rolls record the following under the year 1279:

Grant to William Maffan, an Irishman, that he and his heirs may use English law and custom in the land of Ireland, and not be treated by other laws and customs, against their will, but in life and death henceforth enjoy English liberty. The like to Richard Sperling, an Irishman.[12]

Attempts to obtain access to English law for all Irishmen (excepting those in Ulster), and practical concerns on the part of the English government eventually led to a universal grant, but it was never effective.[13] Irish individuals were consequently forced to petition for this privilege throughout the Middle Ages. A grant of law meant that its recipients were from that moment on only to be tried and sued under English law, although in practice this was difficult to enforce. Record sources such as the patent, close and charter rolls also contain evidence of Irish tenurial contracts and correspondence with the king of England. For instance, the charter rolls record that the lesser noblemen Diarmaid Mac Giolla Mo-Cholmóg (fl. 1195) and his son Seaán or John held lands directly from the king in the area immediately south of Dublin,[14] and there is evidence in the patent and close rolls for correspondence between Feidhlim Ó Conchobhair (†1265) and the king.[15] Gaelic language sources are often as tight-lipped, in some cases even completely ignoring the presence of settlers.[16] But they, too, when read closely, yield a

12 *Calendar of the patent rolls preserved in the Public Record Office. Edward I. A.D. 1272–1281*, ed. H.C. Maxwell Lyte (London, 1901), p. 332 (dated 8 November 1279). 13 See especially A. Jocelyn Otway-Ruthven, 'The request of the Irish for English law, 1277–80', *IHS*, 6 (1948–9), 261–70; Aubrey Gwynn, 'Edward I and the proposed purchase of English law for the Irish, c.1276–80', *TRHS*, 10 (5th ser.) (1960), 111–27; and J.R.S. Phillips, 'David MacCarwell and the proposal to purchase English law, c.1273–c.1280', *Peritia*, 10 (1996), 253–73. See also *CDI*, ii, no. 1400, 5 Edward I [Chancery Files, Bundle 23, Norman French]; *CDI*, ii, no. 1408, 1276–1282 [Royal Letters, no. 2679] and *CDI*, ii, no. 1681, 10 June 1280 (see also *Cal. patent rolls, Edw. I*, pp 380–1). For the universal grant, see *Statutes and ordinances*, pp 324–5 (1331 A.D.). 14 *CDI*, i, no. 356, 12 Nov 1207 (full text: *Rotuli Chartarum in Turri Londinensi asservati*, T.D. Hardy, vol. i, part i (1837), 173) and Kenneth W. Nicholls, 'Inquisitions of 1224 from the miscellanea of the Exchequer', *Analecta Hibernica* 27 (1972), 103–12 at 108. See also James Mills, 'The Norman settlement in Leinster – the cantreds near Dublin', *JRSAI* 24 (1894), 161–75 at 162–3. 15 The following imply that Feidhlim had sent letters to Henry III: *CDI*, i, no. 2039, 28 May 1233 (full text: *Foedera*, ed. Rymer, vol. i, part i, p. 209), and idem, vol. ii, no. 457, 29 July 1255 (full text: *Calendar of Close Rolls of the reign of Henry III: A.D. 1254–6* (London, 1931), p. 213). A letter to the Lord Edward has survived intact, see *CDI*, ii, no. 713, c.August 1261 (full text: *Royal and other historical letters*, vol. ii, p. 199, no. DLXV). 16 E.g., *Topographical poems of O'Dubhagain and Giolla na Naomh O'Huidhrin*, ed. John O'Donovan (Dublin, 1862) and the later edition, *Topographical poems by Seaán Mór Ó Dubhagáin and Giolla-na-Naomh Ó hUidhrín*, ed.

number of 'anglicizations'. Annals and prose tracts, for instance, provide evidence for intermarriages, albeit very infrequently, and, along with genealogical materials, are sources for the use of adopted foreign first names among Irish men and women. In addition to this, Irish-built structures are the focus of a number of bardic poems, and occasionally are claimed to have had foreign features.[17] Physical evidence can on occasion support this, and other material remains bear witness to the use of seals and seal-matrices among the Irish nobility.[18]

DEFINING ANGLICIZATION

Efforts to map the shape and extent of anglicization are hindered by the fact that although the Irish and the English language sources compliment each other in geographical terms, their focus and content do not overlap much. For example, information gleaned from Connacht-based annals does not easily lend itself to a comparison with the proceedings of a court case from Leinster. As a result, it is hard to determine whether adaptations from English culture are particular to a locality or representative for other parts of Ireland as well. However, from the reluctant sources emerge a number of well-acculturated Irishmen. Contrary to what might be expected, angliciza-tion was not restricted to areas under English rule, or even to the marcher or frontier regions. Indeed, many anglicized noblemen lived in areas that were far removed from government control. However, the extent of anglicization among Irish people in the countryside was doubtless significantly less than that among Irish inhabitants of towns, where a foreign presence tended to be far more concentrated. The latter presumably had very different experiences from those of the aristocrats who tended to reside in less densely populated areas. I do not here intend to examine anglicization among townsfolk, but mean to exclusively discuss the phenomenon among the Gaelic royalty and nobility. The disparity between acculturation in town and countryside does, however, highlight a substantial problem with the term 'anglicization': like 'gaelicization', it has a ring of uniformity about it. It is a convenient denom-inator to indicate various forms of adoption from the culture of the English settlers by the Gaelic Irish, but it belies the fact that it was a phenomenon

James Carney (Dublin, 1943). A copy of the Topographical Poems is also found in *Leabhar mór na ngenealach. The great book of Irish genealogies compiled (1645–66) by Dubhaltach Mac Fhirbhisigh*, ed. Nollaig Ó Muraíle, 5 vols (Dublin, 2003–5), iii, pp 244–321.   17 See especially Katharine Simms, 'Native sources for Gaelic settlement: the house poems' in Duffy et al., *Gaelic Ireland*, pp 246–67.   18 Freya Verstraten [Veach], 'Images of Gaelic lordship in Ireland, *c*.1200–*c*.1400' in Linda Doran and James Lyttleton (eds), *Lordship in medieval Ireland: image and reality* (Dublin, 2007), pp 47–74.

that took many different guises for the Irishmen and Irishwomen under its influence. Anglicization covers a range of adaptations, from the adoption of new skills or utensils and weaponry, to making use of the English customs, language and law on a daily basis. Taken broadly, anglicization could include individuals who gathered up foreign weapons from the battlefield and themselves employed these objects in a later encounter. If one takes a stricter definition, being anglicized would involve a greater adaptation, such as being able to speak French or English, or making use of individually acquired access to English law. The seeming lack of evidence might steer the scholar towards the broader of the two definitions, but a more solid case can evidently be made in those instances where there exists proof for more than one adaptation (for instance the use of charters *and* an English personal name),[19] or participation in a potentially anglicizing bond. Bonds such as these included fosterage, gossipred, military and marriage alliances, the latter in particular having a substantial potential for both anglicization and gaelicization.

Anglicization as a process in Ireland has no definite temporal perimeters. Viewing the years 1169 or 1171 as markers of the start of English influence on Gaelic culture arguably implies forcibly assigning the English techniques used in the building of Cormac's Chapel at the Rock of Cashel, and the pre-invasion use of European-style charters among a few Gaelic noblemen,[20] to an artificial pre-anglicized period.[21] The determination of a clear endpoint is equally problematical, because adaptations and acculturation continued to take place throughout the Middle Ages and thereafter. However, without denying English influence on pre-invasion Ireland, one could contend that the twelfth-century invasion was a point at which anglicization really took off, highlighting the strong intensification in this influence. Obviously, continuity in certain trends in pre- and post-invasion Ireland should certainly not be underestimated,[22] but several developments and phenomena increased in

19 For charters see Marie Therese Flanagan, *Irish royal charters: texts and contexts* (Oxford, 2005); for names see Freya Verstraten [Veach], 'Naming practices among the Irish secular nobility in the high Middle Ages', *Journal of Medieval History*, 32 (2006), 43–53. 20 The earliest Latin charter in the European tradition in Ireland precedes the invasion by several years. Flanagan suggests that '[…] it is reasonable to conclude that the introduction of the Latin charter in the European tradition into twelfth-century Ireland was an adjunct of the church reform movement.' Flanagan, *Irish royal charters*, p. 23. 21 Roger A. Stalley, 'Design and function: the construction and decoration of Cormac's Chapel at Cashel' in Damian Bracken and Dagmar Ó Riain-Raedel (eds), *Ireland and Europe in the twelfth century: reform and renewal* (Dublin, 2006), pp 162–75 at p. 166, and idem, 'Three Irish buildings with West Country origins' in *Medieval art and architecture at Wells and Glastonbury*, ed. Nichola Coldstream and Peter Draper (London, 1981), pp 62–5. For the use of European-style charters see below. 22 See especially the work of Marie Therese Flanagan, such as her *Irish society, Anglo-Norman settlers, Angevin kingship: interactions in Ireland in the late twelfth century* (Oxford, 1998).

number quite dramatically from the late twelfth century onwards, while the introduction of others can be shown to be a direct result of the English invasion and colonization of Ireland in that period.

Although lacking in strict temporal boundaries, it is possible to divide post-invasion anglicization roughly into two stages.[23] The first covers the late twelfth and early thirteenth centuries, and was marked by conscious attempts by Irish aristocrats to be included into a wider English, and by extension, European world. This can be illustrated by the increased use of European-style charters (which also necessitated the use of seals), efforts to maintain a personal relationship with the king of England (through letters, military service and holding lands directly from the king), and even, in at least one case, seeking knighthood.[24] The use of charters in the European tradition in this period is a fascinating development. Naturally, this reflects developments in the Irish church, but I believe it is also indicative of a change in attitude on part of the Irish aristocracy. Donating to religious orders through the use of charters was integral to the cultured image of a western European nobleman.[25] The seals of Irishmen correspond to the style used by aristocrats from England, arguably emphasizing Irish aspirations at this point.[26] This idealism was aroused by the prospect of matters such as permanence in lordship, security of tenure and stable succession that the king of England stood for. And perhaps the European world itself was sufficiently enticing. R.R. Davies wrote of knighthood that to outsiders, 'it opened the door into an exhilarating international world of aristocratic fellowship and customs'.[27] This is not to say that all examples of anglicization were driven by this aspiration, or even that the ideal found its origin in the invasion. It was, however, a thriving ambition of many and a powerful influence on acculturation.

The second stage of anglicization started gradually around the middle of the thirteenth century, was in full swing by its end, and continued throughout the later medieval period. This latter period is characterized by the *lack* of that earlier idealism. The use of charters for the granting of lands to religious orders seems to have died out and correspondence and personal contact with the king became more sporadic.[28] Once the colony stopped

---

23 Obviously, there are other potential divisions to be made, but the following split serves to highlight an early and significant development.   24 Donnchadh Cairbreach Ó Briain was said to have been knighted by King John: *Misc. Ir. An.*, pp 86–7, s.a. 1210.   25 Although donations to churches by Irish kings occurred regularly in pre-invasion Ireland (Flanagan, *Irish royal charters*, pp 16–17), the use of charters in the European tradition for donations to (in origin European) religious orders seems to have started in the second half of the twelfth century.   26 Verstraten [Veach], 'Images of Gaelic lordship in Ireland', pp 47–74.   27 R.R. Davies, *Domination and conquest: the experience of Ireland, Scotland and Wales, 1100–1300* (Cambridge, 1990), p. 51. 28 There were exceptions, of course. Domhnall Ruadh Mac Carthaigh (†1302), in an endeavour

expanding and started to struggle, it became clear to most that Ireland was not going to be fully incorporated into a broader European culture in the near future. Also, under English rule, Irish kings, their rivals and main subjects were treated equally.[29] Hence, Irish kings did not find the permanence in lordship they had sought and were not elevated from among their countrymen. In their attempts to gain the upper hand in local politics, the Irish continued to forge alliances with the Anglo-Irish and adopt those elements of the settlers' culture most beneficial to their efforts to gain or maintain political dominance. In general however the Irish seemed to have given up on the idea of being incorporated into that international aristocratic stage of trans-regional knights and nobles, and focussed much more on local political realities. This process was reflected in Irish literature. Aoife Nic Ghiollamhaith has commented that, 'As the thirteenth century wore on, the ideal of the culture-king was superseded by that of the warrior-hero'.[30] Although this earlier ideal of a leader who actively stimulated artistic and academic endeavours and was in tune with cultural developments elsewhere in the western world may have had its genesis in pre-invasion Ireland,[31] it seems to have received a European (or, more specifically, English) slant on the arrival of the English colonists. These changes in their aspirations were influential, as they dictated the 'type' of anglicization the Irish nobles subsequently underwent. Anglicized aristocrats in the second posited stage of anglicization more and more frequently gave English names to their sons and daughters, by which the family displayed an association with an Anglo-Irish family.[32] They also mirrored English military practices, using spurs (which gave an obvious advantage to a rider on horseback), and building structures that were relatively new to Ireland and more difficult to besiege: in short, adaptations aimed at attaining a military advantage. The combined evidence of material remains as well as two poems surviving for a structure built by Aodh Ó Conchobhair (†1309), for instance, suggest it featured foreign designs and included an earthen bank with palisade and a water-filled moat.[33]

to 'acquire the king's friendship by his service', sent a Dominican brother to confer with the king on Domhnall's behalf. Not long after, Domhnall Ruadh received letters of protection 'in coming to the king in England with a moderate retinue, horses, and harness, and in remaining and returning to his own country', to endure for two years. *CDI*, ii, no. 2362, About 13 Edw. I [Chancery files, Edw. I, no. 39] and *CDI*, iii, no. 61, *c*.20 May 1285 (see also *Cal. Patent Rolls, Edw. I, 1281–1292* (London, 1893), p. 165).   **29** Katharine Simms, *From kings to warlords: the changing political structure of Gaelic Ireland in the later Middle Ages* (Woodbridge, 1987), pp 14–15.   **30** Aoife Nic Ghiollamhaith, 'Dynastic warfare and historical writing in North Munster, 1276–1350', *CMCS*, 2 (1981), 73–89 at 80.   **31** See Simms, *From kings to warlords*, pp 11–13 for some radical changes in twelfth-century Irish kingship.   **32** Verstraten [Veach], 'Naming practices'.   **33** The poems are *An tú arís, a ráth Teamrach?*, written by Aonghus Ruadh Ó Dálaigh or Aonghus son of Cearbhaill Ruaidh or Aonghus Ruadh son of Donnchadh son of Aonghus: Edmund Crosby Quiggin, 'O'Conor's house at Cloonfree' in idem (ed.), *Essays and*

Another poem for the same patron, claims Aodh wore golden spurs.[34] Other examples could be added, but hopefully it is evident from the above that the ideals which lived among the nobles in the early period and may have united them to some degree, were by and large absent in the later period.

EXAMPLES OF ANGLICIZATION

A few examples of adapted noblemen and women might further illustrate what is understood by anglicization. An obvious and famous example of an early inter-marriage between the Irish and English concerns a daughter of Ruaidhrí Ó Conchobhair. Few things indicate that Ruairdhrí might have been inclined to look upon the colonists' culture favourably. It was probably out of the need for a secure territorial border that he married his daughter to Hugh de Lacy, the lord of Meath.[35] But although Ruaidhrí himself was not an example of acculturation, by marrying his daughter to that powerful baron he was likely to cause a degree of anglicization in her and in her offspring. And indeed, she seems to have adapted well to her new cultural surroundings. After Hugh's death she remarried, and her second husband was another Anglo-Irish magnate (though not of de Lacy's standing): a man by the surname of Blund.[36] Such a mixed marriage no doubt led to some degree of acculturation by both husband and wife and certainly the children from such unions were often at home in both the Gaelic and English worlds. Ruaidhrí's grandson William de Lacy, for instance, was, according to one source, given the Irish nickname *gorm* (usually translated with 'swarthy'), and at his death received a laudatory obituary from an Irish annalist.[37]

studies presented to William Ridgeway on his sixtieth birthday, 6 August, 1913 (Cambridge, 1913), pp 333–52 at pp 333–4; and *Tomhus muir Chruachna i gCluain Fhraoich*, published in *Dioghluim Dána*, ed. Lambert McKenna (Dublin, 1938), no. 119 and Lambert McKenna, 'Bardic poems', *The Irish Monthly*, 51 (1923), 639–45. See Simms, 'Native sources for Gaelic settlement' in Duffy et al. (eds), *Gaelic Ireland*, pp 246–67 at pp 251–2 for a discussion of the poems. For an illustration and further discussion of the site see Kieran D. O'Conor, 'The morphology of Gaelic lordly sites in North Connacht' in Duffy et al. (eds), *Gaelic Ireland*, pp 329–45 at pp 340–1. **34** Séamus Mac Mathúna, 'An inaugural ode to Hugh O'Connor (king of Connacht 1293–1309)?', *ZCP*, 49–50, 548–75 at 563. **35** The insistence of the Dublin Annals of Inisfallen at calling her 'Rose' seems to be based on a confusion with Hugh de Lacy's first wife, Rose of Monmouth. For the marriage, the possible reasons for this alliance and its consequences see Colin Veach, 'Nobility and crown: the de Lacy family in Ireland, England and Normandy 1172–1241' (PhD thesis, Trinity College Dublin, 2010), pp 68–73. **36** It is possible that her second husband was related to Henry of London, archbishop of Dublin, who was of the Blund family. For Henry of London's possible connection with Walter de Lacy see Eric St John Brooks, 'Archbishop Henry of London and his Irish connections', *JRSAI*, 60 (1930), 1–22 at 6, n. 42. In any case, she must have re-married before Henry became archbishop in 1212 (idem, p. 8), as her son, Thomas Blund, had a wife in 1224: *Royal and other historical letters illustrative of the reign of Henry III*, ed. W.W. Shirley, 2 vols (London, 1862–6), i, pp 499–503 (nos 319 and 833). **37** For

Like marriage, gossipred (*cairdes Crist*, or godparenthood), by which one man stood sponsor at another's child at baptism, was a bond that could lead to close ties between Gael and Gall. An example of early anglicization is the bond made between Feidhlim son of Cathal Croibhdhearg Ó Conchobhair and justiciar Maurice Fitz Gerald in 1235. Judging from his correspondence with the king of England, his visit to the king's court and personal military service in Wales, Feidhlim seems to have been keen to be regarded as a nobleman among the king's subjects.[38] His gossipred with the king's justiciar looks to have been yet another attempt to be included into the international aristocracy.[39]

Both of the above cases are examples from the first posited phase of anglicization. An instance of acculturation from the second phase is found early in the fourteenth century in what is now Co. Clare. One Gaelic source narrates that:

Away to Cork [...] Mahon O'Brien sent Donall his son, that in the strangers' English tongue was singularly expert, to confer with de Clare, and before him to vilify, harm and complain of O'Brien and all Thomond.[40]

So, not only did Domhnall (†1318?) speak English (or possibly, though less likely, French),[41] he was willing to use this skill to the detriment of his Gaelic relatives. What is more, his father Mathghamhain was a consistent ally of Richard de Clare and had established tenurial bonds with him.[42]

Eoghan Ó Madadháin (†1347) might serve as a final and rather striking example of an anglicized Irishman, in which many of the 'anglicizations'

William de Lacy in Ireland see Katharine Simms, 'The O'Reillys and the kingdom of East Breifne', *Bréifne*, 5 (1979), 305–19 at 307–11. His Irish nickname is found in *The book of Fenagh in Irish and English, originally compiled by St Caillin*, W.M. Hennesey and D.H. Kelly (eds) (Dublin, 1875), pp 73 and 77; for the lauditory obit see *Ann Clon*, p. 234, s.a. 1233. **38** Freya Verstraten [Veach], 'Both king and vassal: Feidlim Ua Conchobair of Connacht, 1230–65', *JGAHS*, 55 (2003), 13–37. **39** It certainly failed to give Feidhlim security of tenure: in spite of the bond of gossipred, the justiciar banished Feidhlim from his lands in Connacht in 1236. *ALC*, s.a. 1236, p. 333; *AC*, s.a. 1236, p. 59; *AFM*, s.a. 1236, p. 285. The gossipred in this case may not have been made much before the breaking of the bond as Maurice Fitz Gerald held no lands in Connacht before 1235, but was a substantial landholder in the province from that year. See the grants in *The Red book of the earls of Kildare*, ed. Gearóid Mac Niocaill (Dublin, 1964), nos 3, 4, 22, 23, 24, 25, 27, 28, 31, 48, 49, 65, 67, 74 and 191. Evidence from the annals too points to 1235 as the earliest date for Maurice to come to Connacht (the Annals of Connacht first mention him in the province in 1235, and frequently thereafter: *AC*, pp 50–3, s.a. 1235). **40** Sean Mac Craith, *Caithréim Thoirdhealbhaigh*, ed. Standish Hayes O'Grady (London, 1929), vol. xxvi, p. 135 and vol. xxvii, p. 119. **41** The words used to describe the language concerned are *bérla na ngall*, 'speech of the foreigners'. This later came to mean 'English', but in this period could indicate French also. However, it seems that English was the more prevalent of the spoken languages. **42** E.g., *Caith. Thoir.*, vol. xxvi, p. 135 and vol. xxvii, p. 119 and T.J. Westropp, 'On the external evidences bearing on the historic character of the "Wars of Turlough", by John, son of Rory MacGrath', *TRHS*, 32 (1902–4), 133–98, at 147.

mentioned in the previous section are combined. Firstly, this lord of Síol nAnmchadha (in the Cos Galway and Offaly) probably married a daughter of Sir Raymond an Mhuine de Burgh (†1367). After Eoghan had joined him in a military expedition, he moreover received a grant of English law at the request of Richard de Burgh, the earl of Ulster. And finally, it is claimed in a prose tract written for Ó Madadháin that he had a stone and timber castle built (although we can only speculate as to the possible 'Englishness' of the structure).[43]

THE DISSEMINATION OF ANGLICIZATION

Having established what is meant by 'anglicization', a closer look at the early spread of the phenomenon may be warranted. As was said above, angliciza-tion could be disseminated through the creation of a close alliance with the settlers. Once established, it could also spread within a family. Ruaidhrí Ó Conchobhair's younger brother Cathal Croibhdhearg (†1224), and Cathal's sons Aodh (†1228) and Feidhlim (†1265) are good examples of anglicized noblemen. Cathal attempted to introduce primogeniture for his eldest son Aodh and joined King John on a military campaign in Ulster.[44] Some examples of Feidhlim's acculturation have already been discussed, but it may be useful to note that on top of the above, he also possessed his own eques-trian seal and possibly commissioned an effigy in English style.[45] His older brother Aodh, during his short reign, celebrated Christmas at the justiciar's court and, according to some sources, befriended the epitome of chivalric values, William Marshal.[46]

Acculturation likewise took place over several generations in the Mac Carthaigh family. In 1260, the plea rolls mention a case brought to the English court by the three daughters of Diarmaid Mac Carthaigh, Dearbhfhorgaill, Éadaoin and Raghnailt, married respectively to David de

---

43 *Tribes and customs of Hy-Many, commonly called O'Kelly's country*, ed. John O'Donovan (Dublin, 1843), pp 133 and 140; *Rotulorum patentium et clausorum cancellariae Hiberniae calen-darium*, ed. Edward Tresham, vol. i, pars. i, Hen. II.–Hen. III (Dublin, 1828), no. 93, p. 28. See also Máire Ní Mhaonaigh, 'Nósa Ua Maine: fact or fiction?' in T.M. Charles-Edwards, Morfydd E. Owen, and Paul Russell (eds), *The Welsh king and his court* (Cardiff, 2000), pp 362–81, at p. 365, n. 15. NB: the pleas and perquisites of the Hundred of Síol nAnmchadha were granted for life to Ó Madadháin by William de Burgh (†1333): H.T. Knox, 'Occupation of Connaught by the Anglo-Normans after A.D. 1237', *JRSAI*, 32 (1902), 132–8, 393–406 and 33 (1903), 58–74, at 394. 44 Seán Duffy, 'King John's expedition to Ireland, 1210: the evidence reconsidered', *IHS*, 30 (1996), 1–24, at 10–13 and 15–21. 45 Verstraten [Veach], 'Images of Gaelic lordship', pp 48–9 and 57–8. 46 Brendan Smith, 'Irish politics, 1220–1245' in Michael Prestwich, R. Britnell and Robin Frame (eds), *Thirteenth-century England, VIII* (Woodbridge, 2001), pp 13–22, at p. 18.

Prendergast, Thomas de Kaninges and Robert Cusyn. The very fact that the case was brought to an English court implied access to English law, which, as was mentioned above, was not a given. Irishmen and Irishwomen, even those married to English partners, had to petition to the king to be granted this privilege. What is more, the case itself applied to their situation concepts of English law that were absent from Irish law. The sisters each claimed part of the inheritance of their father Diarmaid, a claim that could only be made through English law, as Irish law would not allow for an inheritance to be passed on through the female line. However, common law did, if no male heirs survived. Diarmaid had had a son Cormac, who had, presumably, died without progeny.[47] Another concept from English law that was applied emerges from the documentary evidence through the court's discovery that Dearbhfhorgaill and Éadaoin were born before their mother and father had been betrothed. This led to the failure of their claims and only the youngest daughter, Raghnailt, succeeded in obtaining her father's lands. In other words, the timing of the marriage of their parents was of the essence and this was a feature peculiar to English common law: canon law regarded such 'mantle children' to be legitimate, and Irish law made no distinction between legitimate and illegitimate offspring.[48] The possible use of primogeniture among the Meic Charthaigh seems confirmed by the fact that the name pool of the family's contenders for the lordship was unusually small. The chance that at any time from the late twelfth to the late fourteenth century, the head of the Meic Charthaigh was called either Cormac or Domhnall was nearly 60 per cent. What is more, any head of the Meic Charthaigh had a father who had been king or lord also.

These facts seem to suggest that anglicization bred anglicization. But although a son following in his father's anglicized footsteps may perhaps seem natural, it was far from self-evident. As has always been the case, many a son disagreed with his father about a stance taken. The author of a poem recorded in the Book of Fermoy, 'Who is it that asserts a right to Cruachan',[49] intended to rouse Muircheartach (†1356) son of Seaán Ó Néill to assert his claim to the kingship of Connacht in right of his mother Úna, daughter of Aodh Ó Conchobhair (1274†). This is quite remarkable, as such an assertion, made in a traditional bardic poem, would again imply the use of English law. The patron's family history makes the claim extraordinary. Muircheartach's Ó Conchobhair grandfather, Aodh, had been known for his

47 NAI, RC 7/1 pp 246–7, 263 and 282–3. 48 *Statutes and ordinances*, p. 33 and Art Cosgrove, 'The Armagh registers: an under-explored source for late medieval Ireland', *Peritia*, 6–7 (1987–8), 307–20, at 312. 49 Royal Irish Academy, MS 23 E 29: 'Cia so agras cóir um Chruachain'. This poem is discussed in Katharine Simms, 'The legal position of Irishwomen in the later Middle Ages', *Irish Jurist*, 10 (new ser.) (1975), 96–111, at 106.

attacks on settlers and his involvement, together with Brian Ó Néill –
Muircheartach's great-grandfather – in the famous Battle of Down (an
assault on colonists in Ulster that was meant to be part of a more extensive
plan to oust the settlers from Ireland). What is perhaps even more remarkable is that Muircheartach's Ó Néill grandfather, Domhnall, was in fact the
author of the Remonstrance mentioned in the starting paragraph of this
chapter, that document that so viciously attacked English presence in
Ireland. However, it is important to keep in mind that individuals were
frequently very opportunistic in their approach to customs. Acculturation
may have brought some perks (for instance Anglo-Irish military backing),
but was sometimes merely a concession and does not of necessity imply
wholesale adoption of English culture, or even a positive view towards
English traditions. The adoption of 'English' weaponry, or the use of a seal
(a very practical item necessary for official correspondence with the English)
should therefore be examined with caution.

WAS THERE A GAELIC IRISH MIDDLE NATION?

If there was a Gaelic middle nation in medieval Ireland, it would have
consisted of a group of at least loosely connected Irishmen and women who,
to a greater or lesser degree, borrowed and adapted English customs, and
some of whom may, in the process, have rejected or distanced themselves
from Irish traditions. Consequently, they would have formed a
group viewed – by its own members as well as by outsiders – as separate from
their English, Anglo-Irish and 'non-anglicized' Irish neighbours. To prove
the existence of a Gaelic middle nation, we need to uncover at the very least
evidence for a common culture. It would be preferable and much more
compelling, of course, to find a statement from contemporaries that would
suggest that the anglicized Irish formed a separate group. Such a testimony
would, however, be hard to find. The king of England tended to make a
distinction between those who were direct tenants and those who were not,
and where appropriate, between 'loyal Irish' and 'Irish enemies' (a distinction
that did not necessarily coincide with 'anglicized' and 'non-anglicized', but
rather was a reflection of political alliances at that particular point in time).
He did not, or so it appears from documentary sources, distinguish between
'Irish' and 'anglicized Irish'. What is more, neither Anglo-Irish annals nor
poetic works show signs of such a division.[50] Foreign observers like Giraldus

50 For poetry see, e.g., Angela M. Lucas (ed.), *Anglo-Irish poems of the Middle Ages* (Blackrock,
1995), pp 150–7 and 207–9; for annals, see especially *The annals of Ireland by friar John Clyn*, ed.
Bernadette Williams (Dublin, 2007).

Cambrensis and Count de Perelhos (no doubt because their focus tended to be on the alien and the bizarre) show little or no interest in anglicized people, and make no mention of them as a group.[51] And finally, the Irish themselves also withhold any explicit information about a possible Gaelic middle nation. Therefore, we have to look more closely into their actions.

With regards to an anglicized culture, a common ideal could have acted as mortar. The wish to be a part of a greater, trans-regional, aristocracy in the late twelfth and early thirteenth centuries may have been a widespread ambition among anglicized noblemen, as was stated above. Although such a common aspiration was not essential, it may have assisted in the formation of a shared culture. With this in mind, one could argue that a Gaelic middle nation is perhaps more likely to have formed in the first rather than in the second stage of anglicization with its focus on local, immediate conditions.

Although the Anglo–Irish forged ties such as those of marriage and, no doubt, godparenthood, among themselves, it seems perhaps doubtful that the anglicized Irish could form a comparable unit of families linked through alliances based merely on a similar approach towards the cultures surrounding them. If intermarriage was a relatively regularly seen phenomenon, and so a marriage unlikely to be build on the ethnic origins of the partners alone, it was without a doubt even less likely to be guided by their attitude towards the presence of colonists in Ireland. However, men living in relative proximity of each other, in similar situations, of like social stature, may have shared views on acculturation, whether they were positive or negative. And indeed, there do seem to have been several marriage links in the early period between families who allied themselves with the English through marriages and military pacts (for what follows, see also the appendix). As is well known, Diarmaid Mac Murchadha married one daughter, Aoife, to Richard de Clare (Strongbow), another, Dearbhfhorgaill, to Domhnall Mac Giolla Mo-Cholmóg, and a third daughter, Órlaith, to the Gaelic king of Thomond, Domhnall Mór Ó Briain. Mac Murchadha's Irish sons-in-law both show varying degrees of cooperation and acculturation. In 1170, Ó Briain received military support from Diarmaid Mac Murchadha's English allies, while the so-called 'Song of Dermot and the Earl' claims that the fact that he became Richard de Clare's brother-in-law led, in turn, to Ó Briain aiding de Clare in a campaign.[52] That Ó Briain was not opposed to

51 Gerald of Wales: *Expugnatio Hibernica. The conquest of Ireland*, ed. A.B. Scott and F.X. Martin (Dublin, 1978) and J.P. Mahaffy (ed.), 'Two early tours in Ireland', *Hermathena*, 18 (no. 40) (1919), 1–16. 52 Goddard H. Orpen, *Ireland under the Normans* (Oxford, 1912–20; repr. Dublin, 2005), p. 64 (original pagination: vol. i, p. 178) and idem (ed.), *The song of Dermot and the Earl: an Old French poem from the Carew manuscript no. 596 in the archiepiscopal library at Lembeth palace* (Oxford, 1892), ii, 2041–8. For a new edition of the same text see Evelyn Mullally (ed.), *The deeds of the Normans in Ireland. La geste des Engleis en Yrlande* (Dublin, 2002), ii, 2039–46.

some degree of acculturation may be inferred from the fact that he married one of his daughters to the English magnate William de Burgh, and another to the anglicized Cathal Croibhdhearg Ó Conchobhair. Domhnall Mac Giolla Mo-Cholmóg, Mac Murchadha's other Gaelic son-in-law, became the first in a long line of anglicized men. He was one of the few Irishmen in this early period to witness an English grant. The family became tenants-in-chief of the king of England,[53] and Domhnall's grandson, found in Latin documents under the anglicized name John fitz Dermot, was married to Clarice, a daughter of Gilbert fitz Griffin.[54] Such links between Gaelic noblemen are surely suggestive of like-mindedness among the people involved. These three men, linked through marriage, clearly saw the potential in befriending the most powerful English barons in their regions, and acted accordingly. In fact, most of the above-mentioned Irishmen and their children were among the relatively small number of Gaelic people who granted lands to religious houses and orders through the use of charters in the European tradition in the second half of the twelfth, and the first half of the thirteenth centuries. Diarmaid Mac Murchadha (who issued charters before and after the advent of the English invasion), Mac Giolla Mo-Cholmog, Domhnall Mór, Donnchadh Cairbreach and Conchobhar na Siudaine Ó Briain as well as Aodh Ó Conchobhair all used European-style charters and seals to authenticate them.[55]

Ties of marriage were of course inseparable from the power-play between families. The correlation between military and marriage alliances is therefore evident. In 1202, a hosting took place by Cathal Croibhdhearg Ó Conchobhair, with the aid of, among others, William de Burgh and two sons of Domhnall Mór Ó Briain: his brothers-in-law, in other words.[56] Although it has to be borne in mind that these marital ties did not guarantee peace between the family members involved, one could argue that they were likely to be the more enduring of military alliances. Once established, a marriage alliance was meant for life,[57] while the ever-shifting nature of political reality

---

53 See above, note 14.   54 John Thomas Gilbert, *A history of the city of Dublin*, 3 vols (Dublin, 1859), i, p. 231; for Clarice, see Brendan Smith, 'The de Pitchford family in thirteenth-century Ireland', *Studia Hibernica*, 27 (1993), 35.   55 For Mac Giolla Mo-Cholmóg see *Crede Mihi. The most ancient register book of the archbishops of Dublin before the Reformation now for the first time printed from the original manuscript*, ed. John T. Gilbert (Dublin, 1897); Flanagan, *Irish royal charters*. Flanagan dated the first of the royal charters to 1161, the last to 1251x1254.   56 *ALC*, i, p. 225, s.a. 1202. Even though in 1200 William de Burgh and the same two sons of Domhnall Mór Ó Briain (Muircheartach and Conchobhar Ruadh) had supported Cathal Carrach Ó Conchobhair, the Anglicized Cathal Croibhdhearg's main rival for the kingship of Connacht. For possible reasons for the English change of alliance, see Orpen, *Normans*, ii, pp 188–9.   57 Although marriage-alliances were sometimes abandoned in favour of politically more beneficial ones. In 1243, for instance, Tadhg, a grandson of Cathal Croibhdhearg, took his mother away from her Mac Diarmada husband and gave her to Cú Chonnacht Ó Ragallaig in marriage. She

in Ireland meant that 'normal' military alliances were often based on a specific, mutual and short-term goal, and consequently more fleeting of nature. Placing too great an emphasis on military and other potentially shorter-term alliances can suggest consistent, long-term strategies where there were none, and thus they may be accredited with a greater significance than is warranted. However significant some military alliances may appear, without any additional evidence, they cannot be taken as proof for the existence of a Gaelic middle nation, as they were not a prerequisite for the formation of a separate nation. And indeed, neither can 'purely Irish' marriages in which both partners were of Irish stock. In case of the Anglo-Irish, the existence of their middle nation implied neither consistency in local or regional policies, nor close-knit alliances within the group. Indeed, factionalism among the settlers was present from the very start of the invasion.[58] What the settlers had in common, and what made them a nation, was their language, culture, and the fact that their origin on the island lay in the prolonged conquest and settlement of the same. But contrary to the usual military ties, intermarriages between Gaelic and English families were instrumental in the mixing of cultures and the acculturation of many, while marriage alliances between two anglicized Irish partners could perpetuate the acculturation. Although they lacked a language and origin distinct from other Irishmen, by continually inter-marrying anglicized families may have been able to create a common culture, or at least a feeling of belonging to a distinct group.

A further distinction could be made if, in the process of taking on some English ways, these anglicized aristocrats had also lost some of their Irish customs in the process, and thus become 'degenerate'. Was this the case? Cathal Croibhdhearg Ó Conchobhair is an obvious example of an anglicized Irish nobleman in the early period. He maintained close contact with the king of England (or his regent) and attempted to install primogeniture to ensure the succession of his eldest son Aodh. But in spite of numerous concessions towards and adaptations from the English, he was far from uncomfortable in the Gaelic world. A relatively large number of bardic poems patronized by him have survived, a sign that he supported the Gaelic institution under which the poets were maintained by those they eulogized in return for their art.[59] At his death it was said that cattle fell sick, an observation building on the ancient Irish notion that the reign of a just king provided the land and

had previously been abandoned by her Ó Conchobhair husband (Aodh), probably between 1202 and 1207. *AC*, p. 77, s.a. 1243.   **58** See, e.g., Peter Crooks, '"Divide and rule": factionalism as royal policy in the lordship of Ireland, *c.*1171–1265', *Peritia*, 19 (2005), 263–307 and idem, 'Factions, feuds and noble power in late medieval Ireland, *c.* 1356–1496', *IHS*, 35 (2007), 425–54. **59** See Katharine Simms' bardic poetry database at http://bardic.celt.dias.ie/.

animals with good health and fertility. He reportedly refused to use a saddle when riding his horse, preferring the Gaelic Irish method of riding bareback. Although Cathal's case may be an extreme example, the paradox or duality was, so it seems, relatively common. Other anglicized Irishmen too, such as Donnchadh Cairbreach Ó Briain and Eoghan Ó Madadháin, had bardic poems written for them. The surviving texts are laudatory and give no sign of their patrons being in any way uncomfortable in the Gaelic world. On the contrary, they by their very existence emphasize these men's engagements with Gaelic traditions and scholarship. The annals demonstrate that many of the anglicized Irish leaders were inaugurated as traditional Gaelic kings too. What is more, motifs found in both bardic poetry and in some of the more elaborate annal entries suggest links with ancient beliefs, such as poet as a lover of the patron, and the fertility of the lands and its people under the rule of a just king, which can hardly have been agreeable to those adhering to the concurrent official beliefs in England.[60]

It is therefore a misconception to assume that the inhabitants of Ireland chose *either* the Gaelic Irish, *or* the English customs and traditions. In reality, they mixed, and that is exactly how the English could become degenerate: they adopted, willingly or not, certain aspects of the culture of their Gaelic neighbours, while still considering themselves to be thoroughly English. However, while generations of settlers lived in Ireland, English culture in England evolved, and so the settlers' culture became a quaint mix of Gaelic customs and antiquated English traditions. The Gaelic Irish who acculturated, however, lived in the midst of their ancestral culture. They gained English ways, but could nevertheless still be up to date on any new development within Gaelic culture (for it is also a misconception that Gaelic culture, over time, did not evolve). In other words, anglicized people were not necessarily degenerate, and among the Gaelic elite, degeneracy was probably a rare phenomenon indeed. It is important to note that, although they might have aspired towards being included in the broader European world, this does not necessarily mean Irish aristocrats were willing to give up their Gaelic traditions. Nor did they need to, as these were often used in settings removed from the official English world.

A sceptic might point out that anglicized lords, when in a Gaelic setting, may have felt the need to emphasize their 'Gaelicness'. And it is true that some Irish families recently risen to prominence had partially fabricated

---

60 For the poet as lover see, e.g., Meidhbhín Ní Úrdail, 'Two poems attributed to Muireadhach Albanach Ó Dálaigh', *Ériu*, 53 (2003), 19–52, verses 16 and 27 of the second poem ('Roinneam, a chompain, chloinn mBriain'), 42–5. For fertility of the land and its animal and human inhabitants see, e.g., the obit for Cathal Croibhdhearg in *AC* s.a. 1224 in which the sickness of large numbers of animals and people are connected to the king's death.

genealogies construed to lend credence to their newly acquired prominence, and likewise had prose tracts written which were meant to lend antiquity to their relatively new claims.[61] But when one compares the surviving evidence, there is nothing to suggest that the anglicized nobles of Ireland were placing any greater or lesser emphasis on Gaelic traditions than those who show no signs of acculturation.

Finally, it may be of interest to note that with but few exceptions the obituaries of anglicized men are generally as laudatory as those of any comparable non-anglicized Irishman.[62] One example comes from the north of the country in 1283, at the death of the husband of Eleanor de Nangle, kinswoman of the earl of Ulster:

Aodh Buidhe O'Neill, king of Cenel-Eoghain and also royal heir of all Erinn; head of the hospitality and valour of the Gaeidhel, and the most distinguished of the North for bestowing jewels, and cattle, and horses; and the most formidable and victorious man of the Cenel-Eoghain in his own time, was slain [...][63]

There are more examples, but one of the most remarkable ones in this respect is the annal entry recorded at the death of Feidhlim Ó Conchobhair:

Fedlim O Conchobair, the son of Mor Muman and Cathal Crobderg O Conchobair, King of Connacht, one who safeguarded and supported his own Province and his friends on every side, who banished and plundered his foes in whatsoever place they were, a man full of honour and valour, of respect and importance in Ireland and in England, died after a victory of repentance and was buried in the monastery of the preaching-friars at Roscommon, which he had presented to God and the order.'[64]

Although this obituary is found in the Annals of Connacht, written by the traditional historians of the Ui Chonchobhair, it is remarkable that Feidhlim's connections with England are not only mentioned, but indeed applauded.

---

61 Kenneth Nicholls has pointed to the fact that much of the perceived continuity in Gaelic traditions was in fact 'the conscious creation of the scholars who provided the intellectual justi-fication for the new Gaelic lords [...]': Kenneth W. Nicholls, 'Anglo-French Ireland and after', *Peritia*, 1 (1982), 370–403, at 392. 62 Exceptions are the various obits of Diarmaid Mac Murchadha, but much of this includes judgments of later scribes included into it: Donnchadh Ó Corráin, 'Diarmait MacMurrough (1110–71) and the coming of the Anglo-French' in Ciaran Brady (ed.), *Worsted in the game: losers in Irish history* (Dublin, 1989), pp 21–34, at pp 21–2. *Expug. Hib.* p. 304, n. 104. 63 *ALC*, i, pp 490–1, s.a. 1283. 64 *AC*, pp 144–5, s.a. 1265.

CONCLUSION

Having summarily surveyed some of the evidence and issues involved, it may be time to move towards a tentative answer to the question 'Was there a Gaelic middle nation?'. It is clear that anglicization in post-invasion Ireland was widespread, although the measure of acculturation heavily varied from period to period, region to region, and person to person. Some men seem thoroughly anglicized (in that there is evidence for their adaptations in several aspects of their lives) while others consciously or inadvertently picked up a couple of 'English habits' through intimate contact with settlers. Some anglicized Irishmen maintained close communication with other anglicized countrymen. In the late twelfth and early thirteenth centuries, a number of Irish noblemen who made varying adaptations towards the English inter-married, not only with the English, but with each other. They also wrote charters in the European tradition, donating lands to European religious orders, while this was a fairly unusual practice which did not persist in Ireland. If one were to call this group of likeminded Gaelic noblemen (and noble women) a middle nation, its existence was very brief and had its heyday much earlier than the 'English' middle nation. The latter was first mentioned in 1297, whereas the former seems to have been linked most to the late twelfth and early thirteenth centuries and seems to have disintegrated before the Gaelic resurgence of the second half of the thirteenth century. Certainly, there was much anglicization after this period. But the similarities and links between the various 'anglicized' Gaelic lords ceased to be as striking and intense. The short-lived nature of this phenomenon may alone be reason enough not to call this group a middle nation.

But what is more, the fact that some of the more anglicized people sought close and frequent contact with Anglo-Irish lords and ladies did not preclude them from engaging in Gaelic traditions and customs, and Irish society did not exclude them. In other words, these Irish noblemen were able to adjust to English or Anglo-Irish customs when required, while remaining firmly rooted and at home in Gaelic culture. This duality seems to have caused no identifiable crisis of identity: more than likely, they merely applied the appropriate customs to the situation at hand. There appears to be no evidence to suggest that they did not constitute an integral part of Gaelic society. The settlers and the king of England may have appreciated angli-cization, but do not appear to have viewed anglicized Irishmen as a group separate from other Irishmen. They did, at least in the early years of the invasion, distinguish between Irish enemies and loyal Irish, but these terms

65 In this context it is also informative to note that, as soon as an Irishman was granted access to common law, he was no longer regarded an *hibernicus* to the law, but was labelled *anglicus*.

could alternate when alliances shifted. In short, there seems to be no evidence that they were viewed as belonging to a separate nation.[65] Neither is there any remaining evidence suggestive of anglicized Irishmen regarding themselves as a distinguishable group. Consequently, it would be difficult to argue that the acculturated noble Irish constituted a distinct, separate Gaelic 'middle nation'.

SOME MARRIAGE CONNECTIONS[1]

European-style charters survive from Irishmen in grey boxes. [2]

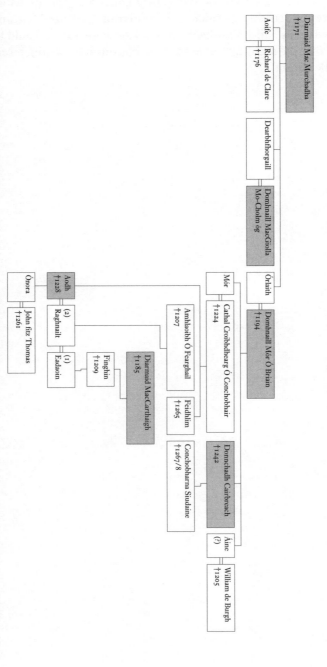

1 References to the marriages: Aoife and Richard: *Expug. Hib.*, 67 and *Song of Dermot*, 1524–37; Dearbhforgaill and Domhnall: *Chartularies of St Mary's Abbey, Dublin: with the register of its house at Dunbrody, and Annals of Ireland*, ed. John Thomas Gilbert, 2 vols (Dublin, 1884), vol. i, nos 4–6; Órlaith and Domhnall: *Song of Dermot*, 2041–6; Áine and William: NLI GO MS 155: Roger O'Ferrall, *Linea Antiqua. Or a genealogical, chronological and historical account of the Gaethelian, Milesian Scottish or Irish people or nation from the beginning of time, to this year of our Lord 1709. In 5 parts or sections*, p. 37 and *Tribes of Hy–Many*, 45; Mór and Cathal Croibhdhearg: 1218 AD: *ALC*, i, p. 259; *AU*, ii, p. 265; *AI*, p. 343; 1217 AD: *AFM* iii, p. 191 and *MCB*, p. 93; Raghnailt and Aodh: *AC*, p. 77, s.a. 1243; Onora and John: Lodge, *Peerage*, ii (1754), 102–5.
2 Flanagan, *Irish royal charters*. NB: Kenneth Nicholls has pointed to a seventeenth-century reference to a charter of the *baile* of Leamore to Cathal Ó Maoil Thuile, made by Cathal Croibhdhearg Ó Conchobhair – Kenneth W. Nicholls, 'Gaelic society and economy in the high Middle Ages' in Art Cosgrove (ed.), *A new history of Ireland, ii: Medieval Ireland* (Oxford, 1993), p. 432. This charter, however, is unlikely to have been in the European tradition and probably more closely resembled Irish charters found in, e.g., The Book of Kells, or later grants like those collected in James Hardiman, 'Ancient Irish deeds & writings chiefly relating to landed property from the twelfth to the seventeenth centuries', *Trans. R.I.A.*, 15 [antiquities] (1825–8), pp 3–96.

Foreign apologues in bardic poetry

KATHARINE SIMMS

Although we know from the accounts of observers that Celtic societies since before the Christian era maintained a class of ceremonial poets or bards, who praised the exploits of living chieftains and commemorated their deaths, in Ireland almost none of this secular praise poetry, as distinct from purely historical or genealogical material, was written down before the thirteenth century.[1] Consequently the expression 'bardic poetry' has become a kind of academic shorthand to refer to the 2,000 or so extant texts of poems composed in syllabic metres in the Classical Irish dialect by a hereditary class of literate, highly trained lay poets in Ireland and Scotland between about 1200 and 1690 AD.[2] Although their work was in many ways traditional, with the majority of the poems designed to be recited at the banquets of either Gaelic chieftains or Anglo-Irish barons, they were produced against the background of two major waves of foreign influence on Ireland, the Anglo-Norman colonization of the late twelfth and thirteenth centuries, and the Tudor-Stuart reconquest and plantations during the sixteenth and seventeenth centuries. Contrary to the views of some earlier romantics, the long and rigorous training of the medieval *filidhe* or bardic poets did involve the arts of reading and writing, and an examination of their apologues can give us some idea of the reading material at their disposal.

Apologues in the context of this chapter are summaries or outlines of pre-existing moral or historical tales that the most highly-educated poets were accustomed to insert now and then into their long eulogies, either to draw a flattering comparison between the patron they were addressing and some hero of the past like Cúchulainn or Alexander the Great, or perhaps more often tactfully to convey a message of contemporary relevance in the form of a parable. Their presence in a bardic poem is a sign of the poet's advanced learning and wide reading, so the majority of extant bardic poems do not contain apologues. In my electronic database listing 1,985 poems,[3] only 657 are noted as containing apologues of any kind.

---

1 On the absence of written texts of praise poems from the pre-Norman period, see Liam Breatnach, 'Satire, praise and the early Irish poet' in *Ériu*, 56 (2006), 63–84 at 81–2. 2 On the poets' training, see Damian McManus, 'The bardic poet as teacher, student and critic: a context for the grammatical tracts' in Cathal Ó hÁinle and Donald Meek (eds), *Unity in diversity* (Dublin, 2004), pp 97–124. On the Scottish praise poets, see Wilson McLeod, *Divided Gaels: Gaelic cultural identities in Scotland and Ireland, c.1200–c.1650* (Oxford, 2004). 3 This database is now

The bardic schools were conducted entirely through the Irish language, and there are few signs of poets with any real knowledge of Latin, while the aristocratic Gaelic warriors who formed their audience, in the thirteenth and fourteenth centuries at least, were probably mostly illiterate, so it is hardly surprising that the bulk of the tales the poets refer to in their apologues are drawn from the saga cycles, and deal with the mythical King Conchobar mac Nessa of Ulster and his warriors of the Red Branch (101 examples, with some poems containing more than one anecdote), Finn mac Cumaill and his Fianna warbands (23 examples), or general 'historical' themes such as the high-kingship of Tara, the Battle of Clontarf, and the successive invasions by which Ireland was supposed to have been populated since Noah's Flood (345 examples).

Nevertheless there are some 134 poems that contain secular apologues of foreign origins in addition to purely religious anecdotes such as stories from the Bible or the apocrypha (154 examples) or tales of non-Irish saints, such as the martyrdom of Catherine of Alexandria, the Life of St Francis or a range of miracles associated with the Virgin Mary (50 examples).

In sorting through and classifying these apologues, I have been much indebted to the work of Liam Ó Caithnia,[4] who lists and identifies the source of most of the apologues available in printed editions of bardic poetry at the time he published his work in 1984. In my own electronic catalogue of the bardic corpus, I applied Ó Caithnia's categories to the additional apologues I came across in unpublished or subsequently edited poems, so that if one excludes the purely religious tales from the Bible, the apocryphal scriptures and saints' lives, only two foreign categories remain – tales originating in classical Greece or Rome, even where these have been mediated through English and French re-tellings or translations (44 examples), and a wider category of 'miscellaneous tales of continental origin' (90 examples). This last heading one might think could have been profitably subdivided into moral anecdotes drawn from preachers' books of *exempla* or examples for teaching purposes used in sermons to the laity,[5] or tales about King Arthur and his Knights of the Round Table, or fabulous anecdotes about animals, either related to Aesop's Fables or to the medieval bestiaries – instructions on how to catch a unicorn, for example.[6] However, as will be seen in what

available at http://bardic.celt.dias.ie where the total of poems listed is 1,968. I have been working from a slightly longer version on my hard disk at home, but the total of apologues involved is not affected.   4 Liam P. Ó Caithnia, *Apalóga na bhFilí, 1200–1650* (Dublin, 1984).   5 See D.L. D'Avray, *The preaching of the friars: sermons diffused from Paris before 1300* (Oxford, 1985), pp 66–71; G.R. Owst, *Literature and pulpit in medieval England* (2nd revised ed., Oxford, 1966), pp 149–209.   6 Rather than the better known method which involved inducing this notoriously fierce animal to lay its head in the lap of a pure virgin and go to sleep, an unpublished poem to Toirdhealbhach Luineach Ó Néill (d. 1595), *Coróin Éireann ainm Uí Néill*, related that it was the

follows, so many of these varied topics seem to be traceable ultimately to the preachers' *libri exemplorum* that Ó Caithnia was probably wise not to make hard and fast distinctions.

I have written elsewhere about my conviction that the tastes and aspirations of the paying patron were more important in deciding the contents of a bardic poem than the personal preferences of the poet,[7] and this seems clearly borne out by the distribution of apologues reflecting the literature of classical Greece and Rome. The research of Liam Ó Caithnia has shown that the bardic poets, perhaps unsurprisingly, given their usual lack of Latin learning, took their stories about Aeneas, the siege of Troy, the wanderings of Ulysses and the wars between Julius Caesar and Pompey very largely from the pre-existing Irish prose translations, or rather adaptations, based on Virgil, Darius Phrygius, Lucan, Statius and so forth, so that where the version of the plot as told in a bardic poem differs from the classic original, it is often because it is following an innovation found only in the Irish prose version.[8] The interesting point about this is that most of these prose translations belong to the Middle Irish period,[9] made by the last generation of native Irish scholars in the much-secularized monastic schools of the eleventh and twelfth centuries who had been educated in both Latin and Irish, and the first dateable use of this material by a praise-poet comes in an address to Eochaid Mac Duinnshléibe, king of the Ulaid, in about 1165, in a passage that compares the mythical King Conchobar mac Nessa and his Red Branch warriors of Ulster with the heroes of Troy.[10] In Welsh bardic poetry, the classical heroes Alexander and Hercules first appear just a little earlier, about the eleventh century.[11]

Yet in spite of the ready availability of these translated classical tales from the mid-twelfth century onwards, only one, or possibly two, of the forty-three

lion's practice to stand beside a tree and then provoke the unicorn to charge and get its horn embedded in the trunk. **7** Katharine Simms, 'Bardic poetry as a historical source' in Tom Dunne (ed.), *The writer as witness*, Historical Studies XVI (Cork, 1987), pp 58–75 at pp 60–6, 71. **8** Ó Caithnia, *Apalóga*, pp 125 (C4a), 126 (C4d, C4g), 133 (C15a, C15b, C15c, C 15e). **9** Gerard Murphy, *The Ossianic lore and romantic tales of medieval Ireland* (Dublin, 1955), p. 17, lists *Togail Troí* (The destruction of Troy), *Togail Tebe* (The destruction of Thebes), *Merugud Ulix* (The wanderings of Ulysses), *Imthechta Aeniasa* (The wanderings of Aeneas), and *In Cath Cातharda* (The civil war of the Romans) all as works of the twelfth century. Robert T. Meyer (ed.), *Merugud Uilix maic Leirtis* (Dublin, 1958), p. xiii suggested a linguistic date in the early thirteenth century for his text. See also, Brent Miles, *Heroic saga and classical epic in medieval Ireland*, Studies in Celtic History, XXX (Woodbridge, 2011). **10** F.J. Byrne, 'Clann Ollamain Uaisle Emna', *Studia Hibernica*, 4 (1964), 54–94 at 61–2, 74, 76, 80. **11** Marged Haycock, 'Some talk of Alexander and some of Hercules – three early medieval poems from the Book of Taliesin', *CMCS*, 13 (1987), 7–38 at 17. Haycock also notes that prose translations of classical tales do not appear in Welsh before about the sixteenth century, giving a chronological gap between the first demonstration of knowledge and its popularization rather similar to the Irish evidence.

poems noted as containing classical apologues date from before 1500. The one certain example is addressed by the fourteenth-century Munster poet Gofraidh Fionn Ó Dálaigh to the young Gerald the Rhymer Fitzgerald, and disguises an originally classical tale as an Irish legend.[12] Otherwise not one can be securely dated before the mid-sixteenth century, and only thirteen are earlier than 1600.[13] I also surveyed poems containing brief allusions to classical literature, instances where a chieftain is referred to as being as brave as Hector or as famous as Alexander the Great, without any actual story about these heroes being given. Of the sixty-nine bardic poems containing such classical allusions, only five date before 1500. Confirmation that there is nothing random about the occurrence of these few medieval allusions comes in the fact that the two earliest ones occur in odes by two different poets addressed to the same man, King Aodh son of Eoghan Ó Conchobhair, who died in 1309, and who displayed other symptoms of being open to foreign influences. He imported English carpenters to build what appears to have been a moated grange of the English type as his chief residence at Cloonfree in Roscommon, and he is described as bearing a coat of arms on his shield.[14] The classical references occur in the two poems in praise of his moated grange. One compares its splendour to Troy in the time of Laomedon,[15] the other states that unlike Troy, Cloonfree will never be betrayed by a woman.[16] The other three references belong to the fifteenth century. The death of King Toirdhealbhach son of Aodh Ó Conchobhair in 1406 was said to be as devastating as the fall of Troy in a single day,[17] a poem celebrating the marriage of Éamonn Ó Broin to Gormlaith Caomhánach compared the bridegroom to Hercules,[18] and the bardic friar Philip Bocht Ó hUiginn pointed out that Aristotle the founder of all scholarship is burning in Hell, and Alexander the conqueror of the world ended in a seven-foot grave.[19] Both these kind of brief references and the actual retellings of

---

12 'A Ghearóid déana mo dháil' in L. Mac Cionaith (ed.), *Dioghluim Dána* (Dublin, 1938 and reprints), poem no. 67 (translated edition in *Irish Monthly*, 47, 509–14). The second possible example is the undated poem 'Féach orm a inghean Eoghain', ed. and transl. in Charlotte Brooke, *Reliques of Irish poetry* (reprint Gainesville 1970), pp 304–6. Since this is addressed to a woman patron it is somewhat more likely to belong to the Early Modern period.   13 See Appendix 1.   14 See Freya Verstraten, 'Images of Gaelic lordship in Ireland *c.*1200–*c.*1400' in Linda Doran and James Lyttleton (eds), *Lordship in medieval Ireland: image and reality* (Dublin, 2007), pp 47–74 at 61–3; Katharine Simms, 'Native sources for Gaelic settlement: the house poems' in Patrick J. Duffy, David Edwards and Elizabeth FitzPatrick (eds), *Gaelic Ireland, c.1250–c.1650: land, lordship and settlement* (Dublin, 2001), pp 246–67, at pp 251–2.   15 E.C. Quiggin, 'O'Conor's house at Cloonfree' in idem (ed.), *Essays presented to William Ridgeway* (Cambridge, 1913), pp 333–52, at pp 340–41.   16 Mac Cionaith, *Dioghluim Dána*, no 119, verse 13.   17 Mac Cionaith, *Dioghluim Dána*, no. 86, verse 13.   18 'Aenta deisi a din Laighin', unpublished poem in Dublin, Royal Irish Academy MS RIA 23/Q/10, fo. 11.   19 Lambert McKenna (ed.), *Philip Bocht Ó hUiginn* (Dublin, 1931), no 16, verse 16–17.

classical tales in bardic verse become progressively more common in the late sixteenth and seventeenth centuries, the existing Middle Irish prose sources being reinforced from the fifteenth century onwards by further Early Modern Irish translations with a classical theme, such as the History of Hercules, based on 'Receuil des Histoires de Troyes' written by Raoul Lefevre in 1464 and translated into English by William Caxton in 1468–71. The Irish version, according to its editor Gordon Quin, seems based on Caxton's printed work.[20]

The late date at which classical apologues appear in Irish poems, like the late date of Welsh prose versions of classical tales,[21] reflects the slow spread of the Renaissance revival of interest in classical Greece and Rome to Northern Europe, not only into the world of the Anglo-Irish barons, but into that of the Gaelic chieftains in the west of Ireland. Of the forty-two sixteenth- and seventeenth-century poems containing classical apologues, only eight are addressed to Anglo-Irish patrons: four to the Burkes of Mayo and Galway, and one each to members of the Barry, Butler, Dillon and Hussey families, while eleven are addressed to the Uí Dhomhnaill, three to Ó Conchobhair Sligeach, two each to the Mág Uidhir, Ó Raghallaigh and Ó Briain dynasties and to the Mac Dubhghaill galloglasses of Connacht with the remainder scattered among a miscellany of Gaelic Irish patrons from Ulster, Connacht and Munster. Since much of the material then used by the poets to supply them with classical references had been available in the Irish language for centuries, it would appear that the change that occurred was a change in taste and level of information among the patrons themselves. Indeed once Trinity College had been founded, and the English government developed a policy of sending all underage heirs of deceased Irish chieftains to study there, the patron might be embarrassingly better-informed than his native bard, and this is something I have discussed elsewhere.[22]

As most of the bardic poets were not themselves proficient in Latin, the channels by which foreign influences reached them were first and foremost the native Irish clergy literate in both Latin and Irish – not only the earlier pre-reform monastic scholars, but as we have seen, later medieval Franciscan friars like Philip Bocht Ó hUiginn and a number of the Ó Cléirigh family of Tír Conaill who produced both clerics and poet-historians.[23] Many Irish clerical families accustomed to filling high church office sent members abroad to study Canon law at Oxford or further afield.[24] Another less obvious

20 E.G. Quin (ed.), *Stair Ercuil ocus a bás: the life and death of Hercules* (Irish Texts Society, Dublin, 1939), pp xiv–xxiv. 21 Above, note 11. 22 Katharine Simms, 'Literacy and the Irish bards' in Huw Pryce (ed.), *Literacy in medieval Celtic societies* (Cambridge, 1998), pp 238–58 at p. 252. 23 Paul Walsh, *The Ó Cléirigh family of Tír Conaill: an essay* (Dublin, 1938). 24 See Canice Mooney, *The church in Gaelic Ireland: fourteenth to fifteenth centuries* ('A history of Irish

channel for foreign contacts were the hereditary medical families, who from the fourteenth century onwards occasionally sent members abroad to universities in England or on the continent.[25] Even where the medical students stayed at home and studied in native Irish medical schools, they learned to read and write Latin in order to consult medical textbooks, though Edmund Campion tells us they learnt it like a vulgar language, ignoring syntax and case-endings.[26] Not only the history of Hercules, but the tales of Guy of Warwick and Bevis of Hampton together with a number of late fifteenth-century prose translations of continental saints' lives and pious homilies were transcribed if not actually translated in the 1460s and 1470s by William Mac an Leagha, a prolific scribe from a Munster medical family, who provided access to English and continental works in Irish versions for Gaelic and Anglo-Irish patrons alike.[27] A manuscript partially written in the house of another member of a hereditary medical family, Niall Ó Siadhail, contains an early copy of the Irish version of the 'Travels of Sir John Maundeville', translated by Finghin Ó Mathghamhna in 1475, which became the source for an apologue by Tadhg Dall Ó hUiginn among others.[28]

The distribution pattern for apologues of miscellaneous continental origin, largely based on the clerical preachers' books of *exempla*, is rather different from that of the classical apologues. Grace Neville has drawn attention to the French historians' agreed definition of an *exemplum* as 'A short story presented as true and intended to be inserted into a speech (usually a sermon) in order to win over an audience through a salutary lesson'.[29] The bardic poets themselves often refer to some incident, real or imagined as 'a sermon', meaning an example that should act as a warning to others.[30] There were a number of Latin anthologies of epitomes of such moral tales in circulation among the clergy of Europe from the thirteenth century onwards, some better known than others, and it was not always easy for Liam Ó

Catholicism' 2, fasc. v, gen. ed. Patrick J. Corish, Dublin, 1969), pp 23, 25–6; H.A. Jefferies, *Priests and prelates of Armagh in the age of the reformations, 1518–1558* (Dublin, 1997), p. 76; idem, 'The diocese of Dromore on the eve of the Tudor reformation' in Lindsey Proudfoot (ed.), *Down: history and society* (Dublin, 1997), pp 123–40, at p. 128.   25 Francis Shaw, 'Irish medical men and philosophers' in Brian Ó Cuív (ed.), *Seven centuries of Irish learning, 1000–1700* (Dublin, 1961), pp 87–101.   26 A.F. Vossen (ed.), *Edmund Campion, two bokes of the histories of Ireland* (Assen, 1963), pp 25–6.   27 Paul Walsh, 'An Irish medical family – Mac an Leagha' in *Irish men of learning*, pp 206–18 at p. 208n.; Robin Flower, *Catalogue of the Irish manuscripts in the British Museum*, ii (London, 1926), p. 470; idem, *Ireland and medieval Europe* (London, [1929]).   28 Flower, *Catalogue* ii, pp 526, 540–41; Ó Caithnia, *Apalóga*, pp 194 (V18), 196 (V22).   29 Definition by Claude Brémond cited here in English translation from Grace Neville, 'Short shrouds and sharp shrews: echoes of Jacques de Vitry in the *Dánta Grádha*' in C.E. Meek and Katharine Simms (eds), *'The fragility of her sex?: medieval Irishwomen in their European context* (Dublin, 1996), pp 87–100 at 87.   30 E.G. Quin (ed.), *Dictionary of the Irish language* (Dublin, 1998), p. 538, col. 192 'sermóin (b)'.

Caithnia to identify a source for a number of the apologues of 'miscellaneous continental origin' that he suspected of being derived from such an anthology of *exempla*.[31] There are altogether ninety poems containing apologues of miscellaneous continental origin listed in my database, and if they are separated into poems on purely religious subjects – that is poems in praise of God and the saints as against moral or didactic verses, or poems addressed to secular patrons or compositions on themes of general interest such as love and death – of the fourteen religious poems with such apologues only one can be definitely dated to a period after 1500, and in the case of that one, the apologue is from Aesop's fables, concerning the crow who tried to hide his ugly appearance by dressing up in borrowed feathers.[32] A number of such foreign apologues occurring in religious poems from the medieval period can be definitely identified as exempla. The fourteenth-century Gofraidh Fionn Ó Dálaigh's tale of the child born in prison, who could not imagine what grass, trees and the sky were like, came from the *Gesta Romanorum* collection.[33] The fifteenth-century Tadhg Óg Ó hUiginn has a tale of a cruel mother who murdered her illegitimate infant. Her hand became indelibly stained with blood, only washed away by her own tears when she confessed and repented. Versions of this story come in the *Gesta Romanorum* and the work of Vincent of Beauvais, and Ó hUiginn refers to using a written source for his tale.[34] Pilip Bocht Ó hUiginn's tale of the vine grower whose vines yielded only a tenth of their expected harvest, and who offered up the whole tenth to God as a tithe, and then was blessed in subsequent years with superabundant crops seems clearly drawn from another continental anthology, perhaps the *Legenda Aurea*.[35]

Bardic poems on religious topics were normally composed by the same lay professional poets who praised the Gaelic chieftains, and again the distribution pattern seems to bear out the hypothesis that the patron's wishes had a strong influence on the contents of the poems. Poems dedicated to God and the saints that were composed after the Council of Trent do not seem to draw on the books of exempla for little moral tales of secular life to adorn their

31 See Ó Caithnia, *Apalóga*, pp 191 (V 11), 196 (V 21), 199 (V 24), 200 (V 25). 32 See Appendix 2. 33 Ó Caithnia, *Apalóga*, p. 195 (V 20). The library of the Franciscan house in Youghal, founded by Gofraidh's patron, the first earl of Desmond, contained a copy of the *Gesta Romanorum* when its catalogue was compiled, 1493–1523. See C.N. Ó Clabaigh, *The Franciscans in Ireland, 1400–1534* (Dublin, 2002), Appendix I, no. 146. The library also held copies of the *Legenda Aurea*, the *Speculum Maius* of Vincent of Beauvais, the *Discipulus* of Johann Herolt, and many other sermon collections and preacher's books: ibid. nos., 13, 31, 104 etc. 34 Ó Caithnia, *Apalóga*, p. 196 (V 21). An attribution to the late sixteenth-century Aonghus Fionn Ó Dálaigh occurs in eighteenth-century manuscripts of the Ó Neachtain circle. The poem is anonymous in the earliest source, Maynooth MS C 97 written by Corc Ó Cadhla 1583–4, and is attributed to Tadhg Óg Ó hUiginn in the Book of O'Conor Don (1631) 35 Ó Caithnia, *Apalóga*, p. 191 (V 11).

narrative, though they still use this source for more obviously religious anecdotes. The famous late sixteenth- and early seventeenth-century poet Aonghus *na Diadhachta* Ó Dálaigh ('Aonghus of the Religious Compositions') regularly drew on medieval exempla as a source for tales of miracles performed by the power of the Virgin Mary, as found in the works of the thirteenth century Jacques de Vitry,[36] the *Legenda Aurea* of Jacopo da Voragine,[37] and the fifteenth-century Johannes Herolt.[38] By the time Aonghus flourished, it is possible he could have accessed such material through printed books. An English translation of the *Legenda Aurea* was first published by Thomas Caxton in 1483. A Latin sermon collection by Johann Herolt was printed in 1509,[39] and an English translation of the sermons of St Bernardino of Siena in 1548.[40] Although poems on purely religious subjects no longer draw on these sources for random secular anecdotes from the later sixteenth century onwards, we find a contrasting pattern when we turn to secular poems containing apologues of miscellaneous continental origin. There are seventy-six examples in all, of which only eight date from before 1500. These eight deal predominantly with the habits of exotic animals, particularly the lion, as a type of the warlike chief who is the patron addressed,[41] but there is also a reference to the mill of plenty, the enchanted mill which grinds out unlimited supplies of whatever the owner desires, which turns up again in modern folktales,[42] and there are two Arthurian tales in the late fifteenth-century elegy for an Anglo-Irish baron, James Purcell, which may have been inspired by the mid-fifteenth-century Irish translation of the Pursuit of the Holy Grail.[43] It would appear then that in the medieval period religious poems draw on the books of *exempla* or other continental works for exotic secular anecdotes more frequently than the poems to lay patrons do, and in the Early Modern period the trend is reversed – religious poems rely less on this type of apologue, secular poems to the chieftains use them quite frequently. Tadhg Dall's tale about the prize for the greatest fool in the world being awarded to a man who agreed to be king for a year and then spend the rest of his life on a desert island can be traced to the anony-

36 Ó Caithnia, *Apalóga*, p. 160 (M 8); L. McKenna (ed.), *Dánta do chum Aonghus Fionn Ó Dálaigh* (Dublin, 1919), no. 48, verses 2–20.   37 Ó Caithnia, *Apalóga*, p. 161 (M 10); McKenna, *Aonghus Fionn*, no. 49, vv. 3–22.   38 Ó Caithnia, *Apalóga*, pp 160–1 (M 9); McKenna, *Aonghus Fionn*, no. 50, vv. 5–39.   39 J. Herolt, *Discipulus de eruditione christifidelium compendiosus...* (Martin Flach 1509). Ó Clabaigh (above note 33) suggests the copy in the Franciscan library in Youghal may have been printed.   40 *Sermons of Barnardine Ochine of Sena* transl. Lady Anne Bacon (R. Carr, London, 1548).   41 'A Dhomhnaill deglamh fa síth' – E.C. Quiggin, *Prolegomena to a study of the later Irish bards* (London [1913]), pp 42–4; 'Dá roinn chomhthroma ar chrích Néill' – McKenna, *Aithdioghluim Dána*, no. 16; 'Ga sealbh as fhearr ar Eas Ruaidh' – unpubl., Book of O'Conor Don, fo. 241b.   42 'Tosach féile fairsinge', Mac Cionaith, *Dioghluim Dána*, no. 120.   43 'Mairg dar chumthach in chumha' – A. O'Sullivan (ed.), *Poems on marcher lords* (London, 1987), pp 22–43.

mous *Gesta Romanorum* collection, as can Eochaidh Ó hEoghusa's tale of the knight who cured the ugly princess of her enchantment by washing her in a stream.[44] Grace Neville has shown that a seventeenth-century *dán grádha* or courtly love poem with a merry tale of the Roman earl who pretended to be dead to find out if his wife truly loved him and overheard her economizing on the amount of cloth she would expend on his shroud can be traced to the thirteenth-century *Sermones vulgares* of Jacques de Vitry.[45] Mícheál MacCraith has linked Eochaidh Ó hEoghusa's tale of the stupefying rain, which turned all the world mad except for thirty philosophers who sheltered in a cave to Bernadino da Busta's fifteenth-century *Rosarium sermonum* and ultimately back to a tenth-century Chinese translation of the Buddhist scriptures, though a more likely source for Ó hEoghusa himself may have been the published correspondence of Sir Thomas More.[46]

This has been a hasty and superficial survey, but bringing it together has altered my own presuppositions about the spread of foreign themes into the corpus of bardic poetry. I had assumed, since so many of the tales of continental origin can be traced back to preacher's anthologies of *exempla* and few of the poets seem to have known Latin, that they may have first encountered these tales while attending mass and listening to sermons by Irish priests who were in a position to read these Latin collections and pass on their knowledge by word of mouth. However the late date and secular patrons to which most of the little tales were directed suggests that Irish poets may have accessed this material chiefly by themselves, reading printed English translations by Caxton and others of the medieval Latin anthologies, while their knowledge of classical and Arthurian material went step by step with the translation of various relevant texts into Irish, to be circulated in manuscript form, both in the eleventh and twelfth centuries before the Anglo-Norman Invasion, and again in the fifteenth and sixteenth centuries in response to the growth of lay literacy among the Irish and Anglo-Irish nobility.

A second conclusion is that the use of this material is not dependent on its availability to the poet at any one period, but on the tastes and expectations of the patron. Fearghal Óg Mac an Bhaird, eleven of whose poems contain secular apologues of foreign origin, a number of them based on *exempla*, did not include any of these in the purely religious poems he wrote for the Franciscans at Louvain, while the fourteenth-century Aonghus

---

44 Ó Caithnia, *Apalóga*, pp 202 (V32), 204 (V36); Eleanor Knott (ed.), *The bardic poems of Tadhg Dall Ó hUiginn* (2 vols, London, 1922), no. 22a. The *Gesta Romanorum* could conceivably have been accessed by the poets through English rather than Latin, as there were medieval English translations circulating in manuscript, S.J.H. Herrtage (ed.), *The early English versions of the Gesta Romanorum* (London, 1879). 45 Neville, 'Short shrouds and sharp shrews' (as above, note 29). 46 Mícheál Mac Craith, 'Cioth na Baoise', *Béaloideas*, 51 (1983), 31–54.

Ruadh Ó Dálaigh, demonstrably aware of the details of the siege of Troy,[47] did not draw on this material for an apologue in a poem to any of his patrons. The poets' choice of subject-matter from one century to the next darkly mirrors, not their own level of education and awareness of foreign influence, but the progress of their patrons' cultural development.

APPENDIX 1

First lines of the earliest poems noted as containing classical apologues, with indications of author, patron, date and subject-matter.

1. *Féach orm a inghean Eoghain*, by M. Ó Gearáin, to 'daughter of Eoghan', undated. **Narcissus in love with own reflection.**

2. *A Ghearóid déana mo dháil*, by Gofraidh Fionn Ó Dálaigh to Maurice FitzGerald, 1st earl of Desmond (d. 1356) and his son Gerald, future 3rd earl. **Old man 'Fiontan' recovers youth by kissing fairy boy.**

3. *Fuigheall formaid fuil Dálaigh*, by Cú Uladh Mac an Bhaird, to Gráinne (d. 1551?), daughter of Maghnus Ó Domhnaill. **Cath Cathardha: Julia wife of Pompey.**

4. *Créad a-nois fhuirgheas Éamonn?* by Tadhg Dall Ó hUiginn (d. 1591) to Éamonn a Búrc. (a) **Cath Cathardha: War between Pompey and Caesar.** (b) **Siege of Troy.**

5. *Fada cóir Fódhla ar Albain*, by Tadhg Dall Ó hUiginn to Somhairle Buidhe Mac Domhnaill. **Caesar's vision of Rome calling him.**

6. *Iad fein chinneas ar Chlainn Néill*, by Tadhg Dall Ó hUiginn to Eoghan Óg MacSuibhne (chief of Trí Tuatha *c.*1570–96). **Siege of Troy.**

7. *Mór iongabhail anma ríogh*, by Tadhg Dall Ó hUiginn to Risdéard mac Oilibhéaruis a Búrc. **Free adaptation of Icarus story.**

8. *Parrthas Fódhla Fir Manach*, by Tadhg Dall Ó hUiginn to Brian Mág Uidhir. **Birth of Hercules.**

9. *Ní deireadh d'anbhuain Éireann/ Críoch Gaoidheal*, by anon. to Walter a Búrc (d. 1590?). **Alexander conquers Greece and the world.**

10. *Seanóir cuilg cairt an Bhúrcaigh*, by anon. to Riocard a Búrc, 2nd earl of Clanrickard (d. 1582). **Hercules conquers isle of purple sheep.**

11. *Ina mbláth leagthar cine Chaoimh*, by Ó Dálaigh Fionn for Art Ó Caoimh (d. 1583). **Hector meets Valour in cave, joins compact.**

47 See above, note 15.

12. *Leis féin moltar Mág Uidhir*, by Maoilín Ó'n Cháinte to Cúchonnacht Mág Uidhir (d. 1589). **Alexander forbade panegyrics on himself.**

13. *Cliath mhínighthe ar mhaicne ríogh*, by anon. to Pilip Ó Raghallaigh (d. 1596). **Achilles' youthful training.**

14. *Fill th'aghaidh uainn a Éire*, by Fearghal Óg Mac an Bhaird for Conn mac an Chalbhaigh Ó Domhnaill (d. 1583). **Four sages on grave of Alexander.**

APPENDIX 2

First lines of religious poems containing apologues of miscellaneous continental origin.

1. *Abb fíoraonda cian ó shoin* – anon., undated and unpublished. Earliest manuscript source Maynooth Library C88, scribe Eoghan O Caoimh, 1704. **Good abbot releases pagan judge's soul.**

2. *Duine do chuaidh do chur síol* – anon., undated, unpublished. Earliest manuscript 16th–17th century (Trinity College Library MS 1340, formerly H.3.19). **Sheep trespass, Vizier imprisons shepherd.**

3. *Lá saoire corp an Choimdeadh* – anon., undated, ed. McKenna, *Aithdioghluim Dána*, no. 94. Earliest manuscript 16th–17th century (Trinity College Library MS 1340, formerly H.3.19). **Jew who stole consecrated Host drowned in its blood.**

4. *Naomtha an obair iomrádh Dé* – anon., undated, ed. McKenna, *Aithdioghluim Dána*, no. 75. Earliest manuscript AD 1631 (Book of O'Conor Don). **Two monks forget the passing of time while conversing of God.**

5. *Peacach ar siol 'n-ár sluaghaibh* – attrib. Máol Muire Ó Leannáin, ed. McKenna, *Aithdioghluim Dána*, no. 80 undated, earliest manuscript 14th century (Book of Uí Mhaine). **The four chaste conceptions: turtle-dove, salmon, etc.**

6. *Maith ra coindmeach coinneamh Dé* – attrib. Gofraidh Ó Cléirigh, undated, unpublished, earliest manuscript 14th century (Book of Uí Mhaine). **The earth as a body: trees its hair, soil its flesh, etc.**

7. *Mairg mheallas muirn an tsaoghail* – attrib. Gofraidh Fionn Ó Dálaigh (d. 1387), ed. Mac Cionnaith, *Dioghluim Dána*, no. 37. **The child born in prison who cannot imagine a better environment.**

8. *Cóir foighide re feirg nDé* – attrib. Tadhg Óg Ó hUiginn (d. 1448), unpublished. **Young monk patiently accepts news of older monk's vision of his damnation and receives salvation as reward for his resignation to God's will.**

9. *Múin aithrige damh a Dhé* – attrib. Tadhg Óg Ó hUiginn (d. 1448), ed. McKenna, *Aonghus Fionn Ó Dálaigh*, pp 65–8. **Tears of penitence wash off bloodstain from infanticide's hand.**

10. *Binn labhras leabhar Muire* – attrib. Giolla Críst Ó Tailliúr, late 15th century, transl. Quiggin, *Prolegomena to a study of the later Irish bards*, p. 35. **Monk experienced years in heaven while listening to a bird sing.**

11. *Réalta na cruinne corp Críst* – attrib. Giolla Críst Ó Tailliúr, late 15th century, diplomatic text in Quiggin, *Poems in the Book of the Dean of Lismore*, pp 18–19. **Vision of consecrated Host as the Christchild.**

12. *Dlighthear deachmhadh asan dán* – attrib. Pilib Bocht Ó hUiginn (d. 1487), ed. McKenna, *Philip Bocht Ó hUiginn*, no. 7. **Vineyard produced only one-tenth expected crop, farmer offered all as a tithe, and was rewarded with bumper harvest.**

13. Olc thuillim mo thuarastal – attrib. Pilib Bocht Ó hUiginn (d. 1487), ed. McKenna, *Philip Bocht Ó hUiginn*, no. 19. **The provident bee works through the summer to store up food for winter.**

14. *Olc a cuitighthear comaoin Dé* – attrib. Uilliam Óg Mac an Bhaird, late 16th or mid-17th century. Earliest manuscript AD 1708–17. Maynooth B 9a. **The crow in borrowed plumage.**

The lost world: post-medieval accounts of the lordship of the Isles

STEVE BOARDMAN

The Hebrides was, perhaps, the area in the medieval British Isles where the political, economic and cultural impact of the 'English empire', as envisaged in Rees Davies' seminal study, was at its weakest. Yet the history of the region, with its independently minded local lords thriving, or at least surviving, in a maritime world subject to the ambitions of the Norse, Scottish and English monarchies and Irish provincial kings deals with many of the same processes of successful, or partial, or abortive political and cultural integration that so fascinated Davies. The complex and fluid nature of claims to 'sovereignty' and social pre-eminence in the Western Isles make the region especially intriguing to those exploring the growth and decline of polities and identities that do not fit easily into the 'national' narratives around which much modern historiography has been organized. The late medieval lordship of the Isles has certainly attracted a fair measure of academic interest in recent years.[1] The scholarly output has been varied in tone and approach, and the conclusions drawn about the nature and key characteristics of Clan Donald lordship rather diverse, often reflecting the particular disciplinary or geographical interests of the author. A unifying feature is that many of the studies have been concerned, directly or indirectly, with the thorny issue of how the lordship related to, and interacted with, the various polities and cultural groups with which it had historic or

---

1 John W.M. Bannerman, 'The lordship of the Isles' in Jennifer Brown (ed.), *Scottish society in the fifteenth century* (London, 1977), pp 209–40; idem, 'The lordship of the Isles: historical background', Appendix II in Keith A. Steer and John W.M. Bannerman, *Late medieval moumental sculpture in the west highlands* (Edinburgh, 1977), pp 201–13; David H. Caldwell, 'The Scandinavian heritage of the lordship of the Isles', in Jonathan Adams and Katherine Holman (eds), *Scandinavia and Europe, 800–1350: contact, conflict, and coexistence* (Turnhout, 2004), pp 69–83; David H. Caldwell and Gordon Ewart, 'Finlaggan and the lordship of the Isles: an archaeological approach', *SHR*, 72 (1993), 146–66; Alexander Grant, 'Scotland's "Celtic fringe" in the late Middle Ages: the MacDonald lords of the Isles and the kingdom of Scotland' in Rees Davies (ed.), *The British Isles, 1100–1500: comparisons, contrasts and connections* (Edinburgh, 1988), pp 118–41; Simon Kingston, *Ulster and the Isles in the fifteenth century: the lordship of the Clann Domhnaill of Antrim* (Dublin, 2004); Richard D. Oram, 'The lordship of the Isles: 1336–1545', in Donald Omand (ed.), *The Argyll book* (Edinburgh, 2004), pp 123–39; Jean Munro, 'The lordship of the Isles' in *The Middle Ages in the highlands*, ed. Loraine Maclean (Inverness, 1981), pp 23–37; Jean and R.W. Munro, *Acts of the lords of the Isles, 1336–1493* (Edinburgh, 1986) [hereafter *ALI*].

ongoing contact: the kingdoms of Scotland, England, and Norway; the inhabitants of Gaelic Ireland; the population of a wider Scottish Gaeldom. Assessments of the relationship between the Scottish crown and the lordship in the medieval period have tended to stress the persistent difficulties experienced by successive Scottish governments in asserting any form of meaningful control over the Hebrides after the establishment of formal sovereignty in the region in the thirteenth century. This view of the Western Isles as an intractable long-term political and military problem for the Scottish kingdom was memorably encapsulated in Ted Cowan's analysis of the campaigns that led to the Norwegian abandonment of claims to overlordship in the Isles through the Treaty of Perth of 1266: 'in acquiring the Hebrides, Scotland had acquired its Afghanistan'.[2] The later medieval lordship of the Isles has often been evaluated within this paradigm of an incomplete or failed integration of the Western Isles into the wider Scottish kingdom, in which the rulers of the Hebrides retained much of the 'sovereign' authority they had exercised before 1266.[3] The sense of partial or complete disengagement from the Scottish realm has been heightened by an awareness that the dominant aristocratic lineage within the Isles had multiple links through military service, kinship, a shared language and social practices, to a wider 'Irish Sea world', which largely lay beyond the ken and the political, legal and military reach of Scottish kings.[4] Moreover, the lords of the Isles maintained regular, if episodic, contact with the English monarchy throughout the late medieval period and, on a number of occasions, presented themselves as allies of the English crown.[5] It is generally agreed that the leaders of Clan Donald held a world view, and operated with a degree of practical independence in the political and military spheres, that was inconceivable for most of the subjects of the Scottish crown – almost to the point where their status *as* subjects of the Scottish monarchy could be called into question.

The freedom of action and political self-sufficiency enjoyed by the late medieval lords of the Isles is often seen as being closely linked to, and partly

2 Edward J. Cowan, 'Norwegian sunset – Scottish dawn: Hakon IV and Alexander III' in Norman H. Reid (ed.), *Scotland in the reign of Alexander III* (Edinburgh, 1990), pp 103–31.
3 See Alex Woolf, 'The origins and ancestry of Somerled: Gofraid mac Fergusa and the Annals of the Four Masters', *Mediaeval Scandinavia*, 15 (2005), 199–213, for a fascinating discussion of the way in which dominant Hebridean lineages of the twelfth and thirteenth centuries sought to link themselves genealogically to the royal dynasty of Man and the Isles.
4 Bannerman, 'The lordship'; Seán Duffy, 'The Bruce brothers and the Irish Sea world', *CMCS*, 21 (Summer 1991), 55–86 and idem, 'The prehistory of the galloglass' in Seán Duffy (ed.), *The world of the galloglass* (Dublin, 2007), pp 1–23; Wilson McLeod, *Divided Gaels: Gaelic cultural identities in Scotland and Ireland, c.1200–c.1650* (Oxford, 2004).   5 *ALI*, lxxiv–lxxviii; Grant, 'Celtic fringe', p. 130.

explained by, a quite deliberate defence of the culture and language of the territories over which they exercised control.[6] For Steve Ellis, 'Clan Donald consciously championed Gaelic values against the *Gaill* and was, for much of the fifteenth century, a virtually independent force expanding into Ulster and Ross'.[7] The evidence for Clan Donald's influence and importance as literary and artistic patrons within the Hebrides and the Scottish west coast, and the strength and range of the familial, political, military, economic and cultural ties that bound them to the aristocratic and scholastic networks of Gaelic Ireland, is indisputable. For some, this means that the lordship should be regarded as the 'centre of medieval Scottish Gaeldom', a rather hazy concept that transforms the extensive evidence for Clan Donald patronage of the Gaelic learned orders into a claim to pre-eminence in the social and political affairs of the various Gaelic-speaking communities of the late medieval kingdom. The same conflation of cultural activity and political ambition is evident in the suggestion in several accounts that one of the key goals towards which lords of the Isles were working was the (re)establishment of a unified, sovereign and determinedly 'Gaelic' polity in the Isles. In this view, the collapse of the lordship at the end of the fifteenth century represented the stalling of a process which had promised the emergence of a Gaelic 'kingdom' centred on the Hebrides. David Caldwell, for example, has suggested that the late medieval lordship closely resembled an 'incipient state' which was 'destroyed by the Stewart dynasty before successfully achieving this transformation'.[8] This model of a quest for political sovereignty as an expression of cultural and linguistic identity makes clashes between the Scottish royal house and the lordship seem, in a sense, natural and inescapable, fired by deep-rooted animosities.

A rather different strand of analysis is evident in the work of John Bannerman and Martin MacGregor, which gives full weight to the cultural distinctiveness of the society over which the lords of the Isles presided, without necessarily seeing in this an implicit political challenge to Scottish kingship or a declaration of separatist intent.[9] Sandy Grant, meanwhile,

---

6 Michael Lynch, *Scotland: a new history* (Edinburgh, 1990), pp 64–70, where the lordship is said to have represented 'a renewed, self-conscious pan-Celtic Gaeldom'; Caldwell and Ewart, 'Finlaggan and the lordship', 163–4; Steven G. Ellis, 'The collapse of the Gaelic world, 1450–1650', *IHS*, 31 (1999), 449–69 and Steven G. Ellis with Christopher Maginn, *The making of the British Isles* (Harlow, 2007), pp 5, 31–33.   7 Ellis, 'Gaelic world', 450.   8 Caldwell and Ewart, 'Finlaggan and the lordship', at 158. See also Caldwell, 'Finlaggan, Islay – stones and inauguration ceremonies' in *The Stone of Destiny, artifact and icon* (Edinburgh, 2003), pp 61–75, at p. 74. See Grant, 'Celtic fringe', pp 132–4 for a discussion of the features that distinguished the Clan Donald supremacy in the Isles from the merely 'aristocratic' power exercised by other regional lords. Ellis, 'Gaelic world', 453, 468.   9 Bannerman, 'The lordship'; Martin MacGregor, 'Church and culture in the late medieval Highlands' in *The church in the Highlands*, ed. James Kirk (Edinburgh, 1998), pp 1–36; idem, 'The view from Fortingall: the worlds of the

locates the development of the lordship of the Isles in the historical context of a kingdom where the emergence of 'hybrid' lordships, displaying features derived from different traditions of landownership and social control, was not unusual. Grant notes the way in which Clan Donald happily adopted new forms of lordship, particularly through the issuing of formal charters, and suggests that the integration of the Isles into a wider political system that was characterized by the widespread delegation of political power and judicial authority was by no means impossible. The barriers that eventually prevented such a process were not cultural as such, but arose from a combination of political happenstance and, ironically, the strength, stability and durability of MacDonald power in the west that made sustained and open defiance of the Scottish monarchy in the pursuit of political and territorial goals a realistic option. In the end, it was the lordship's self-imagining as a 'sovereign' power and the formal structures that underpinned that status that made effective assimilation impossible.[10] The specific political problems souring the relationship between the Clan Donald and the Scottish crown in the fifteenth century have been examined in depth by Norman Macdougall. The rival claims of the royal house and the Clan Donald to the earldom of Ross represented, Macdougall suggests, the lordship's 'Achilles' heel', drawing the lord of the Isles into a damaging, and ultimately fatal, confrontation with the king. In this view, the clashes between Scottish kings and the lords of the Isles again did not grow from, or reflect, longstanding cultural and linguistic estrangement, but in fact arose as the Clan Donald became more directly involved in the politics and political factionalism of the Scottish kingdom and court.[11]

The present essay offers a thoroughly modest, tentative and narrowly-focused contribution to the ongoing debate over the nature of the lordship in the fourteenth and fifteenth century. The main aim is to review a number of texts that provide the fullest comment on the distinctive structures and institutions said to lie at the heart of the medieval lordship. These works, mostly dating from the sixteenth century or later, have proven to be highly influential in framing modern understanding of the lordship, yet they were produced in a context much altered from that which governed the behaviour and shaped the actions of fifteenth-century lords. In particular, their authors had little interest in the methods by which Clan Donald lordship had been imposed (and at times accepted) over wide areas of the Scottish kingdom outwith the Hebrides. The most important of these areas was, of course, the

Book of the Dean of Lismore', *Scottish Gaelic Studies*, 22 (2006), 35–85. 10 Grant, 'Celtic fringe', pp 132–4. 11 Norman Macdougall, 'Achilles' heel? The earldom of Ross, the lordship of the Isles, and the Stewart kings, 1449–1507' in *Alba: Celtic Scotland in the Middle Ages*, ed. Edward J. Cowan and R. Andrew McDonald (East Linton, 2000), pp 248–75.

earldom of Ross. Historians have rightly identified the ambitions of the Clan Donald in Ross as the chief catalyst for political conflict between the family and the Scottish crown during the fifteenth century, culminating in the full-scale assaults on the lordship initiated by James III (1460–88) in the 1470s and James IV (1488–1513) in the 1490s.[12] While the end result of Clan Donald involvement in Ross may have been disastrous, it is not clear how far this was an inevitable or foreseeable outcome of the venture. For periods in the fifteenth century, and perhaps most notably in the last decade of the life of Alexander, earl of Ross and lord of the Isles (d. 1449), it may have seemed possible that the MacDonald earls of Ross would secure an enduring place within the Scottish political elite. Alexander certainly presented himself, and seems to have been treated by others, as a great Scottish magnate, with an elevated and assured social status within the aristocratic hierarchy centred on the Scottish crown. That this position proved to be impermanent should not obscure the way in which the campaign to consolidate the hold on Ross required or encouraged a refashioning of MacDonald lordship. The tendency to treat the MacDonald ascendancy in Ross as ephemeral, superficial and inherently unstable partly reflects the outlook of post-medieval narrative sources produced in a world where Clan Donald power had largely contracted back into the Hebrides. It is also, perhaps, informed by a more modern inclination, outlined above, to see the historical lordship primarily as a political expression of the cultural distinctiveness of the Western Isles in the medieval period.

* * * *

Any evaluation of the late medieval lordship of the Isles is inevitably made more complex by the fact that all of the surviving narrative descriptions of the Clan Donald hegemony postdate its collapse by at least half a century. The chronological distance between these narratives and the events or institutions they describe would, in other contexts, be seen as creating significant difficulties in accepting them as reliable or useful guides. However, there has been a willingness on the part of scholars to admit the potential value of later accounts relating to Hebridean and Highland matters on the basis that some of these obviously incorporated earlier annalistic material, and that the literary and oral culture of Gaelic-speaking areas of the kingdom was capable of preserving fine-textured historical detail that might resurface in, or inform, later textual compilations. Martin MacGregor has provided a compelling and nuanced exploration of the genre of early modern 'genealogical histories',

---

12 Bannerman, *Monumental sculpture*, Appendix II, pp 206–7; Macdougall, 'Achilles' heel?'.

produced in English by Gaelic-speaking authors between the seventeenth and nineteenth centuries, and suggested ways in which these works might usefully illuminate aspects of late medieval society in Gaelic Scotland. One of the significant points made by MacGregor is that the apparently 'medieval' material embodied in these texts cannot be fully assessed without careful consideration of authorial intent and affiliation, the likely provenance or means of transmission of any medieval matter and, of course, the contemporary context in which the early modern manuscript was composed or compiled.[13] MacGregor's note of caution in relation to the handling of non-contemporary sources is important, for recognition of the potential historicity of 'traditional' accounts and the strength of oral culture in the Gàidhealtachd has perhaps encouraged a rather uncritical acceptance of tales first attested in the seventeenth, eighteenth or even nineteenth century as sources of information on the medieval lordship.

The post-1500 accounts of the lordship of the Isles, and much of the modern scholarship reliant on them, lay particular emphasis on the distinctive features of the internal constitution and organization of the lordship. A singular picture of the life-cycle of a typical lord of the Isles has emerged: the rank and title of lord bestowed through an elaborate inauguration ceremony (now assumed to have taken place at Finlaggan on Islay); the exercise of near sovereign authority throughout the Hebrides with the help of a judicial (and perhaps legislative and representative assembly), the 'council of the Isles', which had a semi-permanent meeting place at Finlaggan; burial on Iona, in the graveyard of Reilig Orain, the traditional resting place for the lords of the Isles, and a sepulchre hung about with royal associations. It may be fruitful to examine the provenance and reliability of these later accounts in a shade more depth, since they have played a key role in establishing the view of the lords of the Isles as essentially conservative figures, resistant to external influence, and deeply attached to the 'traditional' forms and expectations of Gaelic lordship.

The first explicit comment on the existence, importance and composition of the 'council of the Isles' came in Donald Monro's account of his travels through the Western Isles during 1549. In his description of Finlaggan on Islay, Monro included a retrospective gloss laying out the earlier significance of the site as a meeting place for the lord of the Isles and a council of fourteen

---

13 Martin MacGregor, 'The genealogical histories of Gaelic Scotland' in Adam Fox and Daniel Woolf (eds), *The spoken word: oral culture in Britain, 1500–1850* (Manchester, 2002), pp 196–239. For an earlier defence of the use of post-medieval sources in studies of the lordship see Bannerman, 'The lordship', pp 209–10. For a particularly stark assertion of a general belief in the value of Hebridean oral culture as a historical conduit see David Caldwell, 'Finlaggan, Islay – stones and inauguration ceremonies' in *The Stone of Destiny, artifact and icon* (Edinburgh, 2003), pp 61–75, at p. 65.

which administered a pan-Hebridean law code reputedly established by the twelfth-century lord Ranald mac Sorley (the progenitor of the MacDonald and MacRuairi families).[14] The work of this council continued uninterrupted, Monro asserted, even when the lord himself was 'at his hunting or at ony uther games', so that 'In thair time thair was great peace and welth in the Iles throw the ministration of justice.' Monro provided a listing of the twelve secular (divided into three groups of apparently varying status) and two ecclesiastical lords who were held to make up the council. According to Monro, the members of the council included the four 'greatest of the Nobles callit lords' (the MacLeans of Duart and Lochbuie, and the MacLeods of Harris and Lewis), four 'Thanes of les living and estate' (MacKinnon, MacQuarrie, the MacNeills of Gigha and Barra) and 'four great men [. . .] of thair royall blude of Clan-donald lineally descendit' (Clan Donald of Kintyre, MacIan of Ardnamurchan, Clanranald and Clan Alastair Carrach of Lochaber).[15] The two ecclesiastical members of the council were said to be the bishop of the Isles and the abbot of Iona.

There are no inherently improbable figures in Monro's enumeration of the fifteenth-century council, but both the make up of the assembly and the power it supposedly exercised in the absence of the lord of the Isles suggests that the account very much reflected the political and social context of the 1540s rather than the situation prior to 1500. As a number of commentators have pointed out, the available fifteenth-century evidence does little to support the notion of a council made up of the fourteen lords detailed in 1549 operating on anything like a permanent basis on Islay, or indeed elsewhere.[16] David Caldwell's suggestion that Finlaggan may have been the

14 R.W. Munro (ed.), *Monro's Western Isles of Scotland and genealogies of the clans, 1549* (Edinburgh, 1961), pp 56–7. For comment on the council in the seventeenth-century *Sleat history*, see below. Monro's work does not, of course, fall within the genre of 'traditional' history as defined by MacGregor. The notion of a distinct law code administered from a central location is clearly important for the idea of the Isles as a 'sovereign' territory. 15 For the identification of MacQuarrie from Monro's 'Macnaie' see Angus Matheson's review of *Monro's Western Isles, SHR*, 42 (1963), 48–51, at 50, n. 1. The suggested council membership could only have been established towards the end of the fourteenth century given the inclusion of two Clan Donald cadet families (Kintyre and Lochaber) descended from John of Islay's marriage to Margaret Stewart. The schema of three distinct groups (deliberately reminiscent of the idea of distinct parliamentary estates?) was clearly not a hierarchy as such, for the order of precedence given to men as witnesses to lordship charters in the fifteenth century tended to intermingle the 'greatest of the nobles called lords' with the 'four great men of the royal blood of Clan Donald'. In the second half of the fifteenth century, the MacLeans of Duart and Lochbuie, and the MacLeods of Dunvegan and Lewis, were normally accorded a position behind the MacDonalds of Dunivaig and the Glens (i.e., Kintyre), and the MacDonalds of Lochalsh (for whom see below), but ahead of MacIan of Ardnamurchan. *ALI*, nos. 88, 96, 113, 120. The leading figures in Clanranald and the MacDonalds of Lochaber do not really feature as witnesses to extant lordship charters. 16 Both in terms of the locations where late medieval lords of the Isles are known to have conducted business, and the personnel surrounding them on these occasions. *ALI*, xlvi–1;

location of an annual midsummer social, political and judicial assembly for the Isles is probably as far as the fifteenth-century record can be pressed.[17]

In terms of the figures or lineages named by Monro as members of the council, it may be instructive to consider the case of two cadet branches of Clan Donald that made no appearance in the 1549 listing. In the second half of the fifteenth century the most important kinsmen and supporters of John, last lord of the Isles, included John's half-brother Celestine (Gillespic) and Celestine's son, Alexander of Lochalsh. For forty years Celestine and Alexander acted as John's principal representatives in and around the earldom of Ross. It is inconceivable that the Lochalsh MacDonalds would not have been considered key members of any 'council of the Isles' between 1450 and the dissolution of the lordship in 1493.[18] In the early decades of the sixteenth century, the last of the Lochalsh line, Donald Gallda (Celestine's grandson), was prominent in attempts to resurrect the lordship, leading risings in 1513–15 and 1516–19 before his death, without heirs, in 1519.[19] Another significant lineage within the fifteenth- and early sixteenth-century Clan Donald was the MacDonalds of Sleat, descended from Hugh, another of John's half-brothers. Unlike the MacDonalds of Lochalsh, the Sleat family was noted for its political opposition to John, playing an especially prominent role in the internal strife that engulfed the Hebrides in the 1480s. The family remained powerful (with its members regarding themselves as potential claimants to the lordship of the Isles) into the sixteenth century, but suffered a major reverse with the death of its then head, Donald Gorm, in 1539.[20] Despite their contrasting roles in the history of the late fifteenth-century lordship, the high status of both families during this period can hardly be doubted. The omission of the Lochalsh and Sleat lords from the list of members of the fifteenth-century 'council' probably reflected the fact that both lineages had experienced a precipitate decline in their influence (with the Lochalsh family effectively dying out in the male line) by the 1540s.

In 1544–5, some four years before Monro's tour of the Hebrides, there had been a concerted campaign to restore Donald Dubh, the grandson of the John, lord of the Isles, forfeited in 1493, to the lordship. The attempted restoration received the support of the English crown, eager to inconvenience the then Scottish government, but it was effectively organized and led by a number of prominent Hebridean families. These men required a mechanism both to legitimate Donald Dubh's claims and to secure their own

Bannerman, 'Lordship', p. 223; Caldwell, 'Finlaggan, Islay', p. 70.   **17** Caldwell, 'Finlaggan, Islay', pp 70–1, 74.   **18** For comment on the importance of Celestine and Alexander, see Stephen Boardman, *The Campbells, 1250–1513* (Edinburgh, 2006), pp 205–8, 254, 262–7. **19** 'The Book of Clanranald' in Alexander Macbain and John Kennedy (eds), *Alexander Cameron: Reliquiae Celticae*, 2 vols (Inverness, 1982–4), ii, pp 164–5 [hereafter *RC*]; *ALI*, 306 (note 4)   **20** *ALI*, 309 (note 18).

position within the prospective revived lordship. The fourteen 'traditional' members of the council reported by Monro bear an uncanny resemblance to the roll-call of Donald's allies in 1544–5.[21] A particularly significant document was drawn up on 28 July 1545, when Donald Dubh commissioned Rory McAlastair, named as bishop elect of the Isles, and Patrick MacLean, described as bailie of Iona and justice clerk of the south Isles, to negotiate an agreement with the earl of Lennox, who was the principal Scottish agent for the English crown. The commission was said to have been issued with the advice of a group of eighteen named secular lords described as Donald's 'barons and council of the Isles'.[22] This seems to have been the first recorded use of the phrase 'council of the Isles' in any extant source before its more famous appearance in Monro's work. When the men named as members of the council in the 1545 commission are matched against Monro's list we find a suggestive concordance. The only secular council member named by Munro that did not also ratify the 1545 commission was MacNeill of Gigha.[23] The two men commissioned to deal with the 1545 negotiations, Rory MacAlastair and Patrick MacLean, would also have been able to claim a place on the council as, respectively, bishop-elect of the Isles and bailie of Iona, the ecclesiastical offices which Monro presented as customarily bestowing membership of the assembly.[24] Patrick MacLean also appeared in a separate communication with Henry VIII's government in August 1545 as 'high justiciar of the Isles' (*insularum supremus iudiciarius*), a rather suggestive title in light of Monro's description of the exemplary justice formerly delivered throughout the Hebrides through the operation of a unified law code.[25] The existence of a class of hereditary judges or 'brieves' (Gaelic *brithem*) in the Isles in the fifteenth century is well attested, while various pieces of legislation enacted by the government of James IV after the forfeiture of the lordship in 1493 more or less confirm the operation of a judicial system within the Hebrides which was quite distinct from the common law

21 A point noted in *ALI*, xlvii–xlviii. 22 *Calendar of letters and papers, foreign and domestic, of the reign of Henry VIII* (London, 1862–1932), xx, part 1, no. 1298. 23 The full list from the 1545 commission was (with lineages mentioned by Monro in bold) **MacLean of Duart, the captain of Clanranald, MacLeod of Lewis, MacLeod of Dunvegan, MacLean of Lochbuie, Angus MacDonald, brother to James MacDonald [i.e., of Dunivaig and the Glens]**, MacLean of Turloske (the brother of MacLean of Duart), Archibald McDonald, Captain of Clan Uisdean (i.e., the MacDonalds of Sleat), **MacIan of Ardnamurchan**, MacLean of Coll, **MacNeill of Barra, MacKinnon, MacQuarrie of Ulva**, MacLean of Ardgour, **Ranaldson of Glengarry**, Ranaldson of Knoidart, MacLean of Kingairloch. 24 The fifteenth-century evidence does not really suggest any regular role for the abbot of Iona or the bishop of the Isles in the lord's council. Bishops of the Isles were very occasional witnesses to lordship charters (*ALI*, nos. 17, 21. This second occasion was, however, suggestive, with the bishop appearing as a witness to a charter issued at Eilean Mor on Finlaggan on 23 June 1427), while an abbot of Iona appended his seal to a grant by John, last lord of the Isles, in 1492. *ALI*, no. 123. 25 *Facsimiles of the national manuscripts of Scotland* (London, 1867–71), vol. iii, p. xxix.

of Scotland.[26] Whether this amounts to evidence for a coherent judicial hierarchy, implementing a single law code, and with an appellate structure centred on the lord's court at Finlaggan during the fifteenth century is less clear, although hierarchy within the judicial caste is certainly implied by the appearance of a 'Hullialmo archiiudice' (William, the arch-judex) as a witness to a charter by Angus Og in 1485.[27] It is difficult, however, to view Patrick MacLean, brother of the lord of Duart, who was not a member of a hereditary legal dynasty, as a likely 'heir' to any high judicial office which had existed in the fifteenth-century lordship. Instead, Patrick's appearance as 'high justiciar' in 1545 suggests an attempt to refashion an older tradition of Hebridean customary law as a tool to aid the assertion of political control in the Isles by the MacLeans and other supporters of Donald Dubh during the 1540s.

In short, while there is no indication that Monro himself was in any direct way an apologist for sixteenth-century claimants to the lordship such as Donald Gallda or Donald Dubh, it seems highly likely that his depiction of the membership and competence of the council of the Isles was influenced by the historical re-imagining surrounding attempts to restore the lordship in the post-1500 period particularly, perhaps, the 1544–5 rising. The use of

26 See *ALI*, xliii–xlv; John W.M. Bannerman, 'The Scots language and the kin-based society' in Derick S. Thomson (ed.), *Gaelic and Scots in harmony* (Glasgow, 1988), pp 1–19, at pp 11–14; idem, 'Lordship', 227; See, for example, the injunction of the Scottish parliament of 1504 demanding that the inhabitants of the Isles should be ruled 'be our soverane lordis aune lawis and the commoune lawis of the realme and be nain other lawis'. *The records of the parliaments of Scotland to 1707*, ed. Keith M. Brown et al. (St Andrews, 2007–2009), 1504/3/45. Date accessed: 24 August 2009. The existence of a separate law code or codes need not, of course, imply an attitude of hostility towards the common law in the fifteenth-century lordship. As Bannerman points out, the hereditary brieves of the Isles were perfectly capable of adapting and utilizing features of the common law where required. Bannerman, 'Scots language', pp 11–14. The lords of the Isles, as holders of estates and judicial offices in other areas of Scotland, were quite aware of legal conventions elsewhere, and their issuing of charters to important vassals from the 1390s onwards implied an adoption of tenurial rights and the establishment of relationships within the Hebrides that drew on Scottish legal practice. This was explicit in a 1409 charter by Donald, lord of the Isles, in favour of his nephew Hector MacLean of Duart, of lands in Coll to be held as fully, freely and honourably as 'aliqua porcio terre in regno Scotie datur a barone liberetenente in feodum'. *ALI*, no. 17. Familiarity with the legal procedures and forms of the common law at the very heart of the lordship is also suggested by an appeal by Malcolm Mackintosh of Moy to have a dispute over offices in Lochaber (a mainland lordship where the king's writ could be expected to apply) decided by the 'most excellent prince our lord James king of Scots or other lawful judge, unsuspect to the parties, assigned to this [matter] according to the common law of the kingdom of Scotland'. This appeal was recorded in three notarial instruments drawn up in Finlagan and the nearby island of Cara in June 1456. *ALI*, nos. 62–4. The location and the terms of the appeal might suggest an attempt to adhere to the strictures of the common law in relation to a tenant protesting against a recognition of lands or offices by his overlord, *RPS*, 1401/2/5. Date accessed: 24 August 2009.   27 See *ALI*, xliii–xlv, 119 and discussion in Bannerman, 'The Scots language', pp 11–14 and Steer and Bannerman, *Monumental sculpture*, p. 128.

the phrase 'council of the Isles' reflected the nature of the political community that supported Donald Dubh's claims, the leaders of Hebridean kindreds, mindful and jealous of their own status, rights and privileges, who had operated in the absence of an effective lord of the Isles for almost half a century. While it is unlikely that the prominent historic role of such a council, its part in deliberating on judicial matters, and its episodic convocation at Finlaggan were invention, Monro's account accorded all these elements a hard-edged precision and formality that embellished fifteenth-century realities.[28] The geographical focus on the Hebrides alone, and the notion of the entrenched institutional influence of the council, may have been less relevant at the height of Clan Donald power in the fifteenth century. At that point the Isles were one part of a network of territories, including the earldom of Ross, which Clan Donald lords governed with the help of a council, usually dominated by close kinsmen and powerful Hebridean lords, but of demonstrably variable membership according to location.

The essentials of Monro's account were widely diffused, not least because they were incorporated into the geographical description of Scotland in George Buchanan's highly popular *Rerum Scoticarum historia* of 1582.[29] The wide influence of Buchanan's work is important, for his history seems to have been the chief conduit by which the existence and function of the council of the Isles became known to the authors of subsequent works produced within, or commenting on, Gaelic Scotland. The appearance of later commentaries from Hebridean authors on the council and its composition cannot, therefore, really be treated as independent corroboration of Monro's account. However, towards the end of the seventeenth century (probably in the mid-1680s), a Hebridean author, now thought to be Captain Hugh MacDonald, ancestor of the MacDonalds of Paiblesgarry (North Uist), compiled a history of the Clan Donald which included a number of observations on the 'constitution of government' of the medieval lordship that had not featured in Monro's description.[30] Despite its late date, MacDonald's work (now usually referred to as the *Sleat history*) has been regarded as an important

28 Although it is difficult to say anything about the educational environment and intellectual world which shaped Monro, his apparent belief in the 'council of the Isles' as an exemplum of the advantages of conciliar rule may also have reflected a more general development in sixteenth-century Scotland, in which the history and virtues of the native Scots of earlier ages (to some extent believed to be preserved in the lifestyle of the Highland Gael) were evoked to identify and measure the failings of contemporary society. Edward J. Cowan, 'The discovery of the Gàidhealtachd in sixteenth-century Scotland'. *Transactions of the Gaelic Society of Inverness*, 60 (2000), 259–84. 29 Monro, *Western Isles*, pp 26–37; *The history of Scotland/ Rerum Scoticarum historia by George Buchanan*, ed. and trans. James Aikman, 6 vols (Edinburgh, 1834–7), i, pp 40, 45 (for Finlaggan as the seat of the 'prince of the islanders' and the existence of a court of fourteen chief men that 'sat daily for the administration of justice'). 30 For the likely identity

source for the pre-1500 period, and the text certainly deserves to be treated seriously as a guide to events and processes in the medieval era, because it is evident that, in places, the history relied on, or incorporated, much earlier narratives.

One of the most significant passages in the *Sleat history* provided a description of the inauguration ceremony by which medieval lords of the Isles were said to have been 'created'.[31] The roots of the lordship in the earlier kingship of Man and the Isles, part of a Scandinavian/Irish aristocratic world where inauguration played a key role in the validation of political power, make it entirely plausible, perhaps even likely, that distinctive 'king-making' rituals remained in place in the Hebrides in the late medieval period. The general tendency, then, has been to accept the account in the *Sleat history* as a useful guide to the reality of inauguration in the pre-1500 Clan Donald lordship. However, a number of difficult questions remain in regard to the portrayal of the ritual given in the *Sleat history*. Most obviously, the provenance and date of composition of the underlying source are wholly unclear. Hugh MacDonald's introduction to the account, 'I thought fit to annex the ceremony of proclaiming the lord of the Isles', suggests that he was drawing on a free-standing report distinct from the chronologically and/or genealogically organized narratives that underpinned the rest of his history.

According to the description presented in the *Sleat history*, the bishops of Argyll and the Isles and 'seven priests' were 'sometimes present' at the inauguration, 'but a bishop was always present, with the chieftains of all the principal families, and a *ruler of the Isles*'. The ceremony involved the lord 'clothed in a white habit' standing on a recumbent stone, his foot placed within a carved footprint, where he received a white rod [from whom is not clear], symbolizing the 'power to rule' and 'his forefather's sword, or some other sword, signifying that his duty was to protect and defend them [the inhabitants of the Isles] from the incursions of their enemies'. Although the account of the inauguration is fairly extensive, it is rather vague in terms of procedure, location and personnel. It also seems to be retrospective, outlining a template that is presented as having governed the conduct of *all* inaugurations in the medieval period. The events described are not tied to the creation of an individual named lord, certain aspects of the process are given variable

of the author see MacGregor, 'Genealogical histories', p. 212.   31 *HP*, i, 23–4. The material on the inauguration was placed between the death of Angus Og MacDonald (d.1314 X 1318) and an account of the career of Angus' son and successor John. The narrative had just laid out how Angus had established the political and military supremacy of the Clan Donald over the MacDougall lords during the early phases of the wars of independence. Hugh obviously considered that this marked the point at which the account of the inauguration became relevant to his unfolding of the story of the MacDonald lineage.

forms (presumably an indication of a backward-looking and summative perspective), and the discussion of the participants in the ceremonial deals largely in generic 'types'.[32] There is thus no real likelihood that the base text was a contemporary (that is, fifteenth-century) or near contemporary account of a specific ceremony: it was almost certainly, even at the point of original composition, a post-medieval production and therefore potentially influenced by the early modern literary corpus dealing with the phenomenon of inauguration in the lordships of Gaelic Ireland or the ancient Scottish realm.[33] Certainly, most of the individual elements mentioned in the account can be shown to have precedents or parallels elsewhere, particularly in Gaelic Ireland: the key point is whether this should be interpreted as an indication of the authenticity of the description incorporated into the *Sleat history*, or a clue that it was an imaginative reconstruction assembled from a range of earlier sources outlining the conduct of inauguration in other lordships.[34] In a potentially circular chain of validation, the *Sleat history*'s description of the footprint stone and the rituals associated with it, the provenance and date of which is simply unknown, has now become part of the corroborating evidence for the use of these stones and the conduct of earlier ceremonies in Ireland and the kingship of Man.[35]

The vagueness of the account extended to the location of the ceremony, for the *Sleat history* does not, in fact, name any specific site for the inauguration rite beyond the assertion that it took place on a stone with a carved footprint.[36] The *History* moves directly from discussion of the inauguration to talk about the 'council of the Isles', introducing the latter subject with the observation that 'Macdonald had his council at Island Finlaggan, in Isla'.[37] There was no link made at this point between the inauguration and the

---

32 The suggestion of variation in the clerical representation at the ceremony, and the statement that the lord might be given his ancestor's sword, 'or another sword', point towards an attempt to encapsulate more than one event. The chieftains of the principal families said to have witnessed the event are unnamed and the white gown worn by the lord during inauguration is allocated to an unidentified 'poet' (whose role in proceedings is not actually specified), although elsewhere in the narrative section of his work Hugh happily identifies 'MacMhuirich' as the poet of the lordship. 33 Elizabeth FitzPatrick, *Royal inauguration in Gaelic Ireland, c.1160–1600* (Woodbridge, 2004), pp 24–5, 191–2. 34 Recumbent flagstones, for example, had a well established role in the rituals associated with the creation or recognition of Irish kings or lords in the medieval period. See Elizabeth FitzPatrick, '*Leaca* and Gaelic inauguration ritual in medieval Ireland' in *The Stone of Destiny*, pp 106–21, at 107–10; W.L. Renwick (ed.), *A view of the present state of Ireland by Edmund Spenser* (Oxford, 1970), pp 6–7 (for the claimed use of footprint stones, the swearing of oaths, and the giving of a 'wand' as part of the inauguration of sixteenth-century Irish lords). 35 See R. Andrew McDonald, *Manx kingship in its Irish Sea setting, King Rognvaldr and the Crovan dynasty* (Dublin, 2007), p. 181 (and Ian Beuermann's review of the same in *EHR*, 124 (2009), 1148–9); FitzPatrick, *Royal inauguration*, pp 117, 120–1, 192. 36 *HP*, i, 24. 37 Ibid. The description of the fifteenth-century council of the Isles provided by the *Sleat history* displays no knowledge of the organization and composition of the council beyond

council, or any suggestion that the two events took place at the same location.[38] Indeed, the only site ever mentioned in connection with the elevation of an individual lord of the Isles was the church of Kildonan on Eigg. Kildonan was named in another seventeenth-century narrative dealing with the history of Clan Donald, the so-called *Red book of Clanranald*, as the setting for the 'creation' of Donald, lord of the Isles, *c*.1390. It was here that Donald was said to have 'received the staff of lordship' (one of the key elements in the inauguration as outlined in the *History*) from his elder half-brother.[39] The inauguration of the lord of the Isles was not, in fact, unequivocally associated with Finlaggan until 1703 and the appearance of Martin Martin's *A description of the Western Isles of Scotland*.[40] It seems clear that Martin's account of the organization of the inauguration was derived from the *Sleat history* or a text that shared the same 'information' on the ceremony.[41] Unlike the *History*, however, Martin's work was organized on a geographical basis, with the author describing individual islands and their antiquities in sequence. It is possible that the proximity of the account of inauguration and the Finlaggan council in his likely source text encouraged Martin to surmise that both were located on Islay. Despite the tenuous (and very late) 'evidence' underlying the identification, Finlaggan's status as the

what one might expect from a seventeenth-century author aware of the general and well-established tradition linking Finlaggan with a medieval judicial/administrative assembly. Instead of Monro's council of fourteen, MacDonald describes the Finlaggan assembly as having sixteen members, divided into a four-tiered hierarchy (although only three strata are actually defined), and he identifies six families that *might* have claimed a place in the lowest social tier of the council. None of the families named correspond with the council membership suggested by Monro.   38 Ibid., 24. Indeed, the need to specify the location for the council might imply that Hugh thought the inauguration took place elsewhere.   39 *RC*, ii, pp 160–1. Unlike most of the 'traditional' histories of the period, the Book of Clanranald, reflecting the assembled lore of the MacMhuirich family, erstwhile hereditary poets for the lord of the Isles, was produced in Gaelic. Although the Book of Clanranald suggested that the 'staff of lordship' was handed over by Ranald after John's death, it may be that Ranald had predeceased his father, and that it was his younger brother Godfrey who fulfilled this role. See Steer and Bannerman, *Monumental sculpture*, p. 127 (no. 49) for discussion. In conversation, David Sellar has raised the alternative possibility that the events described at Kildonan could have been a formal 'pre-recognition' by Ranald of his half-brother Donald's status as their father's heir rather than a full inauguration. This might then explain the epithet 'oighre' (the heir) attached to Donald in fifteenth-century Irish genealogies of the Clan Donald. For comment on the potential significance of Donald's by-name see W.D.H. Sellar, 'MacDonald and the Mac Ruari pedigrees in MS 1467', *Notes & Queries of the Society of West Highland & Island Historical Research*, 28 (1986), 3–15, at 9. This is plausible, although the event as described in the Book of Clanranald is said to have taken place after John's death.   40 Martin Martin, *A description of the Western Islands of Scotland circa 1695* (repr. Edinburgh, 1994), p. 273.   41 Thus Martin specified the use of a recumbent stone, the carved footprint, the presence of the bishop of Argyll and seven priests, the ancestral sword. In his discussion of what he termed the 'high court of judicature', however, Martin followed the Monro/Buchanan tradition in suggesting a council membership of fourteen. I should like to thank Dr Donald William Stewart for his thoughts on Martin's potential sources.

inauguration site for the medieval lordship has now become entrenched as an historical 'fact'.[42]

As recent work on lordship in medieval Gaelic Ireland has emphasized, inauguration was a mutable and malleable ceremony that could be adjusted to reflect and justify the circumstances through which individual lords came to power, often validating a radical redistribution of authority within individual lordships or polities.[43] The most prominent role in proceedings could be claimed by a variety of individuals or groups (these might include members of the wider kindred from which the lord was drawn; prominent vassals; an overlord; members of the clerical or learned orders; or a provincial community), and their part in the justification of the political and social power exercised by a new lord could change, or disappear, over time. In the case of the medieval lordship, the only explicit reference to the act of making a new lord would seem, as indicated above, to relate to Donald's accession to the title *c.*1390. Donald was the eldest son of John of Islay's second marriage, around 1350, to Margaret Stewart, daughter of Robert the Steward.[44] John also had a number of sons by his first marriage to Amy MacRuairi, sister and heiress of Ranald MacRuairi, lord of Garmoran. That Donald became lord of the Isles ahead of his elder half-brothers reflected the fact that his maternal grandfather, Robert the Steward, became king of Scots, as Robert II, in 1371. Exactly when John of Islay decided that his 'royal' sons with Margaret Stewart should succeed to the lordship ahead of the offspring produced in his earlier marriage to Amy is unclear.[45] In the period following John's death in 1387 Donald obtained control of the lordship, though perhaps not without opposition from those who thought that the sons of John and Amy held a superior claim.[46] If the handing over of the 'staff of lordship' at Kildonan was indeed part of an inauguration ceremony, then the

---

42 The certainty surrounding Finlaggan's status as an inauguration site has encouraged physical searches for the 'lost' inauguration stone near the site of the 'council' on Islay. David Caldwell, 'Finlaggan, Islay – stones and inauguration ceremonies' in *The Stone of Destiny, artifact and icon* (Edinburgh, 2003), pp 61–75, at 65.   43 Katharine Simms, *From kings to warlords* (Woodbridge, 1987), pp 16–17, 20, 21–40, 56, 67; FitzPatrick, *Royal inauguration*; Thomas O. Clancy, 'King-making and images of kingship in medieval Gaelic literature' in *The Stone of Destiny*, pp 85–105.   44 *Vetera monumenta Hibernorum et Scotorum historiam illustrantia*, ed. Augustus Theiner, p. 294.   45 See note 39 above for discussion. In June 1376, Robert II and John jointly made a territorial provision for Margaret's children involving the lordships of Lochaber, Kintyre, part of Knapdale and the island of Colonsay. Whether this settlement involved any recognition of the 'Stewart' progeny's rights to govern the wider lordship is not evident, for the main result of the arrangement was that the king's grandsons were established as heirs to the most important territories claimed by Clan Donald outwith the Hebrides proper. Only the grant of Colonsay suggested that the 'Stewart' offspring were to have a substantial interest within the Isles. *RMS*, ii, nos. 567 (Colonsay), 568 (Lochaber), 569 (Kintyre).   46 *RC*, ii, pp 160–1 for the suggestion that the elevation of Donald was 'contrary to the opinion of the men of the Isles'. For the death of John in 1387, see W.M. Hennessy and B. McCarthy (eds), *Annals of Ulster* (Dublin, 1887–1901), iii, p.

crucial symbolic role in that event was played by a man abandoning his putative rights in the lordship in favour of John's family by Margaret Stewart; that is, the ritual was a direct reflection of the political circumstances of the 1380s.[47] It is intriguing to note that this period also produced what appears to be the only reference to the existence of a nominated tanist in the Isles, in the form of Donald's younger brother John Mor, progenitor of the MacDonalds of Dunivaig and the Glens, who was styled as 'the tanist to MacDonald' in the Book of Clanranald.[48] The identification of John Mor in these terms has been taken as an indication that the inheritance of political, social and territorial power within the Isles was, in a general way, governed by the same conventions as applied in the lordships of Gaelic Ireland. However, it may be that the appearance of a tanist was a very particular response to the arguments over who should succeed to the lordship at the end of the 1380s. The granting of a formal place in the succession to John Mor may well have taken place at the same time as the claims of his elder brother Donald to the lordship were vindicated (indeed, it could hardly have occurred before Donald was accepted as lord), and may perhaps best be viewed as a mechanism to confirm the ascendancy of the sons of Margaret Stewart even in the event of Donald's early death without suitable heirs. As it was, Donald lived to *c*.1420x23 and left a well-established adult son, Alexander, to succeed him, so that any rights attached to John Mor as tanist were never exercised. In fact, the range of men with colourable rights to succession to the lordship, already apparently confined to the members of lineages of royal descent by the end of the fourteenth century, may have been further narrowed in the fifteenth century with the acquisition of the claim to the earldom of Ross through the marriage of Donald to Mary Leslie, sister of, and (in the eyes of Clan Donald) heiress to, Alexander Leslie, earl of Ross (d.1402).[49] Rights of inheritance to the earldom were, of course, limited to Donald's direct heirs, and the preference (although not always the practice) in the Scottish realm for property and judicial rights to descend to a legitimate son of a previous lord potentially placed the same constraint on succession to the now linked title of lord of the Isles.

If some uncertainty surrounds the process by which a lord of the Isles was made, there seems to have been little dubiety about the way in which they

19; J. O'Donovan (ed.), *Annals of the kingdom of Ireland, by the Four Masters* (Dublin, 1856), i, p. 709. The 'MacRuairi' offspring were given control of the northern lordships inherited from their mother. **47** It is interesting to observe the Book of Clanranald's description of Donald's brother Ranald as 'high steward over the Isles' (*aird sdiubhor ar Insibh Gall*) at the time of the ceremony, and the appearance of a 'ruler of the Isles' amongst those assigned a role in (or at least present during) the inauguration ritual as envisaged in the *Sleat history. RC*, ii, pp 160–1; *HP*, i, 24. **48** *RC*, ii, pp 159, 213. **49** For discussion see Macdougall, 'Achilles' heel'; Munro, 'Lordship', 26–8; Grant, 'Celtic fringe', pp 127–8.

were remembered after death. Talking of Reilig Orain, the graveyard attached to the abbey of Iona, Monro explained that 'Within this Sanctuarie also lyis [...] the lords of the Iles with thair linages, [...], with sundrie uther inhabitants of the haill Iles, because this Sanctuarie wes wont to be the sepulture of the best men of all the Iles, and als of our Kingis, [...]; because it wes the maist honourable and ancient place that wes in Scotland in those dayis, as we reid'.[50] The burial of individual lords of the Isles in Reilig Orain from the time of Ranald mac Sorley onwards was attested in the *Sleat history* and the Book of Clanranald, with the latter providing a particularly evocative account of the internment of John of Islay *c.*1387: 'his fair body was brought to Iona, and the abbot and the monks and the vicars came to meet him, as it was the custom to meet the body of the king of the Hebrides (*riogh Fiongall*),[51] and his service and waking were honourably performed during eight days and eight nights, and he was laid in the same grave with his father in the church of Oran'.[52] However, by the middle of the fifteenth century, the status of Iona as the primary mausoleum for the lords of the Isles was challenged by the increasing attachment of the lordly line to the earldom of Ross. Alexander, earl of Ross and lord of the Isles (d. 1449) is reputed to have died in Dingwall and to have been buried in the so-called 'chanonry of Ross',[53] the ecclesiastical complex centred on the bishop of Ross' diocesan cathedral at Rosemarkie, although the source of this information is late and slightly problematic.[54] The fact that none of Alexander's sons were buried on Iona would seem to reinforce the idea of a significant break from the tradi-

---

50 Monro, *Western Isles*, pp 62–3. 51 For discussion of this title and its significance see Wilson McLeod, 'Rí Innsi Gall, Rí Fionnghall, Ceannas nan Gàidheal: sovereignty and rhetoric in the late medieval Hebrides', *Cambrian Medieval Celtic Studies*, 43 (2002), 25–48. 52 *RC*, ii, pp 156–7 (Ranald mac Sorley), pp 158–8 (Angus Og), pp 160–1 (John of Islay, d. 1387), pp 162–3 (Donald, d. *c.*1420). The Clanranald history makes no mention of the place of burial of the two Clan Donald chiefs, Donald and Angus Mor, between Ranald mac Sorley and Angus Og. As noted in the quote, John was said to have been buried in his father's grave with no mention of his grandfather or great-grandfather. The *Sleat history* gives all these men burials in Iona. *HP*, i, 13, 14, 17, 23, 34. 53 The 'chanonry of Ross' seems to have been the name given to the ecclesiastical complex associated with the cathedral church of the bishops of Ross at Fortrose. Fortrose was adjacent to an older episcopal centre at Rosemarkie (indeed Fortrose lay in Rosemarkie parish) and in the fifteenth century, Fortrose and Rosemarkie were amalgamated as a combined burgh. The proximity of the two centres seems to have encouraged a rather flexible use of terms to indicate the same location. Thus, Alexander's mother 'Mary [Leslie] of the Ile lady of the Ylis and of Ross' witnessed a property resignation in August 1420, alongside the bishop and the dean of Ross, in 'the kyrke yharde of the chanounry off Rosmarkyng' – presumably the same as the chanonry of Ross. *ALI*, no. 20. Whether the cathedral was a traditional site for the burial of earls of Ross is uncertain, but Rosemarkie was extensively renovated towards the end of the fourteenth century and an extant tomb in this section is claimed to be that of Euphemia, countess of Ross, Alexander's maternal grandmother. 54 Alexander's burial is noted in W.R.B[aillie] (ed.), *Ane breve cronicle of the earlis of Ross including notices of the abbots of Fearn and of the family of Balnagowan* (Edinburgh, 1850), a printed version of a manuscript which, internal evidence might

tional burial patterns of the main lineage in the middle of the fifteenth century, although in the case of John, Alexander's successor as lord of the Isles, there may have been little choice as to his place of interment given that he seems to have died as a pensioner (and effective prisoner?) of the Scottish crown in Dundee in 1503. No such straitened circumstances, however, can explain the choice of John's half-brother, Celestine of Lochalsh, to be laid to rest at Rosmarkie on his death in 1473.[55]

Alexander's decision to abandon the burial church at Iona is intriguing given the terms of an appeal to the papacy made by Abbot Dominic of Iona in 1443–4. The abbot complained that the scandalous behaviour of Finguine MacKinnon, who had illegally secured a position within the monastic community and seized control of some of the church's resources, was causing significant problems. Among the difficulties cited was the resentment the patron of the abbey (presumed to be a reference to Earl Alexander)[56] felt towards MacKinnon, which had caused him to threaten the removal of the relics and bones of his 'progenitors' buried in the monastery,

---

suggest, was written sometime prior to 1615. According to the chronicle Alexander 'deyit in Dingwall, and was buryit at the channerie of Ross, the aucht day of May, ane thousand four hundredth fourtie and nyne yeiris', *Ane breve cronicle*, p. 10. This seems straightforward. However, precisely the same date and place of death (although not burial) was claimed for a previous earl of Ross, Alexander Leslie (d. 1402), ibid., pp 9–10. The picture of two earls of Ross with the same Christian name dying in the same location and, more intriguingly, on the same date (forty-seven years apart) seems suspicious, and it may be that the source has conflated the two men. An early sixteenth-century addition to a calendar associated with Fearn Abbey, which was in fact a likely source for the *cronicle*, seems to confirm Alexander Leslie's place and date of death as Dingwall on 8 May 1402. Robin J. Adam (ed.), *The calendar of Fearn: text and additions, 1471–1667* (Edinburgh, SHS, 1991), pp 21, 86–7. The fact that neither the *Sleat history* nor the Book of Clanranald claim Alexander of the Isles as an Ionian burial makes it seem more likely that he was interred elsewhere, quite possibly at Rosemarkie/Fortrose, although in all probability his date of death was not 8 May. The *Sleat history*, in fact, asserts that Alexander died on campaign in Ireland. While there is no other evidence to suggest that Alexander died in Ireland he is known to have been personally involved in a military expedition there in 1433, with Irish chronicles noting his leadership of a great fleet which was part of an attack by Eoghan Ó Néill on Niall Ó Domhnaill. *HP*, i, 47; *AU*, iii, pp 126–9; *AFM*, iv, pp 894–5. At some point prior to his death in 1448, the celebrated Irish poet Tadhg Óg Ó hUiginn addressed a poem to Earl Alexander which encouraged the MacDonald lord to bring his forces to Ireland, although it is unclear whether the poem can be linked in any way to the 1433 expedition. It is interesting to note that the poem referred to Alexander as 'Iarla Rois' on three occasions, as lord of the Isles once (although the most common epithet was actually 'MacDonald'). Lambert McKenna (ed.), *Aithdioghluim dána*, 2 vols (Dublin, 1939–40), i, pp 114–18, ii, pp 69–71. *AU*, iii, pp 163–4 for Ó Huiginn's death.   **55** For John's death in Dundee see *ALI*, 311 and references there. For Celestine's burial at Rosemarkie (i.e., the chanonry of Ross?), see *RC*, ii, p. 211. Another of John's half-brothers, Hugh of Sleat, was said to have been buried on North Uist. *HP*, i, 49. By the middle of the fifteenth century it would seem that the Clanranald were the most important Clan Donald lineage still using Iona on a regular basis as a burial church. *RC*, ii, pp 166–9.   **56** The initial plea to the papacy listed James II as the lead supplicant (probably a reflection of Earl Alexander's access to royal favour in the minority of King James) and the ambiguous accompa-

and the precious objects bestowed on the institution, to another location.[57] It seems most likely that this particular 'threat', which could be construed as working in Abbot Dominic's interests, was heavily embellished, if not invented, in order to convince the pope of the necessity to take action against the abbot's adversary, and that there was little real likelihood of Alexander removing the remains of his ancestors from the island. However, the fact that Earl Alexander chose to be interred in the Black Isle rather than Iona might indicate that the reported expressions of discontent with members of the monastic community were not entirely empty. Given that Alexander's grand-mother was part of the fourteenth-century Stewart royal dynasty the 'relics and bones' of the earl's 'progenitors' could technically have included not just the remains of former lords of the Isles, but also those of the early Scottish kings reputedly buried on the island. The fiction (for such it seems to have been) of royal interment on Iona had deep roots, reaching back perhaps into the twelfth century, and the supposed status of the abbey as an early royal mausoleum was widely accepted, and promoted, in late medieval Scotland.[58] The claim that most pre-twelfth-century Scottish kings were buried at the abbey was certainly a prominent feature of the sequence of late medieval and early modern chronicles dealing with the history of the Scottish kingdom. The weight of this historical tradition eventually encouraged an interesting piece of retrospective monumental commemoration on Iona itself, if Monro's description of the abbey from 1549 is in any way accurate. Monro claimed that lying within the bounds of Reilig Orain on Iona there were 'three Tombs of stanes formit like little chapellis'. The gable of each tomb apparently held an inscribed stone and, according to Monro, the legend on the stone for the middle tomb read '*Tumulus regum Scotiae*, that is to say, the tomb or the grave of the Scottis kings. Within this tomb, according to our Scottis and Irish chronicles, thair lyis 48 crownit Scottis kings'. Flanking the supposed sepulchre of the Scottish kings were (to the south) a tomb said to contain the remains of four Irish kings and (to the north) a similar

nying phrase, 'and [the] patron of the abbey', could conceivably also have referred to the king. It has been argued, however, that the reference to the abbey's benefactor must have been intended to denote Earl Alexander. *HP*, i, 90. This argument seems sensible given that the most obvious 'relics and bones' interred in the abbey were those of Clan Donald and that Alexander's father Donald, and his son John, were explicitly noted as the abbey's patrons in 1421 and 1467 respec-tively. *Calendar of Scottish supplications to Rome* [*CSSR*], 5 vols (SHS and others, 1934–), i, pp 271–2; v, no. 1201.   **57** *HP*, i, 89–90, *CSSR*, ii, p. 319. For discussion of the background to the dispute see Steer and Bannerman, *Monumental sculpture*, pp 100–2, 106–8.   **58** For brief discus-sion see Edward J. Cowan, 'The Scottish chronicle in the Poppleton Manuscript', *Innes Review*, 32 (1981), 3–21, at 7; Steve Boardman, 'Dunfermline as a royal mausoleum' in Richard Fawcett (ed.), *Royal Dunfermline* (Edinburgh, 2005), pp 139–53, at 140–1. This 'ancient' royal connection presumably underlay Walter Bower's classification of Iona as a 'royal' island (alongside Arran, Bute and Man) in his *Scotichronicon* (1445). *Chron. Bower* (Watt), i, pp 14–15.

monument for eight Norwegian kings. The figure of forty-eight crowned kings of Scotland is clearly derived from the statement found in several medieval chronicles that all Scottish kings between the putative arrival of the dynasty in the kingdom in the sixth-century and the establishment of Dunfermline as a royal mausoleum by Malcolm III (d. 1093) at the end of the eleventh century had been laid to rest on the island.[59] Any attempt to count the number of Scottish kings from Fergus Mor through to Malcolm III's reign as given in the most popular and influential late-medieval and early modern texts would indeed produce a figure of between forty-five and forty-nine monarchs who should have been buried on the island.[60] If Monro did actually see the three 'royal' tombs with their attached inscriptions, then the community at Iona had, at an unknown point prior to 1549, and in the obvious absence of extant individual graves for any of the kings supposedly buried there, erected these communal memorials.

The attachment of Alexander and his son Celestine to Rosemarkie as a sepulchre provides an interesting postscript to the fierce conflict between Clan Donald and their royal kinsmen for control of the earldom of Ross that had been such a feature of the early decades of the fifteenth century. The origins and course of the struggle for control of the province, which pitched Donald and Alexander first against the Albany Stewarts, and then James I (1406–37), are well known and require little rehearsal here.[61] The first four decades of the fifteenth century witnessed a series of political and military encounters between the lords of the Isles and royal or quasi-royal forces which have subsequently been taken as symptomatic of the relationship between the Clan Donald and the Scottish crown and, in some accounts, as part of an extended clash between Gaelic and English-speaking Scotland. The iconic battle of Harlaw (1411), the arrest and imprisonment of Alexander by James I in 1428, the humbling of lordship forces in Lochaber (1429) and the defeat of a royal army at Inverlochy (1431), are all significant episodes, the importance of which cannot be downplayed. However, this period of persistent conflict did not, in fact, result in an irreconcilable breach between the lordship and the wider Scottish polity. The late 1430s and the 1440s, indeed, saw Alexander attain a leading role in the governance of the north after the deaths in quick succession of his principal rival in the region, the earl of Mar (1435), and the alternative claimant to Ross, King James I (1437). MacDonald's military and political ascendancy in Ross in the years

---

59 Monro openly acknowledged that his account of Iona's early fame as a royal sepulchre was derived from written sources, for the main points were 'as we reid'. 60 Forty-five from Bower's *Scotichronicon*, forty-nine from John Bellenden's chronicle. For the assumption that all early medieval monarchs were buried in Iona see, for example, *Chron. Bellenden*, i, p. 286. 61 See Macdougall, 'Achilles' heel'; Grant, 'Celtic fringe', pp 127–9.

after 1437, and his wider prominence in the politics of the kingdom during the minority of James II, are seen to be dependent on the short-term weakness of royal government. Once active kingship was restored, the inherently fragile position of the Clan Donald in Ross came under pressure in the reign of James II and eventually collapsed disastrously in the reign of James III. There is undoubtedly some force to these arguments, but it is also worthwhile to briefly review the attempts by Earl Alexander to secure his hold on the northern lordship by winning acceptance of his rule from local society and royal government.

The evidence for Earl Alexander's increasing concentration on the affairs of Ross and the steady advance of his authority in the region is plentiful and varied. The place-dates of his charters suggest that from the late 1430s and throughout the 1440s, Alexander spent the bulk of his time in his eastern lordships.[62] Moreover, from 22 February 1439 to at least October 1443 (and apparently through to 1447, and possibly even to his death in 1449) Alexander exercised one of the most important judicial offices in the kingdom as justiciar north of Forth.[63] Earl Alexander's conduct in that role may not have been entirely displeasing to the inhabitants of the area under his jurisdiction if the tenor of a letter sent to him by the provost and council of the burgh of Aberdeen on 14 April 1444 is a reliable guide. The communication was concerned with the fate of a number of English merchants arrested by Alexander in Inverness, but the chief interest lies in the way in which the Aberdonians framed their appeal: '[...] for sen, loved be God, heddirtillie [until now] yhe hau al tyme obeit the king alsweil as ony lord of Scotland, and kepit ane hale part til him, for the quhilkis, God will, and yhe sal sone haue grete loving and reward; God forbid that yhe suld, for a litil monee that thir Inglismen has promissit yhou, warpiss your gude name, and the reward and thank yhe have deservide and wonnyn of the king'.[64] While the circumstances may have encouraged a certain effusiveness and exaggeration on the part of the provost and his council, the central point of the appeal related to the issue of potential damage to Alexander's established reputation (his *gude name*) as a loyal and obedient lord, and the presumption of the writers must have been that this was something that mattered to the earl and might elicit a positive response. The earl's high social standing within the Scottish aristocracy in the 1440s, at least partly derived from his relationship to the royal house, was reflected in the place accorded to Ross in a sequence of early to mid-fifteenth-century armorials. Since heralds were acutely

62 *ALI*; Grant, 'Celtic fringe', p. 128; Munro, 'lordship', 29.   **63** See *ALI*, p. 302 for a summary of Alexander's career as justiciar, although curiously this discussion does not include his appearance as justiciar in a document of January 1447. *ALI*, no. 46.   **64** *Extracts from the council register of the burgh of Aberdeen* (Spalding Club, 1844–8), i, pp 10–11.

conscious of the need to rank lords in terms of their social distinction, the prominence of the MacDonald earl of Ross in these collections is striking. The Armorial de Berry, probably compiled *c.*1445, featured the arms of *Le conte Dilles* (that is, 'earl of the Isles', a conflation of Alexander's two principal titles – the arms actually recorded were those of Ross (three lions) within a royal tressure) as the third of the Scottish earls.[65] An equally interesting aspect of this armorial was the appearance of the arms of the MacLeods of Lewis and the MacLeods of Dunvegan among those of Scottish lords below the rank of earl.[66] The MacLeod lords presumably owed their inclusion to their frequent appearances in Earl Alexander's company in Ross.[67] The compilation of the second armorial, the so-called Scots Roll, was probably completed early in the 1450s, shortly after Earl Alexander's death.[68] Here the arms of the MacDonald, earl of Ross (a galley within a royal tressure for the Isles, quartered with the arms of the earldom of Ross), were accorded a place of high honour, immediately following the royal arms and those of the royal dukedoms of Albany and Rothesay. It is perhaps no surprise that papal supplications from men in the north of the kingdom began to highlight their relationship to Earl Alexander, a descendant of the royal house and justiciar north of Forth, as a source of additional prestige.[69]

At the time of Alexander's death the collapse of Clan Donald's position

---

65 J. Storer Clouston, 'The Armorial of Berry (Scottish Section)', *PSAS*, 72 (1937–8), 84–114, plate IV. The adoption of the royal tressure was a common heraldic practice in the fourteenth and fifteenth centuries for Scottish lineages descended from marriages to female members of the royal dynasty, and clearly reflected the notion that such a link bestowed honour and prestige on the bearers of the emblem in a social hierarchy centred on the Scottish royal family. It featured on the seal of Alexander's father Donald in 1410 (and was presumably also a feature of any coat of arms he may have used), surrounding the chief heraldic device of the lineage, the galley *ALI*, 318. The relationship to the royal house was also occasionally specified in Clan Donald supplications to the papacy, presumably because closeness to a kingly line whose status was widely acknowledged added a certain gravitas and authority to the appeal, *CSSR*, i, pp 268–9, 271–2 (Donald as nephew of Robert III). **66** Ibid., plate VI. **67** For the appearance of Torquil MacLeod of Lewis as a witness to charters of Alexander in Kinmylies, Kessock and Dingwall see *ALI*, nos. 26, 34, 47, 50. For John MacLeod of Dunvegan see ibid., nos. 34, 47, 50. **68** Colin Campbell, *The Scots Roll: a study of a fifteenth-century roll of arms* (Heraldry Society of Scotland, 1995), pp 18–19. The Scots Roll also included the arms of MacLeod of Lewis, ibid., pp 26–7. **69** *CSSR*, iv, no. 684 (1 October 1440) James Innes, canon of Moray, 'of baronial race and a kinsman of Alexander, earl of Ross, lord of the Isles and lieutenant of the king', and no. 817 (7 October 1441), Robert Stewart of priest Dunkeld diocese, vicar of St Monivaig, Argyll diocese, 'of a noble race of earls and barons, kinsman of James, king of Scotland and closely related to Alexander de Ylis, earl of Ross and lord of the Isles.' The arms of *le conte de Ros*, following the same quartered arrangement found in the Scots Roll, were also included in an early fifteenth-century collection of coats-of-arms in Bibliotheque de L'Arsenal MS 4790. The arrangement of the Scottish arms (largely dating to the late 1430s) was odd, with the Ross insignia included in a raft of Scottish comital arms inserted, apparently out of sequence, after those of lesser lords. Rosemary Pinches and Anthony Wood (eds), *A European armorial* (London, Heraldry Society,

in Ross and the central highlands could hardly have appeared inevitable. Earl Alexander had cultivated a persona as a responsible Scottish earl that sat alongside, and in his own eyes may have been as important as, his duties and obligations as lord of the Isles. It was certainly not impossible, as the story of the Campbell earls of Argyll demonstrated, for the lords of great Gaelic provinces to become thoroughly integrated into the Scottish political elite without any significant loss of regional power or prestige, and the Clan Donald, after the traumas of the early fifteenth century, seems to have been set on a similar course. The reasons for the failure of this enterprise were complex and varied.[70] It is more than likely that the traditions and attitudes of political, legal and cultural autonomy within the lordship played, as many claim, some part in the final breakdown of the relationship between the crown and Clan Donald. However, as this study has sought to suggest, modern interpretation of the medieval lordship of the Isles has been heavily influenced by a sequence of retrospective early modern texts, most notably the work of Monro, and the late seventeenth-century *Sleat history*, which tended to emphasize the uniqueness and strength of the lordship's internal organization, and thereby made any processes involving accommodation with the Scottish crown seem less likely or viable. Monro's stress on the importance of the council of Isles, partly a reflection of the political conditions of the 1540s, seems to have produced a heightened sense of the centrality of Finlagan as a type of 'proto-capital' and of the formality of the judicial and administrative structures associated with the lordship. The *Sleat history*, meanwhile, preserved an account, of uncertain date and origin, which emphasized the crucial role of formal inauguration in the validation of lordship. Regardless of the accuracy or otherwise of the description as a guide to the conduct of the ceremony, there is little reason to doubt the continued relevance of inauguration as one of the means of establishing lordly power in the medieval Hebrides. However, given the way in which inauguration and its symbolism could be heavily influenced by political context, it would be dangerous to assume a type of culturally driven, almost doctrinaire, and unchanging attachment to particular forms of rule for their own sake. The search for practical responses to immediate problems or opportunities tended to blur the supposed norms governing the distribution of, and succession to, territorial and judicial power across the entire kingdom, not just the Hebrides. In that regard, it is interesting that the event that has left most evidence for the creation of nominated heirs, tanists, and an elaborate inauguration, in fact centred on the elevation of the Stewart king's grandsons to control of the lordship, a process that was, presumably, encour-

1971), p. 166.   **70** Macdougall, 'Achilles' heel' and Grant 'Celtic fringe', for general discussion.

aged by the royal dynasty. Conversely, the fifteenth-century lordly lineage has left us not inconsiderable evidence for their engagement with charter lordship and the common law, extensive interaction with the Scottish aristocracy, and the establishment of an honourable (although as it turned out temporary) position within the Scottish elite as earls of Ross and kinsmen of the royal house.

List of contributors

STEVE BOARDMAN is reader in history, University of Edinburgh. His books include *The Campbells, 1250–1500* (Edinburgh, 2005) and *The early Stewart kings: Robert II and Robert III, 1371–1406* (East Linton, 1996).

DAUVIT BROUN has taught medieval Scottish history at the University of Glasgow since 1990 (since 2009 as professor of Scottish history). He is the author of *Scottish independence and the idea of Britain from the Picts to Alexander III* (Edinburgh, 2007).

JOHN REUBEN DAVIES is research associate in history, School of Humanities, University of Glasgow; he is editor of the *Innes Review*, and apart from writing on hagiography and the cult of the saints, he has published on prosopography, chronicles and charters, especially in relation to medieval Scotland and Wales.

SEÁN DUFFY is a fellow of Trinity College Dublin where he is associate professor of medieval history. He is editor of the *Medieval Dublin* series.

SUSAN FORAN is a postdoctoral fellow at the Centre for Medieval Studies, University of Bergen, where she works on chivalry and national historical writing in late medieval Scotland.

NIAV GALLAGHER is an associate research fellow at the Centre for Medieval Studies, Trinity College Dublin. She lectures undergraduate students in medieval British, Irish and European history. Her research interests lie in the history of the British Isles from the medieval to the early modern period.

JOHN GILLINGHAM is a fellow of the British Academy and emeritus professor of history at the London School of Economics, where he taught from 1965 to 1998. His books include *Richard I* (New Haven, 1999), *The English in the twelfth century* (Woodbridge, 2000) and *The Angevin empire* (London, 2001).

MATTHEW HAMMOND is a research associate at the University of Glasgow and a former lecturer in Scottish history at the University of Edinburgh. He is a co-creator of the People of Medieval Scotland, 1093–1314 database.

KATHARINE SIMMS is a fellow emeritus of Trinity College Dublin, where she was a senior lecturer in medieval history to 2010. She is author of *From kings to warlords: the changing political structure of Gaelic Ireland in the later Middle Ages* (Woodbridge, 1987), *Medieval Gaelic sources* (Dublin, 2009), and numerous articles on the kings, clerics and learned classes in Gaelic Ireland from the thirteenth to the fifteenth centuries.

FREYA VERSTRATEN VEACH holds a PhD from Trinity College Dublin and is an honorary research associate of the University of Hull.

PATRICK WADDEN is currently assistant professor of history at Belmont Abbey College, North Carolina. He has a particular interest in communication between Ireland and its neighbours during the early and central Middle Ages and in how it is reflected in vernacular Irish literature.

Index

(compiled by Áine Foley)

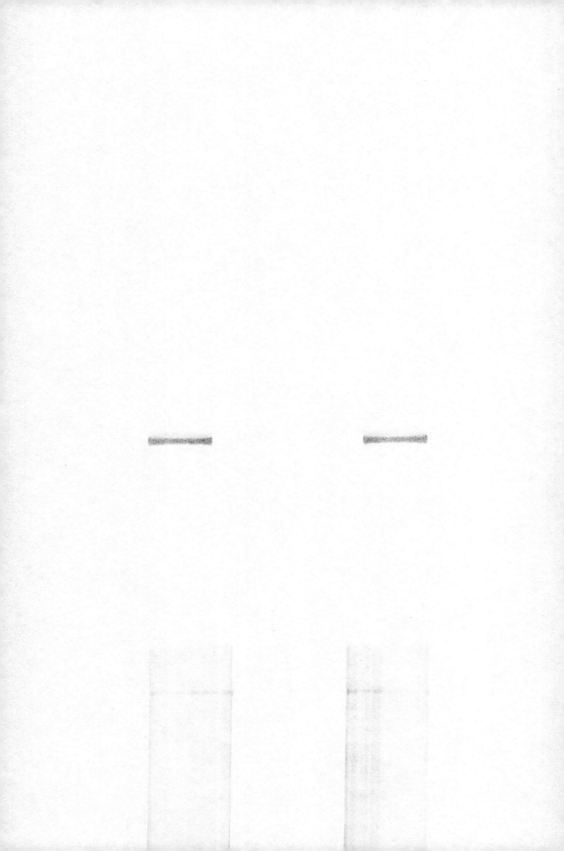